Cover picture:
Maria Coombes at the Queen's Jubilee Pageant
London, BSA Bantam 125 (photo: Mario Costa-Sa)

FOUNDER
C.E. 'Titch' Allen OBE, BEM

PUBLISHER & CHAIR
Mario Costa-Sa Bsc (Eng) MBA
chair@vmcc.net

VICE-CHAIR
Steve Allen
chair@vmcc.net

VICE PRESIDENT
Annie Durrant- Events
events@vmcc.net

VICE-PRESIDENT
Gary Sleeman- Shows
shows@vmcc.net

DIRECTOR
Martin Marmoy
marketing@vmcc.net

EDITOR
Peter Henshaw MA editor@vmcc.net

DESIGN
Louise Hillier editor@vmcc.net

ADVERTISING
adverts@vmcc.net

MEMBERSHIP
Tracey membership@vmcc.net
01283 495100

SHOP
shop@vmcc.net
Terry 01283 495101

LIBRARY
library@vmcc.net
Maddie & Peter 01283 495111

Published by: Vintage Motorcycle Club Ltd
Allen House, Wetmore Road, Burton-upon-Trent,
Staffordshire DE14 1TR
Registered in England and Wales 1570648

Editorial
Peter Henshaw

Photo by: Anna Finch

Welcome to Vintage & Classic Motorcycle: Diary of 1000 Rides. If you are already a member of the VMCC, you'll know that we offer over well over 1000 rides and events, all year round, all over the country. You'll know that these are put on by 85 local sections, staffed and run by volunteers who want to help you get the most enjoyment out of your old bike, whether it's a veteran from the 1900s, a solid British twin of the '50s or a fast Japanese 750. For you, the Diary of 1000 Rides is business as usual for the VMCC – it's all about being out, enjoying our bikes.

If you're not a VMCC member (yet...) then a big hello and welcome to the world of old motorcycles. Maybe you're thinking about buying an older bike for the first time, or adding a couple to your stable. This is where the VMCC comes in. In these pages you'll find reams of useful advice on buying your first classic bike, getting it on the road and keeping it there. There's no lack of bikes to choose from either, and we take a snapshot (and ride) a typical three in the £3000-£5000 range: Yamaha RD250, BSA A65 and Moto Guzzi V50.

To give a flavour of what the VMCC is about, we've also included features from Vintage & Classic Motorcycle, our monthly magazine which goes out to all VMCC members. Britain's biggest gathering of vintage bikes? Tick. A run to Moto Guzzi's historic Mandello factory by a 1000cc Le Mans? Tick. Living with a '60s Triumph T100C street scrambler? (You get the idea). Plus how to spot a fake engine number; track action with a Yamaha TR3 replica; a barn find French moped restored; and as they used to say in adverts for Greatest Hits LPs (remember them?) many, many more.

For us – the VMCC – it's all about the riding, and that's why the heart of this bookazine is the Diary of 1000 Rides – runs, pub meets, autojumbles and events all over the UK. Come and join us.

Peter

Peter Henshaw
Editor, Vintage & Classic Motorcycle

Copyright 2023, Vintage Motorcycle Club Ltd. All rights reserved. No part of this publication may be reproduced or transmitted in any form or by any means, electronic or mechanical, including photocopying, recording, or any information storage retrieval system without prior permission in writing from the publisher.

CONTENTS

Spring run in Glencoe for Richard Cooper's 1958 MV 125 and his wife's 1964 Tiger Cub

FEATURES

6 Triumph T100C
Fresh from the East Coast – 500cc street scrambler back on British roads

12 The Numbers Game
What are the most popular classic bikes? Be surprised...very surprised

16 Le Mans to Mandello
1000cc Moto Guzzi goes home to its birthplace

24 Belgian Fun
Put those pastries away – a Yamaha TR3 race replica takes to the track

28 On the Hammer
Auction reports – what gets good prices, and what are the bargains?

32 The Other Gold Star
The French made a 'Gold Star' too – 50cc with pedals...

36 Forensic Exam
How to tell if an engine/frame number is genuine

54 Buying One
How to buy a classic bike...

64 Your 1st Classic
Why you should....

70 Rule of 3
Three typical choices: Yamaha RD250, BSA Thunderbolt, Moto Guzzi V50

121 Getting on the Road
How to spot a lemon, which tools to buy

EXTRAS

35 All Welcome
The secret to attracting and keeping new members

56 Classic Glossary
How to tell you pre-unit from your Zener diode

60 Section Spotlight
This month – Burton & District

Page 32

VINTAGE & CLASSIC MOTOR CYCLE

Page 24

Page 16

EVENTS

20 Banbury for Beginners
Ever wanted to ride the Banbury Run? Now's your chance

22 Gordon Prime
Honouring ex-WWII despatch rider Gordon Prime (aged 98)

23 The Navigators
Northamptonshire Navigation Rally – what it is and how to take part

38 Founders Relay Rally
Mother of all day rides on 30th April – all 56 checkpoints listed

79 Diary of 1000 Rides 2023
Actually it's more like 1300 rides and events – where to ride and who to meet in 2023

80 Spring Rides
March – April – May

93 Summer Rides
June – July – August

109 Autumn Rides
September – October

117 Winter Rides
November – December

REGULARS

46 Photo of the Month
First signs of Spring...

50 Letters
A tale of redemption...

58 Gem
This month, the AJS Big Port

59 Books
It's 1969, and BSA's selling technique is well on trend

61 Insurance Matters
How VMCC Insurance can help you ride your mate's bike

62 Saved by the weld
Repairing a 1928 gearbox

74 Classifieds
"Ideal club run bike, no oil leaks. £699 ono"

The Vintage Motor Cycle Club
leading the way for 75 years

Welcome to the biggest and best Vintage & Classic motorcycle club in the world.

Please enjoy this personal insight into our 2023 Riding Diary with over 1300 rides, 50 key events and 1000 social meetings all over the UK. Added up, they make you an important part of the largest and growing community of vintage & classic motorcyclists.

Our members' interests span the whole range of motorcycle eras, from the 1900s to the early 1990s and everything in between. From mopeds to superbikes, all are of interest.

From our HQ in Burton-upon-Trent we look after 13,500 members across the UK, many of whom enjoy our riding events plus further opportunities to get involved, which are being added to our website all the time. Full information is at www.vmcc.net

This year the VMCC will be launching regional hubs at locations to include the Ace Café London and Ambergate near Matlock. We are currently looking at venues in Solihull and Wiltshire as well. These will offer a members more opportunity to build a vintage & classic motorcycling community in established areas of interest to the biking community. This includes the ability to drop in any time with café facilities and motorcycle friendly parking – basically the perfect place to start and finish a ride.

We have 85 active sections across the UK with our active members riding and restoring motorcycles which are over 25 years old.

We're an international club too, with 64 motorcycle clubs worldwide affiliated to the VMCC, giving our members a direct international link to fellow vintage and classic riders internationally.

We have the world leading motorcycle reference library service, including the largest and most experienced, DVLA approved, machine dating services, assisting more owners to get an age-related registration than any other club.

If you want to save money, our insurance scheme is worth a look, offering the most competitive insurance rates and high-quality cover for 90% of our members. In surveys, we found that VMCC members pay as little as £30-£50 per bike – our scheme also allows members to insure their modern motorcycle alongside a classic.

The Banbury Run, our flagship event, is the world's largest meeting for vintage & veteran motorcycles, attracting over 500 riders on pre-1930 machines. It's good for spectators as well, truly something for everyone, of any age, interested in preserving and riding old motorcycles.

Maybe you don't own an older bike yet? Try one of ours. The Club has a garage of 16 bikes of all eras available for loan to members, varying from a 50cc moped, CBT qualifying 125s to a 1200cc Yamaha. There is even a Brough Superior and three competition motorcycles which are all available for member use. This is a great opportunity to try out a machine on a ride with your local Section whilst you look for the vintage or classic bike of your dreams.

Many of our sections, notably The Taverners, offer trials and trail riding on classic machines for those who are happiest riding away from surfaced roads. Make contact with any of the Sections listed in the back pages or enquire at www.vmcc.net/join

Please accept our open invitation to come along to our events or meetings, where you will be warmly welcomed. Details of who we are, where we meet and what we offer are all included in this 2023 Diary of 1000 Rides.

Mario Costa Sa
Chair, VMCC

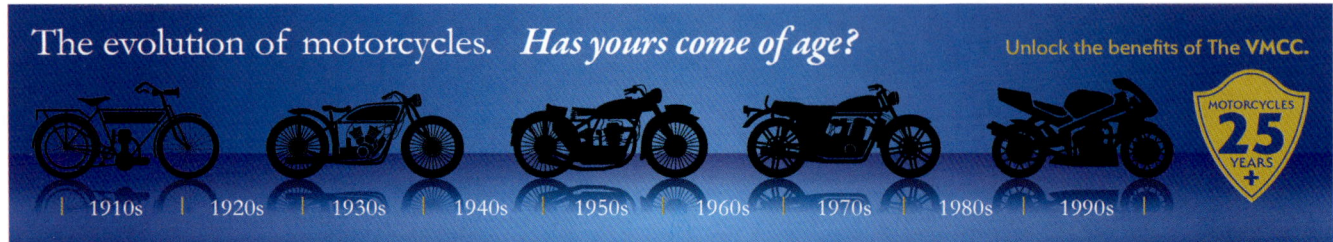

Exclusively for VMCC members at Peter James Insurance

Policy benefits can include:*

- Tailored pricing for VMCC members
- Additional discounts based on length of membership
- Free agreed value
- Free salvage retention
- Member to member cover
- Multi-vehicle options
- Cover for young riders
- Cover for club organised track events
- Up to £3000 cover for tools and spare parts
- Free Helmet & Leathers cover
- No call centre – just friendly and knowledgeable staff

88% of Members Save with VMCC Motorcycle Insurance

VMCC Motorcycle Insurance has been price tested by the VMCC against three key competitors and proven to best value in 88% of sample cases on a sample size of 25 risks†

 0121 274 5355   VMCC.NET/INSURANCE

*Policy benefits, features and discounts offered may vary and are subject to underwriting criteria

†Comparison carried out by the VMCC between January and March 2021.

Peter James Insurance is a trading name of Peter D James Limited, registered in England No 5618022. Peter D James Limited is authorised and regulated by the Financial Conduct Authority (FCA) No: 452647. Registered address: 772 Hagley Road West, Oldbury, West Midlands, B68 0PJ.

DOCIDM168

MY FIRST *Classic*

ASHLEY BOND grew up with Japanese bikes, but hankered after a high-pipe Triumph...

As a teenager, my attention was not immediately drawn to owning a British bike. Back in the late '70s they were rather looked down upon: they never rusted, so the joke went, thanks to abundant oil leaks, and if you saw a bike broken down at the roadside, it would usually be British. So I can't say that owning a classic Triumph was a schoolboy dream, but it certainly became an adult one.

My early bike ownership was rather eclectic. I learned on a Honda C50 step-through, and my first road bike was a pedal-start Mobylette (which looked more like a motorised bicycle). I hated the Mobylette, thanks to its very basic performance and humiliation factor – riding in the gutter. And being overtaken by buses was terrifying! It was rapidly superseded by a bright green Honda SS50 sports moped, a proper 'sixteener special', which I loved. It had fold-over pedals (merely to circumvent the existing law), a 5-speed gearbox and could top 60mph. And to me, it looked like a proper motorbike. Looking back, it's amazing I survived that! Next was a metallic blue Harley-Davidson SS250 (really a rebadged made-under-licence Aermacchi), which I took my test on, much to the chagrin of the examiner. This was followed by a stylish black and red Yamaha SR500 single, which I considered my first 'grownup' bike. I have been Japanese ever since!

Jumping forward a few decades, I began to pay more attention to classic bikes, went to events and began hankering after an old Triumph. And this is where the story of my ownership (I prefer to say 'guardianship') of my now beloved T100C begins – it virtually fell into my lap.

A friend at work asked me to help with the collection of an R75 police BMW that he'd just sold, and a chap came down from Yorkshire to pick it up. We got chatting about old bikes and I professed my desire to own one, "preferably British, ideally 1960s and around 500cc." "Ah," he said, "I might just have the perfect bike for you!"

Right: After a biking career on Japanese machines Ashley knew he wanted a 500cc twin - T100C fits the bill perfectly

Falling in Love

I must admit that I'd never even heard of a Triumph T100C. I was aware of the stunning 650cc TR6C (incredibly rare, especially in the UK). I'd been keeping an eye out for one, though I considered it out of my league at that point, on every level. The T100C turned out to be a sort of younger brother, a smaller 500cc version of the same thing, also with a simple single carb.

When BMW man sent me photographs of the bike a month later I realised he was absolutely right. It did look perfect, gorgeous in fact! The late '60's street scrambler styling and all that chrome. The twin high pipes with polished heat shields, the gold and cream tank and polished mudguards... I jumped on the next train to Yorkshire, and when I got there immediately fell in love.

Close up, one thing that particularly appealed to me was the appearance of being well-used but well looked after – the odd rusty bolt head and light wear, but with the patina that I favour over a full concours restoration look. We struck a deal pretty quickly.

As I got to know the Triumph, it certainly proved to be the perfect bike for me, and an appropriate introduction to classic ownership, though it did take a while to adjust to a right-foot gear change. The engine was simple enough and sounded really tight with no rattles and not a drop of oil leaking. I discovered it already had a Boyer electronic ignition conversion, which made starting a breeze - it has pretty much always started on first or second kick, with rarely any choke.

However, there were some initial minor issues that led to a steep learning curve. Firstly, something fell against it in the garage, causing light damage, and an intermittent ignition issue, with the engine frequently cutting out. This foxed me for some time, until I discovered that there was an electrical short between the battery and the metal seat pan.

Top: As bought, tidy and original
Above: Engine is quiet and oil-tight
Left: Speedo only on the street scrambler Triumph
Below: T100C's trademark, those twin high pipes

That summer, I took it on the Distinguished Gentleman's Ride in London, only to have a catastrophic oil leak in the middle of Westminster Bridge. As I was suitably attired for the ride, I wasn't able to get down on my hands and knees to try and figure it out, nor was my knowledge at the time sufficient to identify the obvious cause. It turned out that the oil return pipe had detached, so oil was being pumped onto the rear wheel instead of back into the reservoir, which took a lot of cleaning up. Both this and the battery short were fixed by my local expert mechanic Tony at Maitland Racing – luckily for me, they are in my neighbourhood.

The Learning Curve

The T100C is a really enjoyable and smooth ride, with enough grunt and a throaty exhaust note to instantly put a smile on any rider's face. The engine is torquey, with smooth acceleration, and certainly responsive enough for 54-year-old machine. It's also surprisingly nimble, with agile handling through traffic. However, I haven't pushed it as it favours low revs, and will happily cruise along in the mid-range at about 50-60mph. Also, what with the chrome and the exhaust note, it certainly turns heads.

Though the Triumph seemed to have been well looked after, and clearly kept in a dry environment in its previous life on the American East Coast, the more I got to know it, the more I noticed small things that needed improving. The fork seal covers turned out to be wrapped in foil, covering up some serious pitting to the chromed originals. The steering lock barrel had been brutally removed at some point, with some damage to the surrounding area. Some bare wires under the seat had been roughly wrapped in electrical tape and left dangling, and on closer inspection the petrol tank had a lot of interior rust. It was this last discovery that persuaded me that it was time to get a professional eye cast over the whole bike.

I took the Triumph to RJM Classics in Bedfordshire, a reliable father and son team, who were genuine and knowledgeable enthusiasts, and judging by the other customers' bikes they were working on, worked to very high standards.

Pay As You Go

We embarked on a period of pay-as-you-go restoration. The front fork internals turned out to be in the same state as the tank interior, so the stanchions were replaced with new seals and

The INTERNATIONAL Classic MotorCycle Show

CELEBRATING 40 YEARS

THE BIG ONE IS BACK!

APRIL 22-23, 2023
STAFFORDSHIRE COUNTY SHOWGROUND, ST18 0BD

MEET Star Guest AGOSTINI! AT STAFFORD

- OVER A THOUSAND BIKES & THE BEST CLUB STANDS IN THE UK
- BRILLIANT TRADE & AUTOJUMBLE
- STUNNING MACHINES FIRED TO LIFE IN THE GP PADDOCK
- SEE THE INCREDIBLE SANDERSON STEAM MOTORCYCLE IN ACTION
- DEATH DEFYING STUNT SHOW FROM 'ON THE EDGE'
- WORLD FAMOUS Bonhams AUCTION
- LIVE MUSIC & BAR
- PLUS MUCH MORE!

TICKET INFO: £15.50 IN ADVANCE
£2.50 SAVING & EARLY ENTRY WITH ADVANCE TICKET
FREE PARKING & UNDER 16s GO FREE

WWW.STAFFORDCLASSICBIKESHOWS.COM
CUSTOMER SERVICES 01507 529529

  @CLASSICBIKESHOWS   @CLASSICBIKESHOW  ON THE EDGE motorcycle stunt show MORTONS ARCHIVE  Bonhams

Left: Fuel tank corrosion was a flaky business

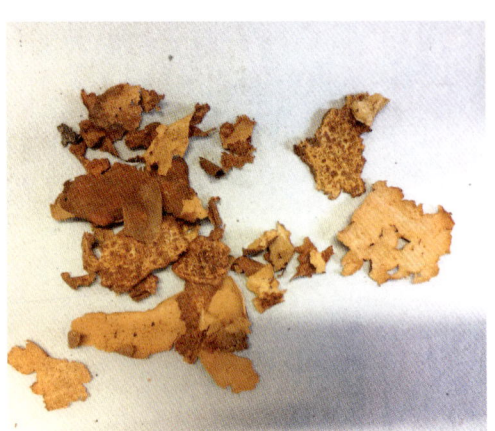

Below: New strap prevents the battery moving about

gaiters, then repainted. The tank was cleaned, treated and lined, and fuel filters installed in the petrol lines on both sides. RJM also took the precaution of cleaning out the oil tank.

Though functional, the carburettor was a well-worn original and was replaced with a new Amal Concentric. All the wiring was tidied up, and a new retaining strap made for the battery as the original had disintegrated with age, though I kept the original buckle, a nice detail. The loose wiring behind the left side panel turned out to be from the factory, a shoddy job from when the older model had the ignition switch in this position. The front brake was cleaned and skimmed by hand, vastly improving its limited performance, while the rear brake rod adjuster needed replacing – incorrect nuts had been used, so the rod itself needed retapping.

The engine proved to be as tight as first thought, and was left largely untouched, though RJM checked the valve clearances, added an oil filter and replaced the gearbox outer cover gasket (which was missing). New exhaust finned rings were fitted and sealed too.

There was a bizarre surprise when the lack of a headlight pilot lamp bulb was investigated. There was actually no provision for one, and on closer examination the whole headlamp turned out to be from a Triumph Stag! A new old stock Lucas unit was located and fitted.

Another discovery came when fitting a new clutch cable when slight play in the handlebars was noticed – the handlebar mounting bracket was cracked in two places, which meant a whole new top yoke.

Details to Do

When I eventually picked the bike up from RJM, it looked a whole lot smarter and rode even more smoothly than before. The very next day I rode it to the Ace Café for a Triumph Day, heading back there for the Vintage and Classics Day (where I was snapped arriving on it – picture in the Journal!)

I decided it was time for something more adventurous, so took the Triumph to the Malle Mile off-road racing event at Grimsthorpe Castle, where it flew around the dirt tracks with ease. I felt like I was in upstate New York under the woodland canopy. While I was there, I met Triumph collector Dick Shepherd, who commented favourably on the T100C's originality, but also pointed out some things which weren't. The seat's Triumph logo, for example, was faded and the seat itself was an old pattern replacement, though a good quality one. The seat logo and a erratically dancing speedo needle remain the only things left to be sorted out. I want to keep the original speedometer, so rather than buy a new repro I found The Gauge Shop, who can restore the instrument and keep its original 8500 miles. Dick has recommended Leighton's for the seat.

New World

I really love this machine, and much as I enjoyed the Malle Mile, have decided I would rather keep it as a smart street scrambler, rather than beating it up at off-road events. So I'm keeping an eye out for a TR5T Trophy Trail – exactly the same engine and a similar vintage, but more appropriate off-road.

Thanks to the Triumph, I am completely committed to classic bike ownership, aided considerably by the VMCC, with my basic technical knowledge improving all the time. I thoroughly enjoy the events and meeting other riders along the way, and seeing some beautifully restored old bikes. I realise I may not be typical of most members in my mechanical knowledge, and I certainly won't be attempting to strip down an engine any time soon, but that doesn't deter me from owning and running an old British classic. In fact, I'm planning to ride mine to the West Kent Run this summer!

If I were to keep any classic bike for daily use, it would certainly be the T100C. It's definitely reliable enough, and every time I'm on it I get stopped at the lights at least once for a chat, such is its head-turning power. Basically, I couldn't be happier with the bike that found me!

Not an out and out scrambler, but the T100C was and is perfectly usable off-road

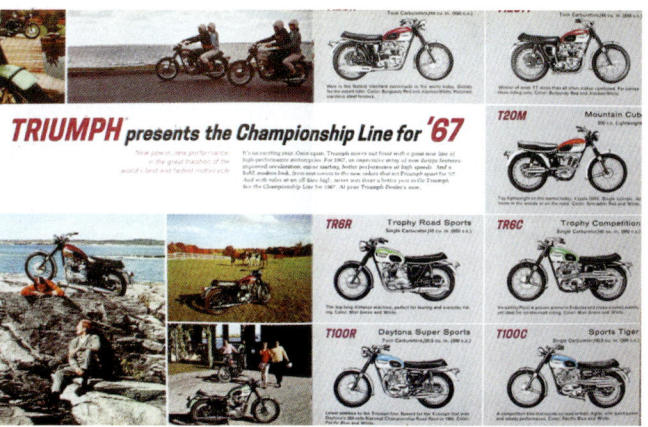

The Back Story

I wanted to find out more about the T100C, so joined the VMCC. The Library was soon able to tell me it was manufactured and assembled at Meriden in December 1967 and shipped to TriCor America, the East Coast distributors of Triumph, for the 1968 model year. I also found out that it was re-imported to Britain in the 1990s and that the gold and cream tank colour is actually from a 1965 model. So either it was a special order (which is possible, as the cooling fins were also painted gold at some point in the bike's life), or it was a replacement tank from an older bike. There is certainly no sign of it having been resprayed from the original '68 colour of Aquamarine. I decided to keep the gold and cream, as it's one of my favourite Triumph colourways.

I also learned what the 'C' suffix meant, the full model name being Triumph Tiger T100C Trophy 500 Competition. Designed at Meriden as a US export model, it has the signature wide bars and high, chromed left side twin pipes, with distinctive heat shields. This original street scrambler design was easily convertible for desert racing, which was very popular at the time in America and a driving market force.

THE NUMBERS GAME

What are the most popular old bikes? How many are on SORN? A new report reveals all.

Early last year (V&C, February 2022) engineer Fred Spaven wrote about the CO2 emissions of old bikes – as you'd expect from Fred, the article was carefully worked out and scientifically rigorous. But he's not the only one who's been thinking about this. A new report – 'Quantifying Classic Motorcycle Emissions' – has just been produced by Loop, an automotive PR company, and has come up with some interesting findings, not just about the carbon footprint of old bikes, but giving a much clearer picture of which bikes we're riding, thanks to detailed stats from our dear old DVLA., amongst other sources.

First off, definitions. Exactly what constitutes a classic vehicle – how old does it have to be? FIVA (the Federation Internationale des Vehicules) reckons anything over 30 years counts as classic, while the DVLA says anything over 40 years old is 'historic' as long as it hasn't been substantially changed for the last 30. As we all know, the VMCC's cut-off has been 25 years since the 1960s. All of these definitions obviously include pre-war, vintage and veteran machines as well.

The Loop report takes FIVA's definition, which adds up to 624,805 old bikes currently registered in the UK, which make up a substantial chunk of all powered two-wheelers on the DVLA database – 31.6% to precise. But of course, more than half of them (nearly 350,000) are on SORN, so the actual on-the-road proportion falls to 14% – our oldies are a minority, albeit a significant one. What really puts it into perspective is looking at the big picture of all vehicles, of whatever age, on UK roads. According to the DVLA, there are nearly 41 million of them, of which old bikes on the road make up just 0.67%. No wonder we're not seen as critical to government transport strategy.

Pop Pickers

Now to the interesting bit. It's probably a reflection of age, but asked to name the most popular classic bike marque, until recently I would have said BSA or Triumph. Wrong, it's Honda, and by a huge margin. There are nearly 36,000 C90s, CB250s and CX500s et al, currently plying British roads – BSA takes the runner-up spot with 28,713.

The reasons aren't hard to find. Since the 1970s (for the last 50 years in other words) Honda have been selling thousands of bikes a year in Britain, whereas the sales of British machines had slowed to a trickle by the mid-'70s, and Triumph's early 1990s revival hasn't worked its way through the system yet. Triumph (of Meriden) takes third place in the top ten most popular classic marques, followed by Lambretta, underlining just how strong the classic scooter scene has been for many years, though oddly Vespa doesn't make it to the top ten.

The other three major Japanese badges fill the fifth, sixth and seventh spots – Yamaha, Suzuki and Kawasaki, in that order – while Norton, BMW and Velocette make up the rest of the top ten. As with Honda, the three Japanese are there

Above: Do you ride a pre-war British bike? The number of survivors is dwarfed by modern classics
Right: Research by FEMA (see page 15) springs few surprises

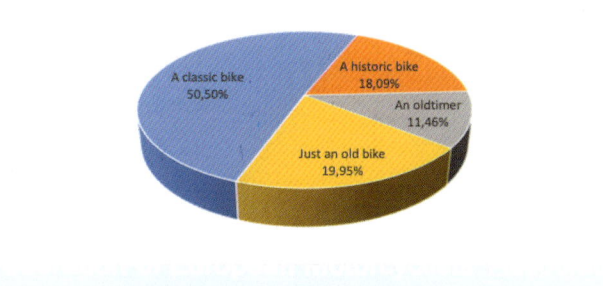

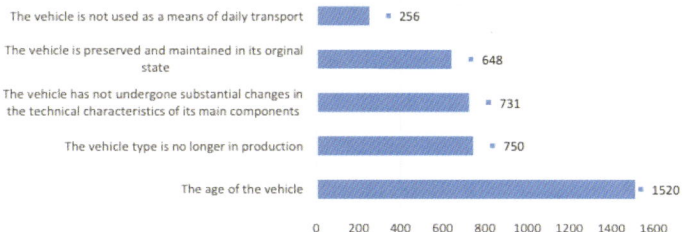

because of big sales over the last 40-50 years, while Norton, BMW and Velocette fans are ensuring that none of 'their' bikes are being scrapped now. Like the Triumphs and Lambrettas, they're all being saved.

But within most popular badges, which are the most numerous models? Hands up who guessed the Honda C90? Clever you – 1278 of Honda's biggest-engined step-through are currently registered for the road, making it Britain's most popular classic two-wheeler. Once again, big sales when new mean a good number are still with us, though of course thousands more C90s will have gone to the great scrapyard in the sky, or been flogged to death as field bikes, until relatively recently. Given the prices they now fetch, it's reasonable to assume that none of the survivors will meet this fate.

Anyway, where were we? Triumph's Bonneville is runner-up (891 on the road, most of them 750cc T140s) while the Tiger, its single-carb cousin, is back in seventh place (457), something else that reflects original sales figures. In between we have the Lambretta GP150 in third place (659) followed by the BMW R80, Honda CB750 and then the VFR750. In eighth is BMW's brick, the K100, with the Lambretta GP200 and Yamaha RD250 in ninth and tenth. As an aside, it's interesting that the RD is the only 250cc bike to make the top ten, which is surprising given that many thousands of 250s were sold in the 1970s and early '80s until learners were restricted to 125s. Maybe, as the ultimate bike for learners (no CBT or any other compulsory training in those days) not many survived... The C90, Lambrettas and RD250 apart, all of the top ten bikes are big 'uns, 650-750cc upwards.

It's worth noting that these figures will not be 100% accurate. Apparently a smattering of Triumph Acclaims and BMW convertibles are recorded by the DVLA as motorbikes... Still, a Bonneville is a Bonneville, right?

Digging deeper into the model specific info, Honda's big hitters are followed by the CBR1000 and 600, with smaller numbers of CB400s, CG125s, XBR500s, C50s and CX500s surviving and licenced for the road. Norton's share is split about equally between 750 and 850 Commandos, and Dominators. Various Kawasaki Zeds also get equal billing and Yamaha's second most popular bike is the XT500. As for BMW, the running order goes: R80, K100, R100, K75 and K1200.

On SORN

When it comes to which bikes are on SORN, there are two interesting differences. All the numbers are bigger, because there are more classic bikes hibernating in garages than ready for the road. This also reflects healthy new motorcycle sales in the late 1970s, peaking at over 300,000 in 1981. Naturally those numbers are dominated by 'modern' classic Japanese bikes, which are far more likely to have been mothballed. Maybe they're not worth restoring/recommissioning just yet, or maybe the generally younger owners have jobs and families keeping them busy.

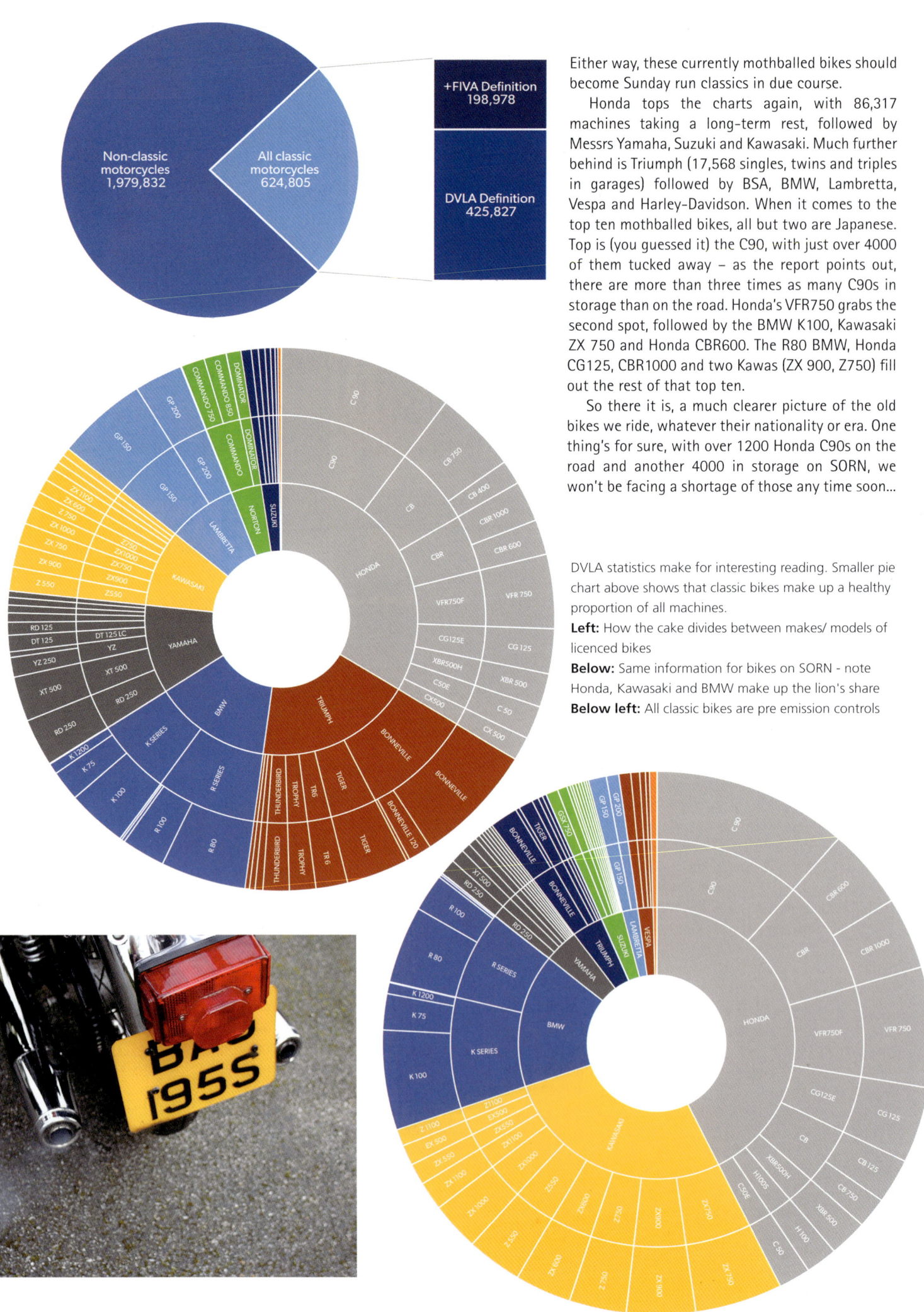

Either way, these currently mothballed bikes should become Sunday run classics in due course.

Honda tops the charts again, with 86,317 machines taking a long-term rest, followed by Messrs Yamaha, Suzuki and Kawasaki. Much further behind is Triumph (17,568 singles, twins and triples in garages) followed by BSA, BMW, Lambretta, Vespa and Harley-Davidson. When it comes to the top ten mothballed bikes, all but two are Japanese. Top is (you guessed it) the C90, with just over 4000 of them tucked away – as the report points out, there are more than three times as many C90s in storage than on the road. Honda's VFR750 grabs the second spot, followed by the BMW K100, Kawasaki ZX 750 and Honda CBR600. The R80 BMW, Honda CG125, CBR1000 and two Kawas (ZX 900, Z750) fill out the rest of that top ten.

So there it is, a much clearer picture of the old bikes we ride, whatever their nationality or era. One thing's for sure, with over 1200 Honda C90s on the road and another 4000 in storage on SORN, we won't be facing a shortage of those any time soon...

DVLA statistics make for interesting reading. Smaller pie chart above shows that classic bikes make up a healthy proportion of all machines.
Left: How the cake divides between makes/ models of licenced bikes
Below: Same information for bikes on SORN - note Honda, Kawasaki and BMW make up the lion's share
Below left: All classic bikes are pre emission controls

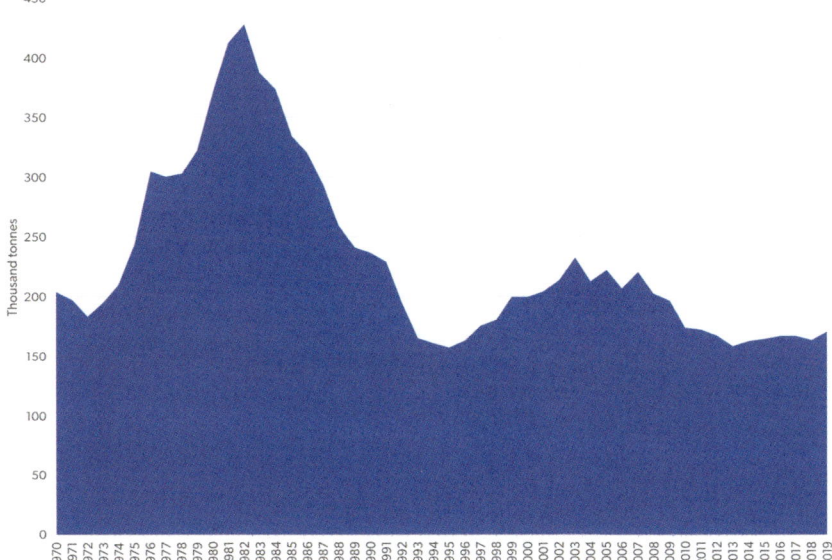

Top: Total fuel use by motorcycles, by year
Above: Total miles ridden by motorcycles, by year
Below: Honda C90 is the most common classic bike, and many are being put to good use

Carbon Footprint

These top tens are all very interesting, but the report's real purpose is to focus on the carbon footprint of classic bikes. And note that's the carbon footprint, measured in CO2e, a collective figure containing all gas emissions (not just CO2) which add to the greenhouse effect, which in turn is causing climate change. It's not a measure of those gases which worsen air quality – carbon monoxide, nitrous oxides, particulates and so on. Motorcycle emissions weren't limited by law until Euro I arrived in 1999 – they've been radically tightened up ever since, and the current standard is Euro 5. Our classic bikes – all of them pre-1999 – will almost inevitably have far dirtier exhausts than modern machines.

Still, that's not what this report is about. By digging into historical data on motorcycle miles travelled and fuel use, the author has come up with a carbon footprint for an average classic bike being ridden for the national average of 700 miles a year (yep, that's all it is). It's 209.9kg CO2e per year. Just to put that in context, add up all classic bike CO2e emissions and they make up 0.05% of all the UK's transport carbon emissions. Great, eh? Except this is a relatively small number of vehicles travelling a mere 700 miles a year, so of course it's a tiny figure – you'd expect nothing else.

On the other hand, take a bike's lifetime carbon emissions into account, and the footprint of old machines looks even smaller. Lifetime emissions include those resulting from its original production as well (known as embodied carbon), and the older a bike is, the smaller this will be per year. So, a flat tank or pioneer machine has less embodied carbon per year than anything younger and their owners can feel accordingly good about their hobby. Unless they trailer the bike to events behind a gas guzzling 4x4. Nothing is simple...

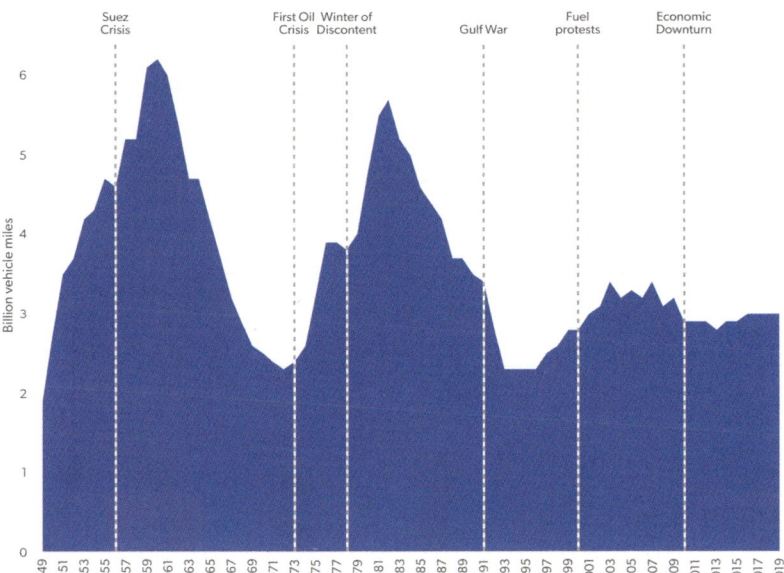

FEMA Survey

Whilst we're in survey mode, here's one by FEMA (Federation of European Motorcyclists), undertaken online in late November last year. And...there were no real surprises. Of the 1614 motorcyclists who responded to the survey (96% of whom were men, average age 56) the vast majority (87%) thought old bikes should be exempt from low or zero emission zones. Just over two-thirds thought the same about MOTs and 71% ticked the same box for road tax. Two-thirds ride less than 1800 miles a year on their oldest bike, and the same proportion have specific classic bike insurance.

Just over half (52.6%) don't ride in winter, though that average hid some big national variations – only one in four French riders take a winter break, but almost 80% of the Swedes (have you seen a Swedish winter?) And finally, 34% of German riders were members of a national motorcyclists organisation, but 57.4% of the Brits – who said we were apathetic?

Travel MANDELLO

Two classic Moto Guzzis make a pilgrimage to the factory – TIM MITCHELL & MARK GREY

Did you know Moto Guzzi is the oldest motorcycle manufacturer in continuous production, dating back to 1921? Each September, the factory at Mandello del Lario, by the shores of Lake Como, opens its doors for the GMG (Giornate Mondiali Guzzi, 'Guzzi World Days') to welcome the Guzzi faithful. There was supposed to be an extra special 100th anniversary celebration in 2021, but due to Covid it was postponed until the following year. Since this was going to be the big one, we were determined to be there on our classic Guzzis.

Each year, university friend Mark and I get week passes from our nearest and dearests for a motorcycle tour. Previously, we've done it on modern bikes and since Mark now lives in Germany, we generally alternate between European and UK tours, sometimes taking in events like the Classic TT or the Spa Classic – otherwise it's all ride, beer & food, sleep, repeat.

Mine's a 1989 Guzzi Le Mans 1000 Mk4 which I've owned since 1990, but recently dressed it up as the retro-styled 1000S. Mark's is an earlier Mk2 from 1979, which he's owned from our university days of the mid-'80s and earlier this year treated to a well-deserved professional engine rebuild after clocking up 60,000 miles. Since both bikes have had recent major overhauls, we took them on a shakedown long weekend in Wales via the Festival of 1000 Bikes at Mallory where several problems were duly found and dealt with.

A classic sports bike doesn't necessarily make the best touring

Opposite page main: Tim's 1989 Le Mans 1000 in touring mode, by the picturesque Lake Brienz
Opposite page inset: Mitchell and Grey channel their inner Fonz at Donington
Right: Fantastic scenery on the road to Mandello
Below: Fish eye view of one of those hairpins – required Guzzi riding technique

machine, and we'd be away for six days, so we were going to need to carry luggage (and tools...). Rummaging around in the loft revealed an old set of leather panniers (complete with a 1986 IoM TT sticker!), plus a tank bag of similar vintage that I could strap onto the pillion seat. Comfort on all-day rides was going to need dealing with but, with an inflatable seat cushion on top of the well-padded Guzzi seat, my legs ended each day in much less pain that they could have done. We'd be using my phone to navigate with, so I wired in a USB socket to keep the phone charged and a handlebar mount to hold the phone in place.

Were we worried about the bikes breaking down? Well not really – the Guzzi V-twins are low tech and solidly built, so mechanical failure is rare and any problems are usually fixable with a basic toolkit. Electrical problems are a bit more common, so a multimeter and battery booster pack were packed just in case.

Forward Base Camp

It's over 800 miles from my home near Cambridge to Mandello, probably a good three days ride each way. Even though I'd taken this bike across Europe a couple of times previously, that was 30 years ago, when my lanky legs folded onto the quite cramped Guzzi's footrests a lot more easily than they do now. I really didn't fancy such a long ride this time, so we cheated a bit. I was planning a family holiday in the French Alps, so combined the two and trailed the bike to "forward base camp" at the ski resort of Les Gets in the north-western Alps. After a few trial runs around the beautiful Route des Grandes Alpes, I was ready to start the ride to Mandello, via central Switzerland where I was to meet up with Mark.

Despite having done several European tours previously, we'd not really ridden much in Switzerland, partly because it's so expensive but mainly because we tend to ride our modern bike tours at a 'brisk' pace and the penalties for speeding in Switzerland are particularly severe. This time, at the more leisurely pace of classic bikes, this was going to much less of a problem, so we took the opportunity to take in plenty of Swiss roads, and particularly the high mountain passes.

Day 1: Les Gets to Brienz – 135 miles

This was fairly straightforward, starting off with a ride round the Portes du Soleil ski resorts to the Swiss border at Chatel, cross

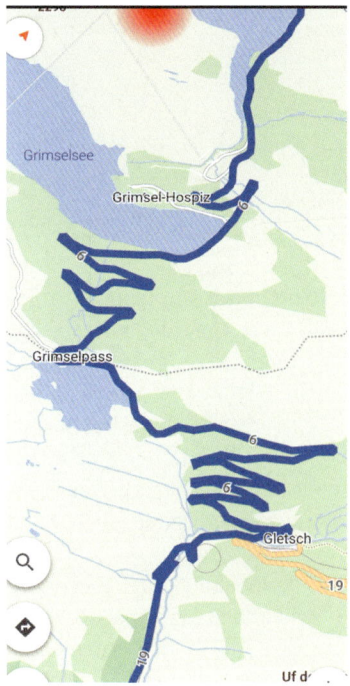

Above: View from the Furka pass – Grimsel pass on the right, Neufenen round the corner to the left
Left: One reason why they enjoyed the trip
Below: Up in the clouds, on the San Bernadino pass
Below right: Between passes, on the way back to Brienz
Opposite page left: Tim and The Master (Carlo Guzzi)
Opposite page right: Celebrity ride-in – that's Ewan McGregor on the Mandello

as its torquey engine and tall gearing are perfect for medium-fast distance riding. The rumble of the engine on acceleration followed by the resonant boom on the overrun, all combined with the tapping beat of the valve gear, create a great aural accompaniment to the spectacular scenery and really let you ride in the flow.

After a bit of a slow but scenic chug round Lakes Thun and Brienz, I arrived in good time for a beer or two before dinner. Mark turned up soon after I did – from his home near Stuttgart, he'd ridden south on the famous Schwarzwald Hochstrasse (Black Forest high road) to the Swiss border, then cross country to Lucerne followed by a climb over the Brunig pass into Brienz.

The family-run hotel we stayed in (the Alpenrose, in the village of Hofstetten) couldn't have been more welcoming. "I like young men, old motorbikes and ooh, the smell of your leather jacket," said the matriarch in her German-accented English. Even though we're not "young men" any more, she and the rest of her family and staff were fabulous hosts.

Day 2: Brienz to Bellano – 175 miles

This was going to be a longer day's ride and much more technical, taking in several passes over 2000 metres with loads of tight hairpin bends on each side. The overnight rain had stopped and the skies were clearing, but the roads were still damp, so we set off cautiously. First up was the Grimsel pass, at 2165 metres, and quite cold at the top even in early September. Seven hairpins in quick succession took us down to the head of an isolated valley, with the Furka pass on one side (which we left for the return journey) and our route to the Nufenen pass following the valley. With mountains rising up on all sides and the zig zags of roads

the river Rhone at the eastern end of Lake Geneva, then it's one road all the way to Lake Thun, which connects with Lake Brienz via the imaginatively named town of Interlaken. That road (no. 11) runs along a series of river valleys, with nice open sweeping bends connecting small villages and ski resorts, with picturesque mountains either side and not much in the way of traffic.

It's easy to get into a nice rhythm riding a big Guzzi twin,

the only signs of habitation, it looked like we'd ridden to the end of the world!

By the time we got over the Nufenen pass (2480m, the highest point on our trip) our hairpin technique was well and truly honed. These Guzzis are long and slow steering, built for high-speed stability rather than agile cornering, so were a bit of a handful. But their linked brakes let us control our speed with the foot pedal (that also operates one of the front discs) making steering a lot easier, and the chugging engine pulls through in pretty much any gear, so we could get into a nice rhythm of braking, pitching into the bend, looking right up through the exit (the essential tip for hairpins!) and powering out. By then, the sun was out and the roads dry, so it was warmer in the valleys but still cold, with snow in places, at the tops of the passes.

Since we were on the only road in the area, traffic was quite heavy with several lorries or buses to contend with. On modern bikes, with their power and instant response, it would have been easy to bang in the overtakes even between the tightest harpin sections, but it was a bit trickier on the big Guzzis. They have flywheels the size of manhole covers, so take a while to spin up, and gearchanges that are about as slick as a dumper truck's, so overtaking requires a lot of forward planning. Fortunately, though, there were short sections of road resurfacing works every few miles with alternating single-file traffic. Normally, this would be a bit of a pain, but for us it meant that we could get to the head of a line of stationary traffic and enjoy clear roads until the next set of works.

A couple more passes – San Bernadino and then Splugen, with its numbered hairpins (there's over 50 of them!) – led us down to Lake Como and Bellano, our base for the weekend, just 10 miles along the lakeside from Mandello. We'd booked an apartment built into the hillside, a short walk from Bellano's lakeside centre, with spectacular views over the town and lake from its balcony.

Days 3 & 4: Mandello del Lario

The plan was to ride the 10 miles alongside the lake to Mandello and as soon as the traffic gridlocked (an estimated 60,000 Guzzisti were expected, six times the town's usual population!), dive off into a side road to find somewhere to park. And it pretty much worked. Loads of bikes, nearly all Guzzis, were heading there with us but it didn't jam up until we were quite close. We managed to find a side street to park in that was only a few minutes' walk from the town centre where the factory is situated. Queues in the hot sun to get into the factory site were round the block and seemed to be moving at a snail's pace, so we gave that a miss and instead wandered around the rest of the attractions that were laid on – display tents of Guzzis old and new, including two of the famous V8 racers, the statue of Carlo Guzzi, a big selection of pop-up bars and eating places, plus all the bikes, parked in any available space, that people had ridden in on.

The next day (Sunday), we took the train in so that we could enjoy a beer or two. By early afternoon, the queues for the factory site had pretty much gone, so we were able to walk straight in and spend a very enjoyable few hours wandering around the production lines and famous wind tunnel. The current models were also on display, along with the new V100 Mandello, which looks as good in real life as it does in pictures.

Days 5 & 6: Bellano to Les Gets via Brienz – 325 miles

The ride back was very similar to the ride there, except that we turned right instead of left at Splugen and returned to Brienz via the Oberal and Furka passes. The weather was fine, just a bit chilly high up, the scenery was stunning and the roads were great – it's easy to get used to such amazing conditions! By then, riding the Guzzis was second nature and we quickly settled into a fast flowing rhythm. The miles just seemed to disappear, and we were surprised by how soon we found ourselves back in Brienz. We enjoyed the same warm welcome at the Alpenrose and parted ways the next morning, with Mark heading north to Stuttgart and me west to Les Gets.

So...

Can you enjoy a touring holiday on classic bikes? In a word, "yes". We had just as much fun as we do on modern bikes, and nothing went wrong. Of course, the pace is a bit slower and we missed the comfort and overtaking ability of modern bikes (and I missed the hard panniers on my Tiger!), but we just planned fewer miles each day. And Switzerland is perfect for this type of tour, where the roads are well suited to the pace of older bikes and the scenery is fantastic. Shame it's so expensive!

Overall, I reckon this trip ranked very highly compared to our previous ones. Although we did fewer miles on fewer riding days, it was more of a challenge on the older bikes. We completed our pilgrimage to Mandello and enjoyed a great adventure. Will we do a similar trip again? I'm pretty sure we will!

BANBURY for Beginners

Ever wanted to ride the Banbury Run but didn't know where to start? PETER JACKSON is your guide
Photos: Kevin Gunstone

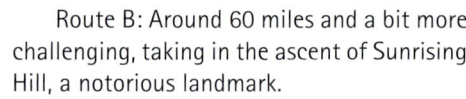

The Banbury Run – the largest gathering of pre-1931 motorcycles and three-wheelers in the world – has been running for many years. Taking in some of the prettiest Cotswold villages and countryside, it is run mostly over country lanes with a few main roads used to connect it all together. The 2022 event was the 72nd in a long series designed to test and showcase the reliability of pre-1931 motorcycles and the skill of their riders, and with up to 500 machines taking part, it is recognised as the leading event of its type worldwide. Last year's Banbury saw some changes in the organisation and a fair number of new riders, so whether you are an old salt or a beginner these notes may help you better understand this great event.

Timed or Untimed?

The first thing to say is that there is a choice between being a timed or an untimed entry. If you choose to be untimed then much of the following does not apply and you can simply set off at your own pace, complete your chosen route at your own pace and even stop for some light refreshment on the way around. If however you choose to be a timed entry then you need to know about Classes, Routes and Concessions, as detailed on the entry form.

Classes

These simply define the age group of your machine. Each class has an allocated average speed as follows.

 Class A: Veteran pre-1915 (average 15mph).
 Class A1: Veteran pre-1915 (av. 18mph).
 Class B: Early Vintage 1915-1924 (av. 20mph).
 Class C: Late Vintage 1925-1930 (av. 24mph).

Routes

These have the same letter designation as class and are designed to be suitable for the type of machine in that class.

 Route A: Around 40 miles and avoids steep hills.
 Route B: Around 60 miles and a bit more challenging, taking in the ascent of Sunrising Hill, a notorious landmark.
 Route C: Similar to Route B but up to 70 miles in length.

The particulars of the routes are not disclosed until the morning of the event. Untimed riders still need to specify a class on the entry form to ensure that they get a route sheet suitable for their needs when signing on.

Concessions

These seem to cause more confusion than anything else, but they are simply a means of allowing a rider to opt for a route more suitable to them or their machine regardless of its age. It is important to note that for timed riders, it is their chosen class which defines the route that they will ride, which will also have the same letter designation. They will maintain the average speed appropriate to the class normally allocated to that route.

Thus a rider of an early vintage machine opting to enter in Class A1 will ride route A and maintain a speed of 18mph – the rider of a veteran machine opting to enter in Class B will ride route B and maintain a speed of 20mph.

The concessions are as follows.
 1: A rider over 60 years of age may enter any class, on any event qualifying machine.
 2: Any rider may enter a class higher than their machine age eligibility.
 3: All riders of machines of 250cc or less, or of any sidecar combination or three-wheeler, may enter one class lower than their machine age eligibility.

Armed with all this information, filling in the entry form should be a doddle.

Maps & Checkpoints

In short, the whole event is arranged around a regularity run. As a rider, you are marshalled to the start from Gaydon at your allotted time and then follow the route sheet given to you when you sign in. Your job is to try and maintain the average speed

There is plenty of time to wander the paddock afterwards

appropriate to your entry with the aid of a watch, speedometer (if you have one), and whatever natural sense of speed you may possess. Other high tech aids are not allowed and outside assistance (other than a push and a bit of spannering) are also not allowed.

To make matters more interesting you will come across at least two checkpoints on the way where you will be timed and have your card marked, hopefully within the margins allowed to qualify for a gold or silver award (3 minutes early to 5 minutes late for gold and 3 minutes early to 15 minutes late for a silver). These time checkpoints are not marked on the route sheet so be prepared to come across one at any time! The final time check is at the finish back at Gaydon and you should note that the final mileage is not disclosed either.

You might gain some clues by examining the maps of the route displayed at the signing-in tent –people have various ways of working out how they will meet their target. But that's all part of the fun and adds to the sense of achievement if you finally make it within your target. Ordnance Survey Landranger Map 151 covers the area of the run.

The Gaydon site has camping facilities for those wishing to stay overnight and this is certainly an advantage if you have an early start and want to get organised in good time for your start.

Bikes are displayed both before and after the event for the public to view and for the judges to examine for concours awards. An autojumble and entrance to the Motor Museum are added attractions for those not actively involved in riding, so why not come along and enjoy a day out amongst the old bikes?

Classes in Full

Class A: Veteran. Machines manufactured before 1st January 1915
Average speed 15mph = 4 minutes per Mile.

Class A1: Veteran. Machines manufactured before 1st January 1915
Average speed 18mph = 3.33 minutes per Mile.

Class B: Early Vintage. Machines manufactured between 1915 and 1st January 1925.
Average speed 20mph = 3 minutes per Mile.

Class C: Late Vintage. Machines manufactured between 1925 and 1st January 1931.
Average speed 24mph. = 2½ minutes per Mile.

One of the following three concessions, which are not available to team entries, can be requested on the Entry Form.
1. Riders of 60 years of age or over may enter any class irrespective of age of machine.
2. Riders may enter any class higher than the machine's eligibility.
3. Riders of machines of 250cc or less and any sidecar combinations or three-wheelers may enter one class lower than the machine's age eligibility.

GORDON PRIME
Celebration Run
16th April 2023

Gordon Prime, who has just passed away aged 98, was a despatch rider during World War II, and in October last year launched 'Bash On Regardless', a book about his experiences. A friend to the charity Age Cymru Dyfed over many years, Gordon was also interviewed for the West Wales Veterans Archive, an award-winning digital archive held at the National Library of Wales, Aberystwyth. At the launch of his book, Gordon briefly described his despatch rider experiences to a large assembled audience, and also of his ambition to see a memorial to despatch riders installed in the National Memorial Arboretum.

This sentiment resonated with those of us involved in organising the Duty to Ride (DTR) initiative. Although DTR is not funded by the VMCC and not part of the Club, it was felt that, as an organisation whose founder and many early members were themselves despatch riders, we do have a role to play in helping to launch the fund and to promote Duty to Ride amongst our members and to the wider motorcycling community.

The Duty to Ride appeal was launched last May to raise funds to create a permanent memorial at the National Memorial Arboretum to honour those despatch riders and couriers, both military and civilian, who had lost their lives whilst riding in the course of their duties.

Although the VMCC has been instrumental in launching this appeal it was always envisaged to be of interest to riders of all ages on all types of machines from all over the world. Any opportunity to raise awareness is welcomed and so when we heard about Gordon Prime and his desire to see a memorial dedicated to DRs, it seemed obvious to organise some event that would recognise his achievements and generate media attention for both Duty to Ride and the VMCC.

Gordon Prime Pembroke Run

Hence the Gordon Prime Memorial Run, organised by the VMCC for both members and non-members including, by preference, military bikes of the period through the beautiful Pembroke countryside. The route will include a parade past the care home where Gordon lived until recently. The date of Sunday April 16th 2023 was chosen, being of special significance to Gordon. It was on this day in 1945 that his closest colleague and friend was killed only weeks before the end of the war.

The ride will start and finish at Carew Cheriton Control Tower Museum, Carew Airfield, Carew, Pembrokeshire SA70 8SX – there is plenty of parking for vans and trailers and overnight camping in caravans and camper vans. The route is being planned by Jim Codd of the West South Wales section and details will be available on both the VMCC Duty to Ride website. The provisional route is to Chapel Bay Fort via Castle Martin, Stackpole, Freshwater West, Manorbier, Tenby, back towards Milton, then back to the start/finish.

We are hoping for a good turnout of predominantly period bikes and hope to have press coverage from local newspapers, radio and television. The event will start at 11am with one minute's silence and playing of the Last Post at Carew Cheriton Control Tower.

Spectators are welcome and can enjoy visiting the museum as well at marvelling at the array of machines taking part. Donations can be made on Just Giving.

Help Needed

We are looking for help to organise this event, ideally from people already in the area and other local groups – British Legion, Military Camps, Motorcycle Clubs etc. to participate and support the event, media coverage (local TV/Radio, newspapers etc.) local dignitaries (Mayor etc.)

Photo courtesy Western Telegraph

More Information
www.vmcc.net
www.dutytoride.org
www.carewcheritoncontroltower.co.uk

Northamptonshire Navigation Rally

Want to ride this Rally in September? WILL CURRY gives a taste of last year's event Photos: Edwin Webb

The aim of the Navigation Rally is to visit a number of checkpoints in Northants, answering questions to prove you've got there. The number of required checkpoints you have to visit depends upon the age of your motorcycle – my 1929 Ariel (Vintage class) had to make 10 unmanned checkpoints and one manned, while a Late Classic class bike (1971-1997) would have to tick off 14 unmanned checks and three manned.

The rally attracts all sorts of bikes and riders from far and wide, and in 2022 nearly half of the 30 entrants came, like me, from outside the Northants Section. I've done several now and enjoyed all of them. Part of the enjoyment is in the preparation – the checkpoint locations are sent out in advance so there is plenty of time to plan a route, though I always take the appropriate OS maps on the day to help with the inevitable unexpected road closures or navigation errors. I rode 130 miles last year, though with lots of stops – you'll have to start the bike many times during the day.

Finding the actual checkpoints can be trickier than it seems – one memorial in a village was hidden amongst three large sycamores. And despite the careful route sheet preparation there were a couple of occasions where the road didn't agree with the route sheet I'd prepared, and that's where the OS maps come in useful. It's worth keeping an eye on the weather forecast too. It was for dry and warm last year, which was true until rain arrived at the penultimate checkpoint. On went my overtrousers, which had no grip on the saddle. I slipped and wriggled uncomfortably while getting hotter and hotter in the non-breathable plastic. Definitely a case of the wrong trousers.

Top: Colin Durnall's well travelled Red Panther – broke down a mile before the start, but he fixed it, did the event and rode home

Above: Edwin Webb's 250cc Morini V-twin topped the Late Classics

There was no award for me in 2022 except a good day out, but others did gain awards. Richard Stone (1929 Velocette KN) bagged the Vintage Cup while Edwin Webb (1980 Moto Morini 2c 250) was awarded the Northamptonshire Challenge Cup for best performance on a Late Classic. Other award winners included John Lourie and his 1925 BSA Round Tank 250, who together got the A. Jed Cup for the greatest combined age of rider and machine. Alison Chew (Triumph Speed Twin outfit) bagged the Alan Burman Memorial Trophy.

So, would I recommend the Northamptonshire Navigation Rally to a friend? Yes, I'd recommend it to anyone!

Alison Chew and Speed Twin outfit won the sidecar/three-wheeler award

Northamptonshire Navigation Rally 2023
Date: Sunday 3rd September 2023
Full details from: Trevor Pinfold
email trevorpinfold168@btinternet.com

Belgian FUN

JOHN BOTTOMLEY took his Yamaha TR3 replica to Spa for the Bikers Classic

Back in 2018 I submitted an article on my project to build a circa 1972 350cc TR3 Yamaha. Over the years I've been fortunate to take part in a few events on the continent – all have more than lived up to expectations. I had always wanted to take part in the Bikers Classic at SPA, but until I built the Yamaha, I didn't really have a suitable bike to ride.

Having ridden the Yamaha briefly in 2018 I entered it for the 2019 Bikers Classic, which was fantastic. So of course I entered for 2020, only to see the UK and Europe go into lockdown with Covid. The Classic was cancelled, and the organisers wouldn't issue a refund but did offer a voucher for the 2021 event.

Meanwhile, I reflected that the one thing which needed improving on the Yamaha was its front brake. The RD 350 front disc is an excellent brake for a road bike, but on the limit at racing speeds, especially on what is a very fast circuit. With the bike performing so well I decided that it was worth investing in a replica 260mm four-leading shoe Yamaha brake that the original TR3 would have been equipped with.

I soon found that there were none around, and the only supplier was Buda Racing in Hungary. I was in luck, they only had one left and had no plans, due to the uncertainties of Covid, to make any more. I paid a 50% deposit, had them build it into a wheel, and just before lockdown hit they finished the wheel and asked for the balance of the cost prior to shipment.

A couple of days after lockdown I received an order confirmation of shipment with a tracking number. All seemed in order and it was possible to track the parcel to an international forwarding centre in Hungary...but then nothing. Worried that I had made an expensive mistake, I chased Buda by phone but they confirmed it was in transit and I had to be patient. Sure enough, after a further couple of weeks I received an email confirming my package was due for delivery by a local UK courier – it was,

Left: Spa is a fast and exciting circuit

Paddock transport was a varied bunch
Below: 4LS front drum fitted and ready to go

to say the least, quite a relief. It turned out that in the early days of Covid it was taking days for courier companies to drive across Europe due to the many and changing conditions.

Green Light

So I had my wheel, but then the work started. The brake arms were fabricated in stainless, which is never easy to form, bend or drill. I decided to make up the cables and all the fittings, in total having to fabricate 30 pieces, which was time consuming but well worth the effort. It was a cleverly designed brake and pleasing on the eye, so although we were still in lockdown I couldn't wait to try it out.

Fortunately I had the chance to use the bike at a Brooklands track day at Castle Combe in 2020 and then at the VMCC 75th Anniversary at Cadwell in '21. This was sufficient to bed in the new linings and realise what a powerful piece of kit this was. Complete with brake, the wheel weighs around 8 kilos and what it has done is give the bike a more planted feel. I have not managed to get it to fade, which was always one of the weaknesses of drum brakes. I was really hoping Spa would go ahead so I could give it my ultimate test.

Finally with restrictions lifting, the 2022 event was confirmed and payment with my 2020 voucher was still possible. The organisers had reduced the event to a two-day track day format with the same amount of riding time on track. There was no endurance racing, though there was a two-day enduro and a trial. The ride around the old circuit was replaced with four laps of the track for anyone who wanted to do that – you simply had to collect a sticker from race control.

Signed On

The journey to Spa was uneventful, apart from customs (see box out) and having arrived we were directed into a holding field until the welcome centre opened. Walking up to it I was greeted by a Yorkshire accent – it was Mick Seward, who I used to ride enduros with ten plus years ago…the motorcycling fraternity is a small world.

Once signed on and equipped with a welcome pack, race number, and transponder it was off to the paddock, another 2-3km away. Getting settled in the paddock can be a bit of a pushing and shoving match but with fewer riders and three differing groups it worked out quite easily. We were next to a German amateur racing team – Red Hot Racing – and in the second level of the paddock so reasonably close to the fast food stalls, bars and toilets. Scrutineering turned out to be a low key affair starting at 5pm. Following UK practice I put my leathers on and was fortunately near the front of the queue. It turned out I was the only person in leathers as all they were interested in was that I had a helmet and leathers. With the scrutineer's yellow sticker on the front number plate and the transponder fitted we were good to go tomorrow.

The Briefing

Saturday dawned with a clear blue sky and the prospect of ideal riding conditions with temperatures in the range 28-30 deg C. This concerned me a little as it was hotter than 2019 and with a track elevation change of 300 feet I was apprehensive about the jetting, which had been troublesome last time – I was right.

The next challenge was the briefing, split into two (200-rider) sessions, carried out by the clerk of the course in four languages, but all very logical and important. Due to the length and accessibility to the track, in the event of incidents they send emergency vehicles onto the track in either direction, riders being given a yellow flag warning on the trackside TV screens, augmented by the marshals waving a yellow flag at each marshalling station. You are obliged to slow in response or risk exclusion from the meeting, and be aware that a service vehicle may be driving towards you or behind you.

The transponders were there to not just provide lap times, but give the organisers info to marshal us into groups of similar speeds after the first two rides. I was allocated a group number (with a sticker for the numberplate), and looking at this I realised why it was important – the lap speeds ranged from 80kph to 150kph! Not only were there some serious guys on the track, but the Spa circuit is just over 7km long and has 20 corners. I was in the middle of the slowest group, which I was very pleased with. The quick boys were mainly on the younger and larger machines of 750-1000 cc capacity.

The final piece of the briefing was a helmet sticker to be placed on the front of the chin guard so that one person could monitor a double row of riders entering the track via the pit lane.

The Yamaha ran reasonably well in the mornings and the carburation was OK, allowing me to pull 9000rpm in 6th gear down the two long straights. Later in the day it wasn't so good and I reduced the main jet by 10 to 250 – I was nervous about going weaker, but this improved things. Part of the problem was advice from people who had raced TR3s back in the day – that was to keep it on the boil through the gears, or in the vernacular 'rev the nuts off it', because the Yamaha two-stroke will not be damaged by revs. I must admit I have found this difficult to put into practice, as I grew up with old bikes that you had to treat with some respect to avoid catastrophic failures. Also, I am not getting any younger and when my gear ratio spread shows 125mph at 9000rpm in sixth gear it does sort of focus the mind.

Above: Yamaha ran well and gave John a good two days at Spa
Left: Drum brake plus fittings wasn't cheap but well worth fitting
Opposite: Ready for the next run, in the cool of a pit garage.

Reflections on Spa

My investment in the new front brake was a great decision, well worth the investment both aesthetically and performance wise. As for Spa, it is described as the most beautiful circuit in the world, which is not an overstatement. The setting is incredible and the sheer size of the track, both in length and width plus the trackside warning flag screens, make it quite a spectacle. Then there's the variety of corners, all of which are fast and flowing, each presenting differing challenges – it takes some time to get into one's head.

Out of the whole circuit, I have to single out Eau Rouge. This is an incredible experience. You charge down past the old pits and take the slight left hander into the uphill right hander at whatever warp speed you dare, coming out at Radillon on to the long straight. 'I got away with that,' you think, before getting your head down for a nearly mile-long stretch of straight tarmac.

The Bikers Classic is well organised, and the atmosphere in the paddock is hard to describe. It buzzes, but it's also relaxed, with no enforcement of rules like wearing helmets, and pit bikes of all sizes and configuration ridden by all. In fact, you must have your wits about you when walking around. Friendly banter, with English as the common language, and riders helping each other regardless of nationality – I had some useful discussions about carburation with the German team next to us.

It's good for spectators too, with easy access to the pits and the pit lane for all, plus of course unlimited supplies of Belgian chips and mayonnaise. In summary, if you want a real bucket list experience then look at Bikers Classic Spa in August for both riders and spectators – I'm sure you would enjoy it.....hopefully I will be there too.

After the event, we decided to avoid the usual mad dash home, stopping in Ghent for a night. I had never been before because like many people I always aimed for Bruges. Ghent is just as scenic with a 10th century castle and a large undergraduate community with more bicycles than you can imagine in a traffic-free city centre (the Spa paddock is good training when on foot...). Definitely worth a visit.

Want to Go?

All information for riders and spectators at bikersclassics.be/en/

Brexit Borders?

So I was booked for the 2022 Bikers Classic, but post-Brexit would I be able to take the Yamaha with me? It appeared that the only way to take non-registered race bikes to Europe was with a carnet with all its costs and bureaucracy. However, it emerged that it was possible to register race bikes with DVLA and make a declaration that they were only for off-road (highway) use. It was then possible to obtain a Q plate number and a V5/C registration document which should be acceptable to the French customs. This had been successful for others, so I decided to go down this route.

With bikes loaded (I took my 250 Ducati as a spare and to ride in the mass parade) I set off with some trepidation to catch an early shuttle. All was well checking in and going through the English and French customs but then I was waved into a side area. Seeing my two shiny, new Q Plates and a van full of the usual stuff one has to carry, the customs officer asked the usual questions: were the bikes mine? (Yes); is all the gear yours? (Yes); did you pack it all yourself? (Yes). He told me to drive the van over to another lane which had a channel running along its left-hand side, leave it running, in neutral with the handbrake off and walk through an adjacent gate.

I took a double take to confirm I had heard correctly. But the van then started to move forwards, and I realised the front nearside wheel was being pulled along the channel. We walked to the exit gate of the lane and were greeted by the customs officer who confirmed that they had just X rayed the van ..... everything was OK. He apologised for the delay and suggested I drove to the front of the boarding queue.

With some relief we jumped into the van and were on our way. Thankfully that was the only hold up we had on the journey – coming back no one was interested in what was in the van, so all the effort in registering the bikes either paid off or was not necessary. Not sure which, but at least I felt good that it had worked. If not I would have had something to argue with them about before they impounded the bikes!

On The Hammer

What's up, what's down? IAN KERR looks at recent auction trends and GEOFF MCGLADDERY reports on two sales

Looking back over the second half of 2022 since my last appraisal of classic motorcycle auctions, the results have been as diverse as usual. In most cases the vast majority of machines are sold on the hammer with a few being sold just after, leaving just a very small number of bikes unsold at the end of the day.

Certainly when you compare the prices achieved, they do tend to be better than those appearing on a well-known on-line auction site, with many machines advertised there not seeming to reach the reserve. In many cases the reserves are unrealistic (too high) and the same bikes keep reappearing, often lowering the starting price before disappearing altogether when the seller gives up.

In professional auctions, it would seem an increasing number of the bids are made by phone and on-line rather than in person. Many of course are now overseas buyers taking advantage of the weak pound in comparison to their own currency, which also provides good business for the motorcycle shipping business. The downside is that some historic machines are lost to these shores forever.

Bonhams underlined the trend, reporting that their October Stafford Sale had bidders from 29 countries taking part. Whilst you would expect these to include European and American bidders, residents in Canada, India and South Africa are now entering the collectors' world.

But it's not just British bikes going overseas. This a two-way process with many dealers and private individuals shipping bikes bought cheaply abroad and offering them for sale here at auction, hopefully making a tidy profit.

Barn Finds & Racers

Barn finds continue to be highly sought after. Despite being offered as found, leaving the buyer to shoulder the time and cost of restoration, many of these are reaching prices not far short of what you would pay for a running example in reasonably rideable

Top: Mixed bunch of classics – Ducati 916, monkey bike and Triumph Hurricane, all eminently biddable
Above: Auctions offer plenty of choice
Below: Barn finds can be worth as much as rideable bikes

Left: Projects hold a fatal fascination for some, hence their healthy prices

Right: One end of the scale – 1936 Brough Superior SS100 outfit being sold by Charterhouse at Haynes Museum, 30th March. Estimated price: £260,000-£280,000

condition. Anybody who has completed a restoration will tell you that costs have gone through the roof, often leaving them heavily out of pocket when selling. If these projects are being bought for some sort of shed therapy, then so be it. Either way, if you have a project you are unlikely to complete, it seems the best place to get top dollar is at an auction!

There is also is a trend for collections coming onto the market – some small, others quite large and specialised. Take the Forshaw Collection of 31 speedway motorcycles, sold by the family after 25 years on display at the Haynes Motor Museum, and auctioned by Bonhams in October. This represented six decades of machines collected by the late enthusiast, engineer and former speedway rider Richard Forshaw, who clearly knew what he was collecting, as shown by the prices attained.

Grabbing the headlines was an American 500cc OHV Crocker hand-built speedway machine which made a staggering £126,500. A 1929 498cc Scott Dirt Track machine also made a very healthy £25,150, while a 1939 500 Excelsior-JAP, doubled its pre-sale estimate to sell for £18,400.

Competition machines from all disciplines always sell well, especially if they have some provenance, like the 1956 Jawa 500cc DOHC Grand Prix bike (one of only four made) which sold at the same sale. Offered with a top estimate of £18,000, when the hammer finally fell it made £88,550.

Silverstone Auctions held their final sale at the combined car and motorcycle show at the NEC in November and had three Dresdas all sell for reasonable money, as did the 1954 500 MSS Velocette Scrambler – believed to be the oldest one in existence – which made £7650. A Royal Enfield 175cc OHC factory prototype seemed quite cheap at £4612, as did a few other unusual machines.

Uppers & Downers

Away from the mainstream, monkey bikes are becoming collectable and making good money, and as I reported last time, Vespa and Lambretta scooters are also selling well, gaining big numbers at the H&H auctions run at the National Motorcycle Museum.

The memorabilia and collectables segment continues to be steady, with items from well-known names making the largest sums, as you might expect. That brings us back to the mainstream market. Brough Superiors and Vincents are still selling well at decent money, although the Vincent Comet seems to be dropping to a more realistic £10,000 bracket.

Triumph twins have also dropped, but not as much as BSA twins, which in some cases are selling as cheaply as AMC and Ariel singles. It's a different story for singles from the Triumph and BSA factories, with prices rising quite steeply.

Small lightweight Japanese bikes are still on the up as people

Above: One of the Canadian import BSA singles (this one a B44) handled by HJ Pugh

Right: One of three Dresdas – this one a T500 Suzuki – recently sold by Silverstone

seek an electric foot to deal with ageing bones, and the Kawasaki Z900 seems to be the one to have if you are looking for a larger machine, with quite high prices being achieved for mint restored items.

As you might expect, any trends that cause prices to rise tends to get people looking elsewhere. Big Italian bikes are creeping up in value, but that didn't seem to put off bidders for a particularly rare Ducati. Even given that 2022 was the 50th anniversary of Paul Smart winning the Imola 200, I don't think anyone would have predicted the final sale result on a 1974 round case 750SS that the factory sold after that win.

Built from the DNA of Smart's bike, this immaculate machine may have been cosseted in a private collection and looked not far short of concours, but many thought that Bonhams pre-sale estimate of £140,000-160,000 was very optimistic.

It was actually slightly the other way, with the bike finding a new owner for £172,500, with bidding coming from all directions, just proving that despite a general tightening of belts, the classic market is still buoyant and that the best prices are still being gained at auction!

Ian Kerr MBE

Photos: Thanks to the following auction houses - Silverstone, Bonhams, Charterhouse and HJ Pugh. And Roger Fogg for the seatless barn find Triumph

Reports from the Floor

H&H Auction – National Motorcycle Museum – 7th December 2022

More than 200 classic machines came under the hammer in this excellent auction. The morning session, dedicated to scooters, met with variable results, with plenty of unsold lots mixing it with some spectacular and often surprising 'big ticket' sales. To give it some perspective, three of the top ten prices of the day were paid for scooters, all of them Lambretta 200 derivatives. Top scooter price of £21,746 was paid for a superb 1963 Lambretta TV200 (GT200). It had everything going for it, a superb and highly accurate restoration with correct numbers and detailed history from new.

Despite sky-high prices on premium models there were still some bargains to be had. An immaculate 1956 Lambretta LD150 Mk2 Tradesman with its Steib combination cost just £4012. Two 'project' Dayton Albatross models each made an identical £944 and would surely keep their new owners in their respective sheds for the rest of the winter (and more!)

The afternoon session, reserved for motorcycles, proved fascinating, with a mix of surprisingly high prices, plenty of bargains and a good sprinkling of 'unsolds'. Let's start with the high prices, and top price of the day – £100,480 paid for a rare 1973 MV Agusta, one of only 583 750S models built. When it was new, MV were at the top of their game, but they were already being challenged in road-going machinery by Honda's game changing CB750 four and Kawasaki's DOHC Z1. Whilst not cheap, these two machines brought ownership of the hitherto unobtainable four cylinders with the reach of mere mortals. There wasn't much to choose between the CB750, Z900 and the MV in performance, but prices were a different story, and in fact the differential has widened. When new, the MV cost four times more than the Honda, but that gap has now widened to a chasm. While that '73 MV went for six figures, a '73 CB750, in excellent condition with V5C and correct numbers, reached just £6495. A Z1 Kawasaki from the same year made £18,880.

In fact, good Japanese machinery seemed to be in abundance at the auction. A picture-perfect 1967 Yamaha YR1 captured hearts and minds to make a well deserved £5900. There was plenty of good British machinery on offer as well, with a rare and highly original 350 Manx Norton making a strong £36,580, a good price for a Manx. A G45 Matchless made a well deserved £28,320. Only 80 or so G45s were ever built and they have been somewhat overshadowed by their more illustrious G50 cousin, but in the right hands they were seriously competitive. Meanwhile, a unique 1929 Rex Acme TT replica was hammered

Above: Collections large and small come up for auction now – this one belonged to the late Ian Dettmer
Left: This 1954 Velocette MSS Scrambler made £7650

down for an impressive £28,910.

Whilst prices for British road bikes were generally flat, there were some bright spots such as a fabulous 1960 Gold Star, a joy to behold and surely worth the massive £17,464 – if not a record for a Goldie at auction, then it's close. A nicely patinated 1938 Ariel Square Four made a strong £13,688, reversing the depressing decline in values for these anachronistic but much loved British bikes.

HJ Pugh – Sunday 19th November – Ledbury

This well attended auction saw over 300 machines cross the block. Reports of the death of the classic bike market are premature, though some trends were visible, notably the high level (17%) of 'not solds.' Some of these were down to over-ambitious reserves but the market also seems weary of unremarkable mid-century British bikes, especially 350s.

The early part of the auction was dominated by the 60 or so BSAs imported from Canada, in various stages of incompletion and dereliction. Given their condition they attracted strong bids and buyers (with strong right legs) fought over the seven B50s with top money – £3946 – being paid for one fairly complete example. A 1971 B50T project still made a very strong £3069 and a Velocette Vogue a creditable £1973, but a superbly restored 1960 Norton Model 99 Deluxe went for a disappointing £5809.

A 1965 BSA Lightning looked very complete and original, while still requiring extensive cosmetic restoration sold for a strong £3946. For exactly the same money you could have taken home Lot 980, a shiny, correct looking 1970 version complete with V5C. "Go figure!" as our cousins might say.

Geoff McGladdery

The full versions of Geoff's reports first appeared in the Herefordshire and Mid Wales Section newsletter

13th May 2023

Devitt MCN Festival of Motorcycling Sale 2023

East of England Arena, Peterborough
PE2 6XE

£3 million of motorcycles sold in 2022*
Four dedicated auctions a year
International client base
Friendly and knowledgeable team

*All prices include a buyer's premium at 12.5%

ENTRIES NOW INVITED | To consign your motorcycle scan the QR code or call +44 (0)1926 691 141

ENQUIRIES
+44 (0)1926 691 141
silverstoneauctions.com

@silverstoneauctions

Stratford On Avon Racecourse,
Luddington Road,
Stratford-upon-Avon,
CV37 9SE

GATES OPEN 9.30am

SUNDAY, 19th MARCH, 2023
Also - 14th May, 25th June, 3rd September

TICKETS ONLY £6

A great day out for any car or motorcycle enthusiast, the Stratford Autojumble offers a vast array of parts, restoration services and related products for a variety of vehicles. From the organisers of Kempton and 'Normous Autojumble. If you're after a certain part, piece or tool for a motoring project, then the Stratford Autojumble is where you'll find it.

❋ Advance tickets on sale now! ❋ 15 and under go FREE

STRATFORD-ON-AVON RACECOURSE

www.stratfordautojumble.co.uk

Customer Services: 01507 529529   @AutojumbleUK   @StratfordAutojumble

VINTAGE & CLASSIC MOTOR CYCLE   31

The Other Gold Star

Did you know that the French made a Gold Star? ROD GRAHAM explains

It all started when my Velosolex friend Malcolm mentioned that he had seen an old autocycle hanging up at a small Brocante (junk shop) in the south of France, near his holiday home. It was very pretty and apparently beautifully made (albeit dirty and yellowish) but its identity was difficult to establish. The fuel tank was mounted on top of the crossbar, rather than underslung, which gave it more of a motorcycle look, and the owner described it as a Paloma. The badge on the headstock read 'Etoile D'Or' (Gold Star) and the engine (which was seized) was a pretty little thing with 'Junior' cast on the flywheel.

Although dry and externally rust free, the autocycle had apparently been caught in a bit of a flood many years ago, after which the owner had sold it to the Brocante with a seized engine. Crucially for us it looked completely original, even retaining its red pinstripes, and was offered to Malcolm at Euro 400. We talked on the phone - maybe it would make a good project for both of us.

It was clearly cycle derived, not a true moped, which dated it to the early '50s, and despite the cycle type tube frame and cycle brakes it had a real style about it. Then we found a colourful 1960s Paloma brochure in English, suggesting that these bikes must have been available in the UK. We were hooked, but couldn't stretch to the asking price. Our offer was Euro 200 was rejected with a friendly but firm shake of the head, until Malcolm and his French neighbour discovered a mutual interest in old racing cycles - new best friends, and Euro 200 accepted.

Top: As arrived, after hanging up for 50 years plus
Left: Junior magazine, March 1954, with two young 'uns about to enjoy a cyclemotor jaunt (possibly). Etoile is on the right
Below: The Levallois-Perret area of Paris was a hotbed of cyclemotor production – this is the Le Poulain factory

Clay Protection

Malcolm jubilantly dropped me a line, "The Gold Star has landed." More good news followed: "Bike is probably better than I thought. Even the original bell works. All rubber items and cables were easy to replace. Engine

Above: Tiny carburettor and clever auto-clutch
Right: Engine finished and installed, complete with Malcolm's very neat chain guards

Above: We like the finned crankcase, very stylish
Right: Malcolm warms the Etoile before its first ride

condition unknown. The only main item missing is the drive side chain cover." But the rest of it was all there, although not yet working, due to it being gummed up with a sticky clay residue.

This would be a Covid project, and we decided to try and keep the original parts, repairing as necessary on a minimal budget. At the end of the summer 2020 lockdown respite, the Etoile D'Or came to the UK in the back of Malcolm's car.

Malcolm is an enthusiastic engineer, and I'm not, so while he set about taking the bike apart and assessing its condition I researched what the engine might be. French websites led me to a manual for the Lavallette Junior, made by F.M.L. (Fabrication Mechanique de Levallois) in the Levallois-Perret area of Paris. This rang a bell, as the address put it on the opposite bank of the Seine to the Velosolex factory. This area seems to have been a hive of motorcycle and autocycle manufacture in Paris, in the 1950s and '60s.

Then, shortly after Malcolm came back from France the second lockdown began. I managed one visit to his house, handing over the Junior manual and picking up pedals and crank, stand, exhaust, seat and a few additional bits to get on with.

Malcolm got on with carefully dismantling, inspecting and cleaning, finding that material deposited in the flood must have quickly coated the whole bike and almost every part. Far from being caught in a "bit of a flood", the whole machine appeared to have been submerged, and the clay residue was everywhere, even inside the bell. The good news was that this comprehensive coating had actually protected the bike to some extent. Malcolm discovered a frame number stamped onto the flat surface of the rear frame, revealed as he carefully scraped off the deposits - S.5310. That made this a 1953 machine and possibly the tenth Etoile made that year.

The sparse publicity for the Junior engine dates from 1954, so ours seems to have been one of the early models to use it. There was no rust inside the engine, so the seizing was mostly likely due to it not being used after the bike was waterlogged. That was more good news, making the prospect of our engine being able to be made into a much better runner than we had thought.

Super NOVA

We decided to acquire a registration and age related number from the DVLA, but we had no formal receipt and no import Inland Revenue NOVA, because originally we hadn't intended to register the Etoile. Autocycle expert Andrew Pattle suggested that, with Brexit approaching at the end of 2020, our change of intention might be accepted, and a retrospective NOVA issued. Andrew's advice, with his encyclopaedic memory of all things cyclemotor/autocycle, was able to put us right on one other thing. The bike was *not* a Paloma but, more likely the product of Singer, a small firm based in St Etienne. Andrew's library of information was able to produce a couple of old magazine

Above: Proud parents? Malcolm and Rod with the whitewalled result

snippets, and everything began to drop into place. We had to remember though, that there had been two different French businesses carrying the same name, not to mention Singer of Britain, which had no connection with either.

Trawling the excellent Sheldon's EMU (cybermotorcycle.com) and the French (Cyclememory.org) websites we were able to pin down the exact model of bike and engine. So, ours is a 1953 Singer (St Etienne), Etoile D'Or model J (for Junior), for which Andrew issued his Age-Related Certificate, dated 7th December 2020.

Singer St Etienne, originally formed in 1902, was based at 18 Rue Desire Claude, St Etienne, in east central France where it made lightweight motorcycles using a variety of engines between late 1952 and '58.

The NOVA process was daunting but straightforward – the key is to get everything ready before you start. I was rewarded with the required NOVA reference along with confirmation that no VAT or late penalty was due. Without both the NOVA and the Age-Related Certificate, an application would not be considered by the DVLA.

Care and caution are certainly needed when making age-related applications, but I had been through this before with my imported Velosolex. It's important to avoid the temptation to fill in more than the minimum necessary on the V55/5 form. The registration was completed by the DVLA on 26th January 2021 and I received the V5 shortly after, along with a note of our allocated number – 260 XVN. Result!

Small & Clever

Meanwhile Malcolm had some spectacular good fortune (not to mention great patience and skill) in stripping and unseizing the engine, which only required a new set of rings. The clutch is very small and clearly of the automatic type (early for 1953), since there is no handlebar lever, and is the key to the operation of the cyclemotor. A strip down of the clutch showed it to be of a clever roll-pin type, operating once a sufficient speed is attained when pedalling off.

The beautiful (and tiny) Zenith 12MS carburettor cleaned up well but was missing a jet. Fortunately, Malcolm's patient searching for the correctly threaded bolt size, and handy work with a small file, saved the day. Ultimately, the missing jet was found to have been the only item gone awol. It's not likely to have broken, but had clearly been removed at some stage and lost, rendering the engine unusable. In fact, that could be the reason why the autocycle remained unused and gathered dust for 50 years plus.

The lovely little magneto, a Dynex Type V 15, has no keyway to align the flywheel. Once cleaned, it produced a spark on a test hand rotation but proved very difficult to get consistency, requiring a regular resetting of the flywheel. Malcolm called his engineering brain into service and, together with an old car ignition coil and a rechargeable battery from a drill, rigged these up in the pannier box with a switch and wired it through.

For the fuel tank, we decided to just clean it out and ensure it was sealed. It is an attractive piece of metalwork, sitting proudly behind the handlebars and bearing the Etoile D'Or name. If there were leaks that could not be easily sealed, then we would leave it in place and run a pipe through from an auxiliary tank. There were indeed some pin holes in the metal towards the bottom of the tank, so an external repair would not be very noticeable, and once Malcolm had applied and carefully filed excess tank filler away, it looked terrific...but still leaked. We decided to try a proprietary tank sealer and, having stopped up the apertures, carefully rotating the tank and allowing the sealer to cure, it worked! One leak-free original tank.

Tyre size matching of old foreign tyres is an area of mind-boggling complexity and contradiction. I obtained one set which apparently showed the correct size but were obviously not going to fit. Fortunately, by forgetting what you 'think you know,' we managed to find a set of the whitewalls we wanted, from the Etoile's homeland – they look stunning and really set the look of the bike off. I can see why whitewalls had been fitted originally.

In early August 2021, Malcolm rang me, excited, to say that he had been able to start the engine using a drill. It had fired up almost straight away and did not seem to be leaking anywhere. I drove over to Malcolm's armed with some exhaust paste, so that we could fit this final part, and after a little huffing, puffing and some swearing, it was done.

We had always set out to maintain the Etoile D'Or's originality – including its lovely colour and red pinstripes – and, in the end, only the piston rings, brake blocks and tyres needed replacing, plus the two chain guards hand crafted by Malcolm. We had achieved what we set out to do, to retain the autocycle's originality, and we're both very proud of the way that this Singer St Etienne Etoile D'Or Model J has turned out.

First Ride

We wheeled the Etoile out onto the driveway and spun the engine with the drill. It fired straight away, once again. After warming it up, we flicked the switch to turn it off and pushed the bike to the roadside. We looked at each other and, as was most appropriate, Malcolm pedalled it off. We guessed that engine would fire easily and, as he reached 3 or 4mph it did, the clutch kicking in shortly after. A smiling Malcolm rode the Etoile D'Or under its own power, for the first time in more than 50 years – it looked (and sounded) great.

All Welcome

CHRIS DELANEY on North Cotswold Section's strategy for new members

Whether we like it or not, things are changing in our club – largely for the better – but one inescapable fact beyond anyone's control is our changing demographic. Inevitably, the last ten years have seen a lot of 1950s and '60s era riders give up riding altogether. In the past, a new crop of British bike enthusiasts would be replacing them, but not any more – our attitude as to what might attract potential members must reflect this.

At North Cotswold Section, we found the best way to start was also the easiest – be friendly and welcoming to everyone. They could be potential, new or existing members, but whatever they ride, they need to feel very welcome. I know on occasion new members' bike choices have been criticised when they turn up, so they never came back. Even now, when I meet someone around my age who rides a '70s bike and isn't a VMCC member, the reason they give is usually a negative perception that the Club is just for old men, or an unwelcoming previous experience. We should make the most of the fact that no other club comes remotely close to ours for providing the opportunity to ride your classic bike regularly.

Tailor the Rides

So, having worked out how to make new members welcome, how do we make our rides and events more appealing? It's not rocket science. Time is more precious to people than ever and spending a whole day at a show or country fair is nothing like as popular as it once was. We have found that runs of 50-60 miles are immensely popular, with a pub at the end or in the middle, along with great routes, proper route sheets and, crucially, a

high number of members leading one or more runs a year. This last point is essential to avoid the risk of all the runs being left to a handful of members. Of course, other run leaders need encouragement and support, as the task can appear daunting to anyone leading their first run.

A lot of our new members ride foreign, especially Japanese, bikes and the wider variety of machines we now get at the start of our runs attracts a lot of interest from other motorcyclists, as the bikes are what they (not what their dads) rode in their youth.

Word of Mouth

In my experience, the system of Allen House directing new members to their nearest section did not work – our section never received one single new lead to follow up. The recent changes by Steve Allen back to regular lists of new and re-joining members is a positive step and welcomed. These monthly lists of new members are checked each month and any local new members contacted, as we used to do, but the response has never been great. What has worked for us has been our website and Facebook presence, where we publish loads of pics of our runs and include links to contact us. Instagram is a new venture, and we'll see how that goes.

The most success, however, still comes from word of mouth and interested people approaching us at the beginning and end of runs, so we now vary the start venues more, to increase our visibility, and it works.

Let's make them all welcome.

Forensic Exam

Is that frame and engine number genuine? Forensics can help, as KEN GERMAN explains

This is clearly a question a lot of vintage and classic motorcycle owners have asked themselves at one time or another, especially if the digits in question are rusty, faint or simply non-existent.

Thankfully our marque specialists and machine examiners are experts on some of our really old machines, but what about classic bikes, where the problem of frame and engine identity seems to be a growing concern to members, especially those who own or intend to purchase a bike with suspect numbers.

Have a Good Look

The first job is to clean the numbers and the area around them – take an initial picture, and keep doing that because the processes described can themselves be destructive, albeit in a minor way. That said, some methods of erasure such as chisels and drills make restoration difficult if not impossible.

Any stamping is a visible deformation of the metal surface, with the molecules underneath affected or bruised, often extending up to eight times the depth of the original stamping. So even if the original digits have been ground off, it may be possible to recover them, with the aid of a chemical etchant. Of course, only part of the originals may be exposed, and difficult to read thanks to grind marks, but they could still help to establish or negate the true provenance of a machine.

Is the paint around the frame number original? This will normally be baked on by the factory. If it can be removed with Acetone or cellulose filler then it's not original paint and usually indicates someone has removed it for some reason and made good with spray paint afterwards.

Does the stamping look original? Fortunately in the VMCC we have marque specialists who can advise us on what the stampings should look like for comparison and give an opinion on any digits that we find.

On classic machines of the 1970s and 1980s, end marks at the beginning and end of the frame and engine numbers were used for security reasons as an anti-tampering measure. These were basic however and frequently erased or replicated where necessary.

Is the metal surface original? Most frame and engine numbers were stamped into specially prepared surfaces on blank metal, either milled flat or textured in some way. In either case no

▲ Cleaning revealed the real last five digits of this number to be 00607

▲ Here alterations have been made at different times – the last two digits were stamped in after a weld inclusion was made.

▲ Freehand attempt to cover the last three digits – they are faint, but you can just make out the original '357'

▲ A simple change to two digits – the true sequential number should read 007176

▲ Partial recovery of digits – first digit could be a 2, 3 or 8, the last could be P, B or R.

grinding or polishing marks should be visible.

Have the numbers been ground off? If paint has been removed and the serial digits exposed then any tampering should be fairly apparent. If it appears the area has been ground away there should be a 'dishing' to the surface where the digits would have been – feel the surface with your fingertips, does it feel dished?

Attempts to Deceive

If a serial number has been restamped or altered in any way then this should also be apparent. Whilst classic machines had symmetry to their stamping earlier vintage machines have not and were likely done by hand – this is where assistance from experts can prove most valuable.

On some examples of tampered numbers, the area has been ground away and welded over prior to re-stamping. Indication of this may be gas bubbles or weld pits seen in the molten metal surrounding the digits.

Attempts to deceive or confuse have included 'stitching in' a different number, or filling in with car body filler. Valuable stolen machines with frame numbers stamped on the frame knuckle have been stripped and the frame disassembled and rebuilt using a donor knuckle or blank. That's a lot of work but value and rarity can clearly make it worthwhile.

Is the engine/frame number in the correct place? I've seen quite a few cases where bogus numbers were stamped on, just a few inches away from the correct stamping position, now hidden by paint. Some bikes have received as many as five different frame numbers, particularly on the front downtubes.

Examination

Many motorcycle frames were made of mild steel and before starting any examination it's important to note and photograph any markings you see around the area of the frame, removing any oil, grease and resprayed paint from the surface to be worked on.

Wipe the area with Acetone or Fry's Reagent (a mixture of deionised water, Cupric Chloride CuCl2 and Hydrochloric Acid HCl) on a cotton swab across the surface and repeat several times. The swab may be left on the area for a while and changed at regular intervals.

Illuminate the area from various angles whilst examining the surface and record any characters or partial characters that appear. It may be necessary later in the examination to carefully remove the rough surface with abrasive paper, but not more than necessary.

A 6-volt battery (not 12-volt!) electro-etching process can speed things up. Connect the positive terminal to metal and the negative to a swab containing Fry's Reagent. Get it the wrong way round and you will electroplate the surface, but this can be reversed by re-connecting the terminals in the correct order!

On engines (and a few frames) made from aluminium alloys the best etchant where erasure or alteration has taken place is a Sodium Hydroxide Solution, also known as Lye or Caustic Soda, again on a cotton wool swab. This should be done several times and after each attempt the area should be cleaned with acetone.

Professional forensic scientists would when necessary consider using nitric acid to enhance any part letters and numbers found

Spot the anomaly? Single digit change on a Ducati engine and frame number

Above: Erasure, dishing and restamping on this Honda frame number
Below: Kawasaki engine number restamped in a non-factory font – notice the different shape of the zeros

– not a substance found in many of our garages but it is still available to the public complete with important advice as to its use.

So what are you likely to find? Unlike the police who are using forensics to search for evidence that a machine might be stolen, most of us will be wondering whether our machine is genuine, or if not what its real identity could be.

Armed with information about the type of font used, the position of the letters and numbers, spacing and symmetry, depth and appearance, either taken from a genuine similar machine or on advice from a marque specialist, you too are in for some detective work – knowing the correct font may be invaluable to getting a good result.

Fake Avoidance

It is unlikely that any added or altered digits will have been made with the same set of stamps. After cleaning the area thoroughly (with paint stripper if necessary), pick out the debris in each digit, using a wire brush if needed. Firmly press Blue Tack into the numbers and slowly peel it away. If additional or overstamping has taken place then the difference in dimensions (depth and width) of the die should be apparent.

Digits that are stamped into magnesium alloys can be tested with Ammonium Persulphate in more or less the same way and thermal recovery could also be considered to uncover erased digits on cast iron, though this needs oxy-acetylene to heat and relax the area.

It's a humbling thought that in the decade before 1997 one million motorcycles were stolen, 585,000 of which were never recovered. There are clearly many fakes out there and it attests to the importance of the VMCC's experts and the valuable advice they offer, why the Club's trusted certification of authenticity is so important.

FOUNDERS RELAY RALLY
30th April 2023

STEVE ALLEN is your guide to the Founder's Relay Rally

The Founder's Relay Rally is back by popular demand and will be held on Sunday April 30th 2023. There are 56 checkpoints covering England, Scotland and Wales. To reduce costs to the Club there will be NO plaques produced. All check point details are printed below and are also available on the website (www.vmcc.net/Founders-Relay-Rally) where there is also a copy you can download. There is no charge to enter this event, simply select the check points you wish to visit and plan your route – no entry fee or registration required either.

If you wish to record which check points you have visited use the Check List printed in this Journal (see page 44) or download a copy from the website (www.vmcc.net/Founders-Relay-Rally). Copies will also be sent to participating sections to hand out, and each section will be sent sheets of VMCC stickers to affix to your check list.

Area: Anglian
Section: ANGLIAN SECTION
Check Point: Bottisham Airfield Museum
Address: Wilbraham Road, Bottisham, Cambridgeshire CB25 9BU
Directions: The museum is 3 miles outside Cambridge. Exit the A14 on Junction 35 signposted for Bottisham and Stow cum Quy. Follow the A1303 towards Bottisham and Newmarket. Take the 2nd right turn onto Wilbraham Rd and the museum is 100 yards on your right.
Check-point Open: 10.30-16.00
What 3 Words: voted.with.tiredness

Area: South Midlands
Section: BANBURY SECTION
Check Point: The Dirt House
Address: The Dirt House, Southam Road, Little Bourton, OX17 1RH
Directions: On the A423, just north of the town. Travelling from Banbury, follow signs for Southam and Coventry A423 – the pub will be found on the right-hand side approximately 1 1/2 miles out of Banbury (look for VMCC sign). When travelling towards Banbury the pub is on the left-hand side of the A423 at Little Bourton approximately 1 1/2 miles before Banbury (VMCC sign).
Check-point Open: From 08.00
Description: Pub on east side of A423
Grid Reference: SP 456 441

Area: Anglian
Section: BEDFORDSHIRE SECTION
Check Point: Shefford Town Memorial Association Clubhouse
Address: 10 Hitchin Road, Shefford, Bedfordshire, SG17 5JA

Directions: Get the Woolpack pub on your left, go along 50 yards and turn right up the drive, go another 50 yards and the clubhouse is on the left. Coming into Shefford from A6001/B659 roundabout, follow road to mini roundabout. Turn left, Woolpack Pub on your left. After 50 yards turn right down the driveway.
Check-point Open: 08.45-17.00
Grid Reference: TL 14950 38750 TL 149387 X514950 Y238750

Area: North West
Section: BLACKPOOL & DISTRICT SECTION

Check Point: Richard and Linda Lancaster's Farm
Address: 21 Bryning Lane, Wrea Green, Lancashire,
Directions: On entering Wrea Green keep the village green on your left and head towards Warton down Bryning Lane. Check point is on the right.
Check-point Open: 10:00

Area: South West
Section: BOURNEMOUTH AND NEW FOREST SECTION

Check Point: The Carpenters Arms Pub
Address: Carpenters Arms Pub, 103 Burley Road, Bransgore, Hampshire, BH23 8BA
Directions: From Ringwood, south on B3347, SP to Christchurch. Ride 5 miles to Winkton, turn Left at Winkton, SP to Bransgore on Burley Road. Straight on 2 miles, Carpenters Arms pub on left-hand side. From Lyndhurst on A35 to Cat and Fiddle pub turn right SP Bransgore, then 2 miles, at Bransgore turn Left SP Winkton. Pub on right after 720 yards.
Check-point Open: 10.00-17.00

Grid Reference: 50degs 46min 37.4 sec N 1deg44 min31.9sec
What 3 Words: animates.waddle.trek

Area: South West
Section: BRISTOL SECTION

Check Point: Avon Valley Railway
Address: Avon Valley Railway, Bitton Station, Bath Road, Bitton, Bristol BS30 6HD
Check-point Open: 09.00-17.00

Area: South East
Section: BROOKLANDS SECTION

Check Point: Manor Farm Tea Room
Address: Manor Farm Tea Room, Wood Lane, Seale, Farnham, Surrey GU10 1HR
Directions: Turn off A31 (Guildford to Farnham) heading west, signposted Seale. Turn left at T-junction then left again after 350yds into Wood Lane and the Tea Room car park. For a more scenic route turn off A31 earlier, signposted Puttenham, and follow the unclassified lane to Seale.
Check-point Open: 09.30-16.00 (café 10.00-16.00)
Grid Reference: O.S Map: Sheet 186, ref: SU 895 479

Area: North Midlands
Section: BURTON AND DISTRICT SECTION

Check Point: Arnwood
Address: The Davy DOT Museum, Arnwood, Coton in the Clay, DE6 5GY - near Burton upon Trent
Directions: Pat & Ann Davy A515 Draycott-in-the-Clay RAB SP Coton-in-the-Clay, Fauld. 3/4 mile on right. A511 Tutbury mini RAB SP Fauld, Draycott 3 1/2 miles left. Museum & refreshments - donations to TTRA.

Check-point Open: 09.30-16.30
Grid Reference: 128 169/292

Area: Scotland
Section: CENTRAL SCOTTISH SECTION

Check Point: Boating Station
Address: "Boating Station" Clunie Bridge Rd, Pitlochry, PH16 5JY
Directions: From the south leave A9 and follow main street until the 'Green Hotel' sign on left, follow Clunie Bridge Road left (VMCC EVENT sign). Follow the road until the boating station. From the north, leave A9 signposted for Pitlochry, almost immediately watch for the sign for the Green Hotel on your right and take the turn into Clunie Bridge Road, then as above. From Braemar and Blairgowrie by the A924, when you reach Pitlochry High Street turn right carry on to Green Hotel sign, (VMCC EVENT sign) – take the turn into Clunie Bridge Road then as above.
Check-point Open: From 10.00
Grid Reference: GPS -56.707 - 3.751

Area: North West
Section: CENTRAL LANCASHIRE SECTION

Check Point: John Proctor's Farm
Address: Birks Farm, Long Lane, Barnacre, Garstang, Preston PR3 1RN
Directions: Use google maps or sat nav
Check-point Open: 10.00-15.00

Area: North West
Section: CHESHIRE CATS

Check Point: J&S Accessories
Address: J&S Accessories, Chester Rd, Northwich
Directions: On A556 between Northwich and Kelsall, travelling West – approx. 2 miles from A49. Turn left into Waste Lane. Cheshire Cats banner.
Check-point Open: From 09.30
What 3 Words: ///total.baguette.blaze

Area: South Midlands
Section: CHILTERN SECTION

Check Point: The Full Moon Pub
Address: Cholesbury Lane, Hawridge, HP5 2UH
Directions: From Chesham follow signs to Cholesbury up the Vale, follow road up the hill and pub is on the left as the common opens up. From Tring follow the signs at the double roundabout to Wigginton, turn right in Wigginton SP Champneys, just past Champneys turn right on Cholesbury road, follow the road to the T Junction and turn left, the pub is on the right.
Check-point Open: From 10.00
Grid Reference: SP 93547 06971
What 3 Words: scorpions.tenses.candidate

Area: Scotland
Section: CLYDE VALLEY SECTION
Check Point: Big Red Barn
Address: The Big Red Barn Café, South Melbourne Farm, Elsrickle, Biggar
Directions: Elsrickle, 5 miles North of Biggar; on the Edinburgh Road at the crossing of the A702 and A721. Left on A416 from Berkhamstead at Lychrome Road. Right on A416 from Chesham at Lychrome Road. Right at Lychrome Road on Lye Green Road (from Bovingdon). Left on Lychrome road on Lye Green Road (from Chesham).
Check-point Open: From 10.00
What 3 Words: ///breathed.washroom.broke

Area: South West
Section: CORNWALL SECTION
Check Point: Louis Tea Rooms
Address: Louis Tea Rooms, Kit Hill, Callington, PL17 8AX. 01579 389223
Directions: Well signposted off the A390 between Tavistock and Callington.
Check-point Open: 09.00-16.00
Grid Reference: SX 38188-70797

Area: South West
Section: CORNWALL SECTION
Check Point: The Olive Tree Coffee House
Address: The Olive Tree Coffee House, Bar and Bistro, The Wharf, Bude, Cornwall. EX23 8LG. 01288 359577
Check-point Open: 10.00-17.00

Area: South West
Section: CORNWALL SECTION
Check Point: The Portreath Arms
Address: The Portreath Arms, The Square, Portreath, Redruth, TR16 4LA. 01209 842259
Check-point Open: Sunday Licencing Hours

Area: South West
Section: DEVON SECTION
Check Point: The Thatched Inn
Address: The Thatched Inn, Pump Lane, Abbotsham, near Bideford EX39 5BA
Directions: In Abbotsham village which is signposted and just a few minutes off the main A39 Bideford western bypass.
Check-point Open: From 10.30
Grid Reference: Ordnance Survey: SS 42478 26631. East 242478 North 126631
What 3 Words: rider.object.rates

Area: South West
Section: DORSET SECTION
Check Point: North Dorset Railway
Address: North Dorset Railway, St Patricks Industrial Estate, Station Rd, Shillingstone, Blandford Forum, DT11 0SA
Directions: North Dorset Railway is just off the main A357 at the north end of the village of Shillingstone. If you find the Co-op store on the main road, Station Road is opposite. Turn into Station Road and go to the last car park.
Check-point Open: From 09.30
Grid Reference: 50.90464217772308, -2.2516927733791436
What 3 Words: brittle.hippy.blueberry

Area: Anglian
Section: EAST HERTS SECTION
Check Point: Broadlakes Social Club
Address: Broadlakes Lodge Social Club, Shenley Lane, London Colney, Herts AL2 1DQ
Directions: Shenley Lane B5378 2.5 miles north east of Radlett. Leave Radlett A5183 Watling Street, turn right B556 Harper Lane, cross first roundabout and continue following B556 to roundabout, take 1st exit B5378 Shenley Lane crossing over M25, follow approximately 0.75miles. Broadlakes Clubhouse set back on the right.
Check-point Open: 08.45-16.15
What 3 Words: coherent.pens.impact

Area: North West
Section: EAST LANCS SECTION
Check Point: Bancroft Mill
Address: Gillians Lane, Barnoldswick
Directions: Access from the A59 and follow the brown tourist signs to the mill. Can also be accessed from the B6251.
Check-point Open: 09.30-16.30

Area: South East
Section: EAST SUSSEX SECTION
Check Point: Snow Mann Test Day
Address: Bo-Peep Hill, Bo-Peep Lane
Directions: Coming from Lewes on A27 take the next turning on the left opposite Common Lane. There will be a road closed sign but ignore that and continue up the lane until you reach the Snow-Mann event. Refreshments and toilets available plus you can watch some of the competitors.
Check-point Open: 09.30-16.00

Area: North East
Section: EAST YORKSHIRE SECTION
Check Point: Ernie B's Cafe
Address: Market Weighton Road, Holme on Spalding Moor
Directions: Beside the A614 2 miles south of junction with A1079.
Check-point Open: 10.00-16.00
What 3 Words: hologram.local.pack

Area: Anglian
Section: ESSEX SECTION
Check Point: Thaxted
Address: Margaret Street Car Park, Margaret St, Thaxted, Dunmow CM6 2QN
Directions: Entering Thaxted on B184 from the South. Follow High Street up a steep hill with a church on the left at the top. Road bears right, then turn immediate right into Margaret Street. Entering Thaxted on B184 from the North, Margaret Street is on the left. If you pass church on the right you have passed Margaret Street.
Grid Reference: 167 - Lat310 Lon615

Area: South Midlands
Section: FLAT TANK SECTION
Check Point: Bealesville
Address: 'Bealesville,' Hartland Hill, Minsterworth, Glos GL2 8JX.
Directions: This is adjacent to The Severn Bore Inn on the A48 which runs down the west side of the River Severn from Gloucester to Chepstow. It is 4 miles south down the A48 from A40. Coming from the south, 2 miles north of Westbury on Severn.
Grid Reference: SO 754153 (map162)
What 3 Words: dispensed.going.trout

Area: Wales
Section: HEREFORDSHIRE & MID-WALES SECTION (East)
Check Point: Hotspur Cafe
Address: Hotspur café, Shobdon airfield, Leominster, HR6 9ND
Check-point Open: 10.00-16.00

Area: North Midlands
Section: IRONMASTERS SECTION
Check Point: Motorhome in layby on A5
Address: Opposite Bradford Arms, Ivestsey Bank, Holyhead Road, Wheaton Aston, Staffordshire
Directions: Travel along the A5 towards Wheaton Aston (either westerly or easterly). Our motorhome will be parked in the layby on the west carriageway just past the crossroads opposite the Bradford Arms pub.
Check-point Open: 09.00-17.00
Grid Reference: SJ 83252 10720 52.693826, -2.247663
What 3 Words: https://w3w.co/descended.splint.polices

Area: Anglian
Section: KINGS LYNN SECTION
Check Point: Swaffham Norfolk
Address: The Butter Cross (Market Place) Town Centre, Swaffham, Norfolk PE37 7AB
Directions: Town centre position on the A1065 main highway
Check-point Open: 09.30-15.30
Grid Reference: 132 FT 81810 09060

Area: North West
Section: LAKELAND SECTION
Check Point: Station Cafe, Alston.
Address: Station Cafe, The Railway Station, Alston, Cumbria.
Directions: Just off the A686 on northern outskirts of Alston town.
Check-point Open: 11.00-15.30
Grid Reference: NY717546
What 3 Words: supper.engineers.promise

Area: North East
Section: MID LINCS SECTION
Check Point: The Happy Cafe
Address: Sandtoft Airfield, Sandtoft, DN9 1PN
Directions: This can be reached from the A161 via Belton or from the A1146 nr Hatfield. From A18, Scunthorpe to Crowle, take A161 to Belton, Sandtoft is sign posted from the roundabout in Belton, follow road to Café. Sandtoft is sign posted from the A18 Doncaster to Crowle Road, follow road to Café.
Check-point Open: 10.00-16.00
Grid Reference: 104 75.5/08.1

Area: South Midlands Section: NORTH COTSWOLD SECTION
Check Point: Vegetable Matter
Address: May Lane, Ebrington, Chipping Campden, GL56 6NJ
Directions: Vegetable Matter is a Farm Shop and Café three miles from Chipping Campden, home of the North Cotswold Section.
Check-point Open: 09.00-16.00
Grid Reference: SP 18347 39433 Map 150 GPS 52.05340, -1.73417
What 3 Words: shape.plausible.sagging

Area: Scotland
Section: NORTH EAST SCOTTISH
Check Point: The Gennel Durris
Address: The Gennel Durris, Banchory, Kincardineshire AB31 6DP
Directions: From the A957 Stonehaven to Branchory Road take the road signposted Woodlands of Durris. After 1.5 miles turn right up track to Gennel.
Check-point Open: 09.30-17.00

Area: North West
Section: NORTH WEST SECTION
Check Point: Wrakes Farm
Address: Wrakes Farm, Long Lane, Thornton, Merseyside, L29 5XB
Directions: Checkpoint off A565 at Wrakes Farm on Long Lane, signposted for Homer Green, on A565.
Grid Reference: 100 401900 (E) 100 333600

(N)

Area: Anglian
Section: NORTHAMPTON SECTION
Check Point: Milligan's Kitchen
Address: 28 Burton Rd, Finedon, Northants NN9 5HX
Directions: Follow through Finedon towards Kettering on the A6 – last building on the right behind the car wash.
Check-point Open: From 09.00

Area: North East
Section: NORTHUMBRIAN SECTION
Check Point: Bradley Burn Farm Cafe
Address: Wolsingham, Bishop Auckland
Directions: 2 miles east of Wolsingham on the A689.
Check-point Open: 10.00-16.00
Grid Reference: OS sheet 92 105363
What 3 Words: weeded.withdraws.snuggle

Area: Anglian
Section: NORWICH AND DISTRICT SECTION
Check Point: Wymondham Market Place
Address: Wymondham Market Place, Norfolk
Directions: From the traffic lights B1172 and Station Road, turn into Wymondham on Avenue Road, turn first left, Market Street, follow the road for 400 yards to market square on the right. If coming from any other direction, follow signs for town centre.
Check-point Open: 09.30-17.30
Grid Reference: TG 1107001472

Area: North Midlands
Section: NOTTS AND DERBY SECTION
Check Point: The Horse and Groom
Address: Main Street, Linby, Notts
Directions: From A60, take the B6011 signposted Papplewick and Linby. Continue for 2 miles and venue is on the right in Linby village. From Junction 27 M1, head East to the A611. Bear right at the traffic lights. Straight ahead at the first roundabout and left at the second roundabout immediately afterwards on to the B6011, signposted Linby. Bear left at the roundabout after the level crossing and TAKE CARE on the uneven road surface. The venue is 200 yards further, on the left.
Check-point Open: From 10.00

Area: North West
Section: PENNINE SECTION
Check Point: Hollingworth Lake Visitor Centre
Address: Rakewood Rd, Littleborough, Rochdale OL15 0AS
Directions: Aim for Hollingworth Lake B6225 (brown tourist signs) and turn by the Wine Press pub (white building) onto Rakewood Rd. The visitor centre is 100 yards on the left.

VMCC signs will be installed at the junctions.
Check-point Open: From 10.00
Grid Reference: SD942152
What 3 Words: outer.search.beside

Area: North Midlands
Section: SHEFFIELD AND SOUTH YORKSHIRE SECTION
Check Point: McDonalds
Address: McDonalds just off M18 Junction 1 Bawtry Road, Bramley, Rotherham, S66 1YY A631
Directions: Travelling west on A631 from Jct 1 M18. Within 100 metres turn left into Morrisons complex. McDonalds on left-hand side within 150 metres of A631.
Check-point Open: From 09.00
Grid Reference: 217. 5036835 81406

Area: South West Section: SOMERSET SECTION
Check Point: Burcott Mill
Address: Burcott Mill, Wells Road, Wookey, Wells
Directions: Take A371 out of Wells towards Cheddar, after 1/2 mile fork left, signposted Wedmore B3139. After 3/4 mile left into Burcott Mill, which is opposite the Burcott Inn.
Check-point Open: From 09.00
Grid Reference: ST420456
What 3 Words: cabbages.pegs.zones

Area: South Midlands
Section: SOUTH COTSWOLD SECTION
Check Point: The George Inn
Address: The George Inn at Cambridge, Gloucestershire
Directions: On the A38, south of the A419/M5 Junction 13. www.thegeorge-cambridge.co.uk, email thegeorge@quality-inns.co.uk.
Check-point Open: 09.30-17.00 (pub 09.00-22.00)
Grid Reference: Lat Long 51.73345, -2.36438

Area: South West
Section: SOUTH DORSET SECTION SECTION
Check Point: Rainbow Cafe
Address: Rainbow Cafe, East Knighton, Dorset DT2 8LF
Directions: On the A352 Dorchester to Wareham Road, approx. 8 miles East of Dorchester.
Check-point Open: 09:00-17:00
Grid Reference: SY811857
What 3 Words: steady.himself.verse

Area: South East
Section: SOUTH HANTS SECTION
Check Point: The Brickmakers
Address: The Brickmakers, Church Rd, Swanmore, Hampshire, SO32 2PA
Directions: Take the B2177 Winchester Road between Wickham and Bishops Waltham. At Waltham Chase turn north east into Lower Chase Road and continue 1 mile to the T-Junction with Church Road. Turn right at the junction, The Brickmakers is 100yds on the left.
Check-point Open: From 09.00
Grid Reference: SU 57537 16560
What 3 Words: ///guideline.diet.twinkled

Area: Anglian
Section: SOUTH LINCS AND PETERBOROUGH SECTION
Check Point: Stibbington Diner
Address: 2 Old Great North Rd, Stibbington, Peterborough
Directions: From the A1 look for brown signs for Nene Valley Railway and then follow signs for Services. To avoid the A1, access from B671 Wansford to Elton Road, follow signs for Stibbington, then follow signs for Services.
Check-point Open: 09.30-10.30 manned, after 10.30 unmanned
Grid Reference: TL087982
What 3 Words: agreeable.standing.stow

Area: Wales
Section: SOUTH WALES SECTION
Check Point: Caerphilly Mountain Snack Bar
Address: 469 Mountain Road, Caerphilly, Glamorgan.
Directions: At the junction of the A469/B4263 on top of the mountain between Cardiff and Caerphilly.
Check-point Open: 10.00-16.00
Grid Reference: 51.55966, -3.21892
What 3 Words: call.gets.tiger

Area: Scotland
Section: STIRLING CASTLE SECTION
Check Point: Crieff Visitor Centre
Address: Front car park, Crieff Visitor Centre, Muthill Rd, Crieff
Directions: On A822 heading North from Braco and Muthill into Crieff take first left when you get into the 40mph limit. Heading South from Crieff to Muthill and Braco it's the last turn on the right before you leave the 40mph speed limit.
Check-point Open: From 09.30
Grid Reference: 56.3633° N, 3.8522° W
What 3 Words: almost.crowned.stowing

Area: South Midlands
Section: STONEHENGE SECTION
Check Point: Breamore House Countryside Museum
Address: Breamore House Countryside Museum, Upper Street, Fordingbridge SP6 2DB
Check-point Open: 09.00-16.00

Area: South East
Section: SURREY AND SUSSEX SECTION
Check Point: Southern Counties Historic Vehicle Preservation Trust
Address: Southern Counties Historic Preservation Trust Centre, East Hill Lane, Effingham Road, Copthorne, West Sussex RH10 3HZ
Directions: On the B2037, 600 yards from the Curious Pig in the Parlour and 500 yards from The Old House. East Lane is a turning off Effingham Road
Check-point Open: From 09.00
What 3 Words: skinny.bunk.leader

Area: Wales
Section: SWANSEA & DISTRICT SECTION
Check Point: M&P Motorcycle Shop, Gorseinon
Address: Phoenix Way, Gorseinon Penllergaer SA4 9HN.
Directions: At J47 on M4 take exit on the A48 to Gorseinon then onto the A4240. Take a left at the first traffic lights. The shop is on the right at the end of the road.
Check-point Open: 10.00-16.00
What 3 Words: pies.fled.lights

Area: South West
Section: SWINDON MOONRAKERS SECTION
Check Point: The Rat Trap (Car Park at rear)
Address: The Rat Trap,
Highworth Road, Stratton St Margaret, Swindon, Wiltshire SN3 4QS
Directions: Off A419 on to A361 Swindon, change to B4006.
Check-point Open: 8.30-15.30
Grid Reference: 173 176876
What 3 Words: blown.single.milky

Area: National
Section: TAVERNERS SECTION
Check Point: Stone Hurst Family Farm and Motor Museum
Address: Bond Lane, Mountsorrel, Loughborough, Leicestershire, LE12 7AA
Directions: In the centre of Mountsorrel village along Loughborough Road. Car park entrance via Bond Lane opposite car dealership. Look for The Taverners red marquee once in the car park.
Check-point Open: From 09.00

Area: North East
Section: WAKEFIELD AND WEST YORKSHIRE SECTION
Check Point: Squires Cafe Bar
Address: Squires Cafe Bar, Newthorpe Lane, Nr Sherburn in Elmet, Leeds, LS25 5LX.
Directions: Squires Cafe Bar is on the B1222 at Newthorpe near Sherburn in Elmet in West Yorkshire. Just off Junction 42 on A1(M).

Check-point Open: 09.00-16.30
Grid Reference: Sheet 105 ref 468 321

Area: South Midlands Section:
WARWICKSHIRE SECTION
Check Point: Long Itch Diner
Address: Long Itch Diner, Southam Rd, (A423) Long Itchington, Southam
Directions: On A423 1/2 mile south of Long Itchington, 1 mile north of Southam junction A423/A426. Very visible from the road, a former petrol station.
Check-point Open: 10.00-15.00

Area: South West
Section: WESSEX VETERAN & VINTAGE SECTION
Check Point: Silton Village Hall
Address: Silton Village Hall, Silton, Nr Gillingham, Dorset
Directions: Take B3092 from Gillingham towards Milton on Stour. At Milton turn Left SP Bourton. Follow this road for c2miles then look for VMCC arrow pointing you to the checkpoint.
Check-point Open: 09.30-16.30
Grid Reference: 785 303
What 3 Words: simulations.replayed.hopes

Area: South East
Section: WEST KENT SECTION
Check Point: The Pavilion
Address: The Pavilion, Gamecock Meadow, London Road, West Kingsdown
Directions: The Pavilion is on the south side of the A20 London Rd, 1 mile south of Brands Hatch Circuit entrance and 100 yards before The Gamecock pub.
Check-point Open: 09.30 to 16.00
Grid Reference: 188 575629

Area: South Midlands
Section: WEST WILTSHIRE SECTION
Check Point: The Bell Inn
Address: On the B4039: The Bell Inn, High Street, Yatton Keynell, Chippenham SN14 7BG
Check-point Open: 09.00-17.00
Grid Reference: OS Map Reference ST 866 765
What 3 Words: tango.monkey.rucksack

Area: Wales
Section: WORCESTERSHIRE SECTION
Check Point: Cob House Countryside Park
Address: Cob House Countryside Park, Wichenford, Worcestershire WR6 6YF (on the B4204 Worcester-Martley)
Directions: FROM WORCESTER: A443 (signed Tenbury), in 1 m L onto B4204 (signed Martley). Cob House is 4.2m on left. FROM BROMYARD: A44 to Worcester, in 5.9m turn L onto B4197 (signed Martley 3), in Martley R onto B4204 (signed Worcester), Cob House is 1.8m on R. FROM TENBURY: A443, in Great Witley R onto B4197 (signed Martley 3½), in Martley L onto B4204 (signed Worcester). Cob House is 1.8m on R. Grid Reference: OS ref 150 SO778585

FOUNDERS RELAY RALLY
Checklist

When you've visited a checkpoint, add a sticker to the appropriate box.

ANGLIAN SECTION
Bottisham Airfield Museum ☐

BANBURY SECTION
The Dirt House ☐

BEDFORDSHIRE SECTION
Shefford Town Memorial Association Clubhouse ☐

BLACKPOOL & DISTRICT SECTION
Richard and Linda Lancaster's Farm ☐

BOURNEMOUTH & NEW FOREST SECTION
Carpenters Arms Pub ☐

BRISTOL SECTION
Avon Valley Railway ☐

BROOKLANDS SECTION
Manor Farm Tea Room ☐

BURTON AND DISTRICT SECTION
Arnwood ☐

CENTRAL LANCASHIRE SECTION
John Proctor's Farm ☐

CENTRAL SCOTTISH SECTION
Boating Station ☐

CHESHIRE CATS
J&S Accessories ☐

CHILTERN SECTION
The Full Moon Pub ☐

CLYDE VALLEY SECTION
Big Red Barn ☐

CORNWALL SECTION
Louis Tea Rooms ☐

CORNWALL SECTION
The Olive Tree Coffee House ☐

CORNWALL SECTION
The Portreath Arms ☐

DEVON SECTION
The Thatched Inn ☐

DORSET SECTION
North Dorset Railway ☐

EAST SUSSEX SECTION
Snow Mann Test Day ☐

EAST HERTS SECTION
Broadlakes Social Club ☐

EAST LANCS SECTION
Bancroft Mill ☐

EAST YORKSHIRE SECTION
Ernie B's Café ☐

ESSEX SECTION
Thaxted ☐

FLAT TANK SECTION
Bealesville ☐

HEREFORDSHIRE & MID-WALES SECTION (East)
Hotspur Café ☐

IRONMASTERS SECTION
Motorhome, layby on A5 ☐

KINGS LYNN SECTION Swaffham Norfolk	☐
LAKELAND SECTION Station Cafe, Alston	☐
MID LINCS SECTION The Happy Café	☐
NORTH EAST SCOTTISH The Gennel Durris	☐
NORTHAMPTON SECTION Milligan's Kitchen	☐
NORTH COTSWOLD SECTION Vegetable Matter	☐
NORTH WEST SECTION Wrakes Farm	☐
NORTHUMBRIAN SECTION Bradley Burn Farm Café	☐
NORWICH AND DISTRICT SECTION Wymondham Market Place	☐
NOTTS AND DERBY SECTION The Horse and Groom	☐
PENNINE SECTION Hollingworth Lake Visitor Centre	☐
SHEFFIELD AND SOUTH YORKSHIRE SECTION McDonalds	☐
SOMERSET SECTION Burcott Mill	☐
SOUTH COTSWOLD SECTION The George Inn	☐
SOUTH DORSET SECTION Rainbow Café	☐
SOUTH HANTS SECTION The Brickmakers	☐
SOUTH LINCS & PETERBOROUGH SECTION Stibbington Diner	☐
SOUTH WALES SECTION Caerphilly Mountain Snack Bar	☐
STIRLING CASTLE SECTION Crieff Visitor Centre	☐
STONEHENGE SECTION Breamore House Countryside Museum	☐
SURREY AND SUSSEX SECTION Southern Counties Historic Vehicle Preservation Trust	☐
SWANSEA & DISTRICT SECTION M&P Motorcycle Shop Gorseinon	☐
SWINDON MOONRAKERS SECTION The Rat Trap	☐
TAVERNERS SECTION Stone Hurst Family Farm and Motor Museum	☐
WAKEFIELD AND WEST YORKSHIRE SECTION Squires Cafe Bar	☐
WARWICKSHIRE SECTION Long Itch Diner	☐
WESSEX VETERAN & VINTAGE SECTION Silton Village Hall	☐
WEST KENT SECTION The Pavilion	☐
WEST WILTSHIRE SECTION The Bell Inn	☐
WORCESTERSHIRE SECTION Cob House Countryside Park	☐

VMCC *Photo of the Month!*

Is Photo of the Month becoming our weather report? Last month we carried a record number of snowy pictures and March seems to have fast forwarded straight into spring/early summer, with lots of sunshine and blue skies. (The fact that some of these photos were taken last year might have something to do with it, but we're hoping it bodes well for benign weather this month).

Either way, Photo of the Month carries on into the April issue with the same theme – **'Back on the Road.'** With any luck, that's where many of us will be.
If you want to enter, it's free and easy – just email your photo (or photos) to editor@vmcc.net. The best of the selection will be printed in the Journal, and the winner picked by professional photographer Philip Lee Harvey. Good luck!

THIS MONTH'S WINNER – MAC MACKENZIE Picked by Philip Lee Harvey

Accord to Mac Mackenzie, the novelty of his 1915 Triumph Model H, purchased last year, still hasn't worn off. As you can see, he's really entering into the spirit of flat tank ownership. His wife took this picture in their local village last December.

Philip says:
I often work with professional stylists on my shoots, whose job it is to make sure that the clothes worn in the photographs don't distract from the message and actually enhance the overall look. This well composed, naturally lit image is a great portrait. I very much like the restricted colour palette and the use of the lane to guide you through.

Below: Very nice shot by Chris Delaney of his 1980 Tiger 750, which he rather likes – and quite right too. We featured Chris's Tiger in a previous issue of V&C. "Taken one spring morning in Harvington near Evesham on my North Cotswold Section Blossom Run in 2019. We were in the pub opposite, not the church behind, I'm afraid. Not much of a view but the light hit the bike so well!"

Above: Dave Stevenson took this last summer at an evening meeting of the Wakefield Section. Location is the Reindeer Inn, Overton, and the chimney seen through the trees is the National Mining Museum winding engine boiler.

Left: Just to prove what we already know, that you can tour on an old bike... Scott Johnson rode his BSA M20 3000 miles through the Pyrenees and Alps before heading home to Glasgow. " I get through the winter by looking at the photos taken while biking in the better weather, if there is such a thing in Scotland."

Above: New VMCC member Chris Greenhalgh was out on his '86 BMW R100RS just after lockdown when he took this. Road is the one between Stainforth and Arncliffe.

Above: Ben Measures pops a wheelie at the Taverners Trial at Eaton Lodge last year. The bike is a 1948 Ariel 350.
Left: Memories of last summer... John Hodgson's 1956 Sunbeam S7 Deluxe enjoying the sun outside a Cheshire church.

Left: A sylvan glade...or something. Taken by Richard Miles while out for an early evening ride on his two-speed Scott last year.

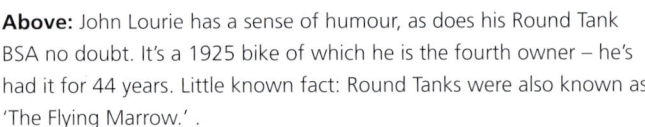

Above: John Lourie has a sense of humour, as does his Round Tank BSA no doubt. It's a 1925 bike of which he is the fourth owner – he's had it for 44 years. Little known fact: Round Tanks were also known as 'The Flying Marrow.'

Above: John Hawkins 1961 Velocette Venom in the snow
Left: Urban cafe scene - Cafe Kothel in Glasgow, taken by Gordon Mowat
Below: "Not the ideal bike for the route, but the only one that was running properly at the time!" writes Gordon Maclean of his 1977 Kawasaki Z1000 A2, taken on a recent club run on what's known locally as the gated road, a dilapidated link between Killin and Glen Lyon, over the hills.

ENTER FOR APRIL

We have a new theme for March and April's Photo of the Month – **'Back on the Road.'** (As you'll have gathered, the themes aren't compulsory, but giving them a go does gain brownie points).

So no prizes for guessing that we'd like some road shots now that our bikes are getting back on tarmac – long, straight piece of road stretching out behind the bike, or maybe something nice and twisty. And of course 'roads' don't have to be tarmac – green lanes, desert pistes and mountain tracks are all equally acceptable. All bikes and three-wheelers must be VMCC eligible. Pictures sent as part of articles for V&C will also be considered. Pictures may be used elsewhere in the Journal, and/or in VMCC advertising. Entries will be sent on to our judge, professional photographer Philip Lee Harvey.
Send your entries to: editor@vmcc.net
Good luck!

HANCO ENGINEERING
BESPOKE ENGINEERING SERVICES

We deliver expert metal fabrication services for a wide range of clients. We work with every client to figure out together the most suitable, cost-efficient solutions, and we guarantee a top-quality end result.

Our Services
- casting repairs
- weld build up
- Rolling
- Welding
- brazing
- bespoke fabrication
- Engineering
- frame alterations

Got a project in mind?
Call Us Today 07597066318

WANTED

 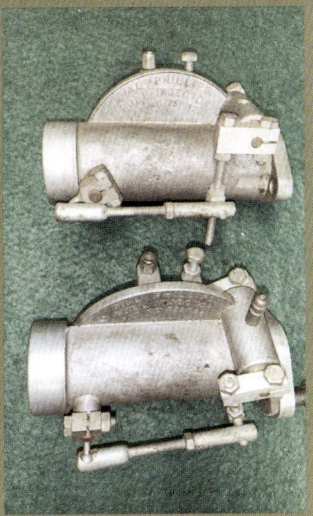

Wanted all GP and TT Amal carbs and other unusual motorcycle Amal carburettors cash paid Braintree 07775 998628 or email photos to motorcyclebuyer7788@outlook.com

---

Motorcycle-Only Events in the South East!

South of England Classic Motorcycle Show & BikeJumble
Sunday 26 March — Theme: The Roaring Twenties & Thirties!
At The South of England Showground, Ardingly, Near Gatwick, RH17 6TL

Ashford Classic Show & BikeJumble
Bank Holiday Monday: 10 April
Ashford Livestock Market, Ashford, Kent, TN24 0HB

Romney Marsh Classic Bikejumble
Sunday 7 May
Hamstreet, Nr Ashford, KENT TN26 2JD

Book your tickets online & beat the queues
Visit www.elk-promotions.co.uk

Romney Marsh Classic Show & Bikejumble
Sunday 25 June

Ardingly Summer Classic Show & Bikejumble:
Sunday 30 July

Romney Marsh BikeJumble with Ride-In Show
Sunday 17 September

South of England Classic Show & 'jumble
Sunday 29 October

ELK Promotions, PO Box 85, New Romney KENT TN28 9BE 01797 344277. Details Subject to Change

Check www.elk-promotions.co.uk BEFORE travelling!

Rare Triumph Bonneville T120RT 1970: "the first 750cc":
Superb condition, fully restored bike in correct original colours (Astral Red/Silver).
- Manufactured May 1970 and immediately despatched to Triumph Baltimore.
- 200 standard 650cc 1970 Bonnevilles were converted to 750cc and homologated for AMA competition in the US.
- AMA Motorcycle Hall of Fame Museum, Ohio letter confirming authenticity.
- Full professional restoration following repatriation to U.K.
- VMCC authenticity certification and owner registered the bike with DVLA May 2021.
- Ridden 90 miles following restoration and owner's ill health now forces disposal.

All paperwork and Owner's Handbook and Workshop Manual are included. £20,500. **Call 07768 827563**

The 2023 Flat-Tank Cotswold Weekend, 10th & 11th June

Runs for all machines over the two days, including a Vintage and Veteran Road Trial on Saturday and a Regularity Time Trial *(ACU permit #200389)* on Sunday. Route options to suit any bike, and all are welcome. Based in the Forest of Dean.

Details from Rob Rendell ear@globalnet.co.uk, 01452 863470, or at www.vmcc-cotswold.org

LETTERS

★★★★★★★ STAR LETTER

Best in Snow

I thought you might like to see photo I took a few years ago when the temperature was about -10 degrees C and my Morgan was coping with winter quite well.

I had arranged to meet an ex-work colleague for a pub lunch shortly before Christmas but it went very cold and snowy. The Mog is great fun in the snow as it keeps going when most other cars are stranded, even the 4x4s if they are on road tyres. The narrow front tyres cut through snow and gave reasonable control while the knobbly on the back (fitted for this run) was running on reasonably fresh snow that hadn't been polished to ice by four-wheelers.

I enjoyed a very pleasant run through the countryside and at one point I caught up a white Transit, slithering about across the road and struggling to keep going. In fairness to the driver, he was very courteous and on the next straight waved me past. I happily carried on, thinking that it's not often I can travel at twice the speed of White Van Man in my 80-year-old tricycle.

Dave Anscombe

Have Logbooks...

I have been having a clear out, found two old brown logbooks and wondered if the bikes are still in existence and if so, perhaps the owners would like them? I have checked the DVLA website and neither of the registration numbers are listed.

They are: 1) a 197cc Francis-Barnett dated 6th August 1957, reg 291 KPU, initial owner Mr Arthur Gunton of Basildon, Essex and 2) a 350cc MAC Velocette dated 7th July 1952, reg RPL 479, initial owner Colin Jones of Woodford Green, Essex.

Keith Rose

Following days of work preparing the 1924 BSA combo ready for its 167-mile Coventry 2 Brighton Run in April, Dave Whitehead persevered to start the beast and it repaid him by almost choking him to death
Bob Badland

Rumi Smoothie

I enjoyed the article (V&C, February) about retrieving a Rumi Formichino (Little Ant) scooter from the USA. I am the proud owner of a 1954 Rumi Turismo Lusso, the motorcycle from which the Formichino is derived.

I bought mine about seven years ago, having retained since schooldays the memory of the noise a Rumi makes. I used to walk to school past a Rumi dealership and always stopped to listen if one was being fired up. The dealer liked to demonstrate the smoothness of the engine by balancing a three-penny piece on edge on the crankcase and revving up the engine.

A useful source about Rumis is the UK Rumi Club. Go to www.rumiclub.co.uk

Nick Granger

Hare Wins

On the mention of a Tricati (V&C, January) I recall an article in the 'Green 'Un' entitled 'The Tortoise and the Hare.' The Tortoise was Mick Potter on a Tricati who finished last in the Junior of 1968 and the hare was Agostini, who won on an MV. The article failed to mention the Triumph engine which had been used in my motoball bike before I sold it to Mick (who tweaked it!)

On another subject, could any member tell me more about John Yallop, whose obituary appeared in the VMCC Journal of August 1990. Around 1982 he wrote an account of fitting Rudge four-valve cylinders and heads to a Harley-Davidson before World War II.

Barry Yallop

Trouble Free

I was very interested in Paul Smith's article about his Honda CX500 apparently overheating, as I have had this problem for a little while. As the CX500 is a reliable machine I rarely have to do any work on it other than the normal servicing, even though it has almost 145,000 miles on the clock. Consequently I know very little about it as I work on the basis of if it isn't broke, don't fix it. On the other hand, I am totally au fait with my older British bikes, having rebuilt them several times.

Trevor Pinfold

In Henn's Defence

Referring to David Crouch's letter in the September Journal. In defence of Geloman, Christian Henn is in Germany and has been dealing from there for many years. He has had problems with what he calls 'cyber crooks' from Spain and has had to change his website address. His email is henn@geloman.de. I have used him and had fairly instant response.

Ken Lee

Answers on Belts

Richard Frank has a problem finding a 1-inch belt for his New Hudson (Letters, January) but I can get 5/8" belts quite easily for my two lightweights (1922 McKenzie and 1923 Atlas). I believe that 5/8" belts are used by lots of agricultural diggers. What I can't get is a belt fastener in that size, because most belts are now endless.

My Atlas is a special with chain-cum-belt transmission, which I built to use an endless belt, outboard of the primary chain. The belt is a bit worn now but has never given trouble, and I can adjust the tension in seconds. The McKenzie belt runs from the (rather small) crankshaft pulley to the (very large) rear belt rim and needs a joint. In heavy rain it only slips but also picks up water and drops it onto the mag. What fun! Also, the belt fastener is now decidedly tired and could do with replacing.

I recently found a good 7/8" fastener (Dunlop, grey finish) if anyone needs it? If anyone has a 5/8" fastener please let me know.

The Project Origin Royal Enfield featured in recent editions apparently uses a twisted rawhide belt with a figure of eight crossing midway. I'm interested to know how this belt is joined and how the fastener copes with the jockey wheel and potential chafing where the belt crosses over. I also look forward to more news about this wonderful machine.

Derek Langdon

Scarborough Plans

Scarborough Week will be 11th-17th June. To book, ring the Arosa Caravan Site on 01723 862166. We have made a booking to visit the Dick Craven Motorcycle Museum on the Tuesday (13th June). Also during the week Arosa will be doing a spit roast and barbeque, plus there will be a video and talk by the Air Ambulance.

Route sheets will be given for the whole week and the site fee is £15 per night. Any further information, ring Tony Cowley on 01302 884085.

Tony Cowley

Left: September 2022 marked the return of the very popular Cornwall Rally at Monkey Tree Leisure Park on the outskirts of Newquay. There were 68 entrants, many with two or three bikes plus 125 people on site.
Peter Lee

I Shall Return

In the January issue, new VMCC member Colin Cade wrote to tell us that he had bought a Honda CB500, identical to the one he had in 1972. However, things didn't go according to plan...

I bought the first CB when I was 24 years old, 14 stone, fit and working on building sites installing commercial air conditioning. The bike was beautiful, and I could not believe it when I managed to find an identical model last year. The trouble is, 50 years later I am pushing 75, weigh under 11 stone and have no upper body strength. I had trouble just getting it on the centre stand.

Riding it was great but I realised that I no longer changed gear instinctively, and I had to think about every one else on the road. I am used to driving at speed in my car, a Nissan Skyline R34 GT Turbo which is pretty fast, but I did not feel in control of the bike on corners the way I should – lack of confidence I guess. To add to the problems, arthritis in my feet means I cannot change gear without pain.

Sadly, I decided I had better sell the Honda back to the shop I bought it from. I got a reply within the hour, he made an offer which I accepted, cash was transferred instantly and he soon collected the CB500 and took it away. I was sorry to see it go, but I expect he has a buyer lined up. I hope so, for it is a lovely bike. I always got good comments from everyone I met while out on it.

The dealer said, "The money is in your bank, why not get a nice 125 instead?" That set me thinking – why don't I do my CBT as well? That would give me the skills and confidence back. And wearing decent footwear instead of trainers would help with the arthritis. So, later on in the year when I am fit again, I'll look into that.

Colin Cade

Sorry to hear that Colin, but glad that you've decided to get some training and come back on a 125. You would be very welcome to do a try before you buy with a Club Garage 125 (Ed)

Massey Memories

In Gems (V&C, February) I was very interested to read about the Massey-Arran company and your request for any information. My late father owned a 1922 Blackburne-engined Massey. As you say, a high-quality product that must have been one of first to feature front and rear hub brakes, albeit of tiny dimensions, made by Messrs Webb (presumably the fork manufacturers?). I can be contacted via the editor.

Jonathan Hill
Dorset Section

More Massey

After reading the article on Massey-Arran in the December issue, I am sending a photo of one of these machines which my father, Leonard Cardy, raced in the 1920s. He competed in grass track and sprint events in East Anglia. The Massey-Arran had a Blackburne engine – he contacted Blackburne and learned that his engine had been used for practice in the TT.

I rode my first Banbury Run in 1959, riding our first vintage bike, a 1923 Douglas – my father rode a 1926 500cc ohv AJS, and I still own both of these machines.

There was a small mistake in your article as AJS took five of the first six places in the 1921 TT but the Massey-Arran finished fifth, not sixth.

Tony Cardy

Ossas Three

I look forward to the calendar coming through the post every December, not only as a yearly planner but to see the splendid VMCC members' motorcycles featured within. You might like to feature this picture of my three Ossa trials bikes next year. On the right is an Ossa 250 MkII Mick Andrews Replica 1974, road registered with excellent help and service from the VMCC Library. In the centre is a 1975 Ossa MkI Explorer (also road registered with Library help) and on the left a 1977 Ossa 250 MkIII TR77, which is currently in the process of being registered.

Paul Hulme

Pioneer Postmortem

The joint VMCC/MSCR Girder Fork event date has been changed from 5th-7th May to 12th-14th May – the original date clashed with the Coronation. I apologise for the change but His Majesty did not consult with the VMCC or myself. Not wishing to have my head cut off (or lose potential entrants) I decided to make the event a week later.

I was interested to read of Mike Wild's Dreadnought ride in the Veteran Car Run. When VMCC President in 2005/6 I rode the bike in the Pioneer Run, collecting it from Geoff Davies who gave me a brief lesson in riding the beast. The first impression was its saddle height, high for a rider of 5'10". I also changed the twin levers so that they opened back towards the rider.

On the run, the machine chugged along at first but gradually lost power and suddenly at Verralls Garage in Handcross it stopped altogether. A postmortem revealed that the exhaust cam was failing to open. There was no back up then, so I hitched a lift on a spectator's BSA to Madeira Drive, where my van was waiting. I took the poor old Dreadnought back to Allen House where I believe the cam wheel was repaired.

I have ridden the London-Brighton route on a 1914 Sun with 269cc Villiers engine – the actual machine (I think) which took part in the very first event for 'Old Crocks' back in 1930.

Geoff Brazendale

WHERE ARE THEY NOW?

Matchless 350 532 KPK

I wonder if anyone could identify the Matchless my mum is sitting on? I think it was a 350 single and the picture would have been around the late '60s as she passed her bike test in 1966 on my 1964 Honda C50 cub, the same bike I started out on!

Mum also rode my 1964 Norton Dominator 650SS in full Paul Dunstall cafe racer trim, which was stolen from a lock-up I had rented to do some work (oh, the joys of living in south east London). She had a go on my first CB500 Four as well, and loved it.

Colin Cade

Scott & Manx Norton

Does anyone know the whereabouts of these two bikes? 1927 Scott YF6144 and 1948 Norton Manx JGO 875. Swaps? 07931 466650.

Jerry Larke

Good news Jerry, both Scott and Manx are still listed by the DVLA, with the Scott on SORN. (Ed).

BSA A10 RSL 312

I'm looking for my old BSA A10, 1959/60, RSL 312 as I'm interested in purchasing it back. Please get in touch. 01670 514898.

Frank Smith
59 Green Lane
Morpeth, Cumbria NE61 2HB

The A10 is still listed by the DVLA, currently on SORN (Ed).

Norman Trials UKP 881

Can anyone help with finding an ex-works Norman please? The reg was UKP 881 and the pictures from 1956 show my father Bob Simmonds riding the bike in trials – hope this jogs some memories. A big thank you to all.

Peter Simmonds

Buying One

How to buy a classic bike, and three typical options – OLIVER HULME

There are plenty of places to buy a classic bike – dealers, social media buy-and-sell groups or via a club – but the same comments apply to all of them.

Setting your heart on a particular make and/or model means less searching but it also reduce the pool of bikes to choose from. So it's worth having a bit of flexibility built into your choice. You may want a Bonneville badly, but if a Tiger or maybe a BSA Lightning comes up that is local to you at the right price, it could make more sense. Being broadminded about your choice will make buying easier.

Visit the seller. Buying unseen might save you a bit of hassle in the short-term but can be a disaster too. There are many tales of people getting far less than they expected to get when the machine arrives. Ideally, find a friend who knows about the model you're looking at and take them along.

First, does the bike run? You'll find plenty of sellers who will announce that the bike turns over on the kick start but "hasn't been started". Ask yourself why not, as a running bike is always going to be worth more. And is it advertised as 99% complete? You can be sure that it isn't.

Check the provenance. Use the DVLA vehicle check website to make your first tentative steps. Does the bike come with a V5c registration document? Many bikes are advertised as "no V5", which raises questions about legality. A V5c for a legitimate bike from the DVLA will cost the seller only £25 and arrive in a few days, so why isn't the seller adding extra value by getting one?

Does the bike have its original registration number? Lots of classic dealers will sell the old number on and re-register the bike. If they have, it reduces the bike's sale value.

Simpler days – that BSA will have seen a lot of life since then

Will your mum still sign the HP form for you?

Check the engine and frame numbers. The idea of 'matching numbers' applies to several British makes, though by no means all. Triumph used this system but BSA didn't follow suit until the mid-1960s, while AMC had its own arcane numbering system. Japanese bikes also usually come with something close to matching numbers, and the frame and engine will have similar digits. Whatever the system, do check that the numbers are stamped on correctly and haven't been over-stamped or otherwise tampered with. They should be neatly stamped, just as they were at the factory. Later Triumphs had a stamped Triumph logo behind the engine number, to make tampering more difficult. Frames sometimes get restamped too, by the unscrupulous.

Non-matching numbers will affect the value of the machine, but if you don't mind the lack of originality, you could bag a bargain. Remember, you are buying an old machine, and there's every chance that an engine could have been legitimately swapped at some time in the past. You could still be left with a perfectly fine, rideable bike, just not original.

Stay in Budget

Work within your budget. Are the tyres good? If they aren't, how much are replacements? Do the chain and sprockets have life in them? Is there anything important missing? Tinware on British bikes is often unobtainable from normal sources and you'll need to hunt it down. Missing parts on Japanese and Euro bikes are even more of a concern as replacements can be extremely expensive – watch out for details such as cracked lenses and torn seats.

Is the bike oil tight? This is less of an issue on a British bike, as, "they all do that, sir", or some of them at least. Is the oil clean or dirty and is it circulating? Have a peek into the oil tank to find out. On a Japanese bike big oil leaks can be more of a concern. Exhausts can be expensive, especially for multi-cylinder Japanese bikes – a repro Honda 750 system will cost well over £1000.

So the bike runs, but is it smooth? If the engine sounds lumpy, there's going to be a reason. Is the gear shift smooth or crunchy? Different models will have lighter or heavier gear shifts and clutches, but a super-heavy clutch indicates problems with the cable or the mechanism.

Take a look at the wiring. Is it looking good and clean, or peppered with crimp connectors? Do all the warning lights and the rev counter work? Have the right fasteners been used throughout the bike? Nuts and bolts may be metric instead of Whitworth, or cheap items from a DIY store. If the fastenings are stainless steel, then the owner hasn't been afraid to spend money.

Has work been carried out and if it has, are there receipts? We have all heard tales of a smart looking bike bought with claims of extensive engine work that turned out to have loose bolts inside the engine, missing circlips and masses of chemical metal and sealant used to cover up bodges.

Will the seller let you ride the bike? This is a thorny issue. A dealer might let you ride it round a car park if you ask very nicely. A private seller might too, usually on condition that you hand over the full asking price in cash first, or maybe leave the keys for the car/bike you arrived on. Riding pillion with the seller won't really tell you anything. Most of the time you'll need to trust your instincts about the machine on offer.

Don't expect any come back if something goes wrong with the bike soon after you've bought it. We are in Buyer Beware territory here. Inevitably you will hear more horror stories than happy ones. A dodgy deal is always more fun to describe than one where you bought the right bike and the right price, and it ran perfectly.

Going home to think about it is a good idea. It might upset the seller a bit, as they want to do a deal there and then, but don't be rushed into a decision, always be prepared to walk away. There are plenty of suitable bikes around and another will be along in a minute. If you see any major issue you don't like the look of, walk away. If it's a minor concern, ask if the seller will cut the price a little. But remember that a dealer may be less able or willing to do a deal as this is their business, they pay tax on their sales and work on very tight margins to compete with private sellers.

The Classic Glossary

Don't know your pre-unit from your zener diode? Our brief guide to old bike terminology is here to help

Advance/Retard Unit
Usually two spring-loaded bob weights that move the points cam forward and backwards depending on the speed of the engine, to automatically adjust the ignition timing. You'll find them on bikes with cb points, occasionally on machines with early electronic ignition systems. Much older bikes have a manual advance/retard lever on the bars.

Alternator
Standard battery charger on British bikes from the early '60s, plus all Japanese machines. The alternator provides alternating current (AC), which is variable and needs a zener diode or regulator/rectifier to control it.

Camchain Tensioner
Common on Japanese motorcycles, a spring-loaded plunger that tensions the camchain. Often referred to as 'automatic', but that doesn't mean it can be forgotten.

Contact Breaker (cb) Points
Before everything went to electronic ignition, these provided the right spark at the right time, two small contacts opened and closed by a cam. Need to be in good condition with the correct clearance.

Overhead cam (OHC)
Camshaft/s mounted on top of the cylinder, usually driven by chain and operating the valves via rockers or directly. DOHC = double overhead camshafts. OHC and DOHC were popularised and made affordable by the Japanese, but they didn't invent it.

Overhead valves (OHV)
OHV engines have the valves mounted in the cylinder head, operated by pushrods housed in tubes on the outside of the cylinder, or cast within the barrels. These operate the rockers which open and close the valves. Standard for British bikes of the 1960s and '70s.

Pre-Unit
Engine is in a separate casting from the gearbox, connected usually by a primary chain within a chaincase. Largely superseded by unit construction by 1965.

Primary Drive
Drive from engine to the gearbox via a clutch, usually by a chain on British bikes – by chain or by gears on Japanese machines. On transverse V-twins, flat-twins or flat-fours from the likes of BMW, Honda or Moto-Guzzi among others, the drive comes straight from the crankshaft into a clutch and then to a gearbox.

Regulator/Rectifier
A more modern version of the zener diode, but it does the same job. Commonly a combined unit, solid-state regulator can be used to replace the zener diode on older machines.

Rockers & Tappets
Rockers are levers that operate the valves by moving up and down on a shaft in the cylinder head, operated by pushrods or by a camshaft. At the end of the rocker where it meets the top of the valve there needs to be a tiny gap, known as tappet clearance, to ensure that the valve is closed.

Side Valve
The side-valve engine had largely died out by 1960, only Velocette persevering with it on the LE flat twin. The valves are mounted on the side of the cylinder, operating on a cam shaft below, and into a flat cylinder head with a combustion chamber. Simple and extremely hard wearing, are not very powerful or economical, but very long lived.

Sludge Trap
Used on many British motorcycles, a small space inside the flywheel which acts as a centrifugal oil filter which prevents dirt, sludge, and unwanted debris from entering the crankshaft and working its way into the journals and con-rod bearings. If it gets blocked it can have catastrophic consequences and should be cleaned out when an engine is dismantled.

Tickler
A button on the carburettor that floods the fuel inlet with petrol and helps cold starting. Use in conjunction with a choke or when the engine is warm.

Unit Construction
Engine and gearbox in a single casting. On British bikes the gearbox was separate within that casting and had its own oil supply while Japanese machines tended to contain the gearbox and engine bottom-end in the same casting, sharing an oil supply.

Wet Sump, Dry Sump
Wet sump engines keep their engine oil in the crankcase while dry sump engines have separate oil tank. British motorcycles are usually dry sump, while most Japanese bikes are wet sump – though some Hondas such as the CB750 are dry sump.

Zener Diode
If the alternator creates too much voltage it will fry the coils and boil the battery. The zener diode uses this up as heat, as a safety valve. That stylish finned item under the headlight of some British bikes is the zener diode.

ACU Member Update

The ACU sent out the following update for all of its members on 16th January

Club Membership

Users can now add multiple club memberships in the 'Club & Team Affiliation' section of their profile. If you wish to add club memberships to your profile, please follow the steps below:

1. Log in to acu.sport80.com using your email address and password
2. Click 'View Profile' and select 'Club & Team Affiliations' option
3. Click 'Add Club & Team Affiliation' button (top right)
4. Select 'Club Membership'
5. Complete the form, selecting the relevant club. The club you select will be sent an email requesting approval of the club membership record.
6. This update means that each club you are affiliated to can separately approve your club memberships. Also that payments made on the club websites will generate new items in the Club & Team Affiliations section of your profile.

Club Websites

Several enhancements are being made to this module, in line with user experience feedback of ACU members, the main items of the first version batch upgrade being:

All member profiles in your account will display in the club management system.

Users can specify which member to purchase a club membership for when buying through the club website. As an example, a parent who is a licence holder can manage multiple memberships to cover other members of his/her family.

Promoters and clubs will be able to access the club management system to set up websites (and for promoters to sell memberships in the way clubs do). These enhancements will work in tandem with the changes made to the club membership records of the ACU Membership System (as specified above). This means individual members can join and make payment to multiple clubs, and subsequently be included in all their club member lists.

Ongoing Projects

Other items we have identified as the top priorities based on user feedback currently being worked on include:

1. Automated creation and distribution of Event Permits.
2. Clubs to be able to approve or reject 'Club Membership – Approval' records from within the system (rather than just by e-mail).
3. The ability of events organisers to control whether they sell One-Event licences for any given event.
4. Changes to the way Approval Required e-mails behave, giving the organisations that make the approvals more control.
5. Allowing event organisers to fully preview event entry forms from the Event Admin Panel.
6. These projects will not apply to everyone, but we hope that by listing them here, we are providing transparency in terms of what is underway and that there is a significant amount of work in progress.
7. The ACU continues to work with Sport:80 to enhance and evolve the membership system as per the requirements of those who use it. Thank you again for your continued feedback and patience during this seismic change.

VMCC contact for ACU enquiries:
Annie Durrant, Vice President – Major Events
07484 647046
events@vmcc.net
vmcc.net/ACU

Gems from the Library:

The AJS Big Port

When we think of good sporting 350s from the 1920s, the flat tank AJS Big Port – named for its distinctively large downpipe and port – is probably one that springs to mind. It was said to be based on the 350cc AJS on which Tom Sheard won the 1921 Junior TT race – Howard Davies famously won the Senior TT in the same year, the first time a 350 had won the Senior. A production ohv 350 was shown at the 1922 Olympia show and went on sale the following year. Given the racing pedigree, it's no surprise that the production Big Port, with a three-speed close-ratio gearbox and light weight (just a little over 200lb) had a very lively performance.

This made it a big hit with sporting riders who used it competitively at Brooklands, hill climbs and the like, and the model is still a very popular machine today. Ivan Rhodes, best known for Velocettes, often extols the virtues of a Big Port. They had a letter designation according to year, so a Big Port B4 was a 1924 machine. The picture shown is from library's copy of the 1928 catalogue, the three-speed, 3.39hp OHV TT Model K6. The Big Port was in the catalogue for over nine years with many changes. By the time it reached the end of the line the heavier 'S' models with a saddle tank and separate oil tank had lost some of their sporty lightweight character.

Ed Grew

The A.J.S. 3.49 h.p. Overhead Valve Model K 6.

Reading Matters

BSA's on-trend advertising, and how to race a classic

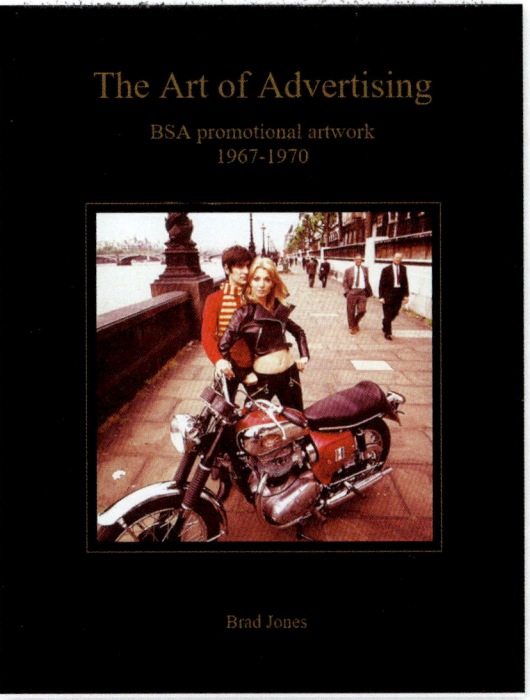

The Art of Advertising

In the late 60s, following the lead of its Japanese rivals and the realisation that sales trends in the crucial North American market were undergoing a drastic transformation, BSA hired a Californian-based photographer to revitalise its by now decidedly staid advertising material. The result was a series of well thought out and striking images that began appearing as advertisements and posters from spring 1967 and throughout much of 1968. With a standard now set the company went on to mimic this style for the remainder of the decade – sometimes successfully, sometimes not – more often than not achieving that critical visual appeal.

Packed into this large-format high quality 85-page book are original posters, advertisements – even of the rarest Bantam of them all, the BSA Bushman – and selected brochure images accompanied by campaign background details, much of which, until now, have been overlooked.

Well researched by the French-based American author Brad Jones, this specialist book will certainly appeal to serious restorers of BSAs of this period and makes an ideal addition to Jones' previous excellent books on the marque: 'BSA Motorcycles – the final evolution' and 'From the inside – BSA/Triumph's Umberslade Hall research establishment revealed.'

Jonathan Hill (Dorset)

Title: The Art of Advertising – BSA promotional artwork 1967-1970
Author: Brad Jones
Publisher: Spangle Publishing 2021
www.bsa1971.com

Racing Classic Motorcycles

Let's be honest, who hasn't ever dreamt about winning a world championship race or an Isle of Man TT? For most us, it remains just a dream. But what does it actually take to turn dream into reality?

Andy Reynolds' excellent softback book – just reprinted by Veloce – lays it out in a brutally honest style which makes clear the sacrifices needed. In 240 pages he details all aspects of racing, highlighting the successes and the dangers – physical and financial – of motorcycle racing, as well as the dedication needed to compete.

Andy Reynolds is well qualified to write on this subject, having raced the best classic machines between 1976 and 2016 at the highest level. Born in West London, he started his working career in engineering and was something of a rocker, like many others collecting a few points on his driving licence. All that changed when he joined the police, which supported his racing aspirations all over the UK and Europe including his beloved Isle of Man – he lapped the TT course at over 100mph during practice for the 2008 Senior Classic MGP and the following year achieved a well deserved third place. Well known for his machine preparation, Andy was able to ride an impressive list of bikes including Aermacchi, Seeley AJS and Matchless, Petty Norton, Manx Norton, BMW, Velocette, Paton, Honda K4, and Norton-JAP.

As one might expect given his police background, the book's text is factual, not flowery. Andy details his career on two wheels in 24 chapters in the same meticulous manner he prepared the bikes, including his times in the VMCC, Velocette Owners Club, the CRMC, and the Federation of British Police Motor Clubs. It's all written with an amazing humility and modesty – like all the greats, Andy Reynolds was just pursuing his own goals in a decent and professional manner and making a lot of friends along the way as result!

Anybody who wants to race a classic bike should read this book before embarking down that slippery financial slope. Certainly, it is one of the best books ever written about racing at grass roots level and something of bargain at £15.99.

Ian Kerr MBE

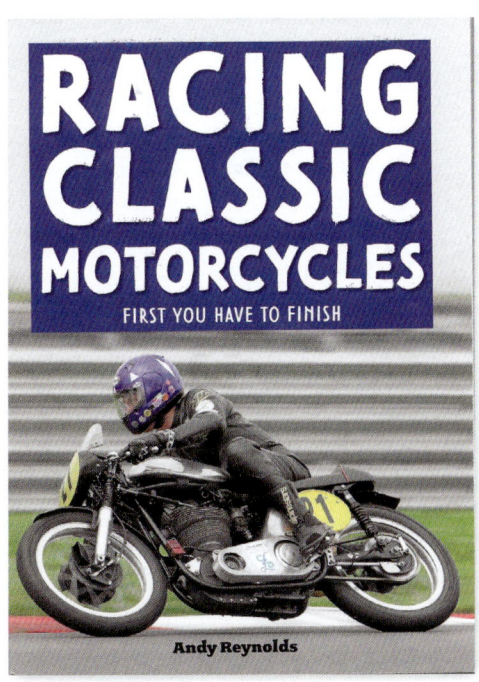

Title: Racing Classic Motorcycles
Author: Andy Reynolds
Price: £15.99
Publisher: Veloce Books
www.veloce.com
E-mail: enquiries@crowood.com
www.crowood.com

SECTION SPOTLIGHT

MICK DUGHAN (Section Chairman) profiles the Section closest to VMCC HQ

Firstly let me make it clear, we are not Allen House. You would be surprised how many members from other Sections think we are, but Allen House just happens to be on our patch.

The Section was established in 1971, and some of our founder members are still quite active considering they are now in their 80s. Once Covid restrictions were eased in 2021 we held a run to celebrate 50 years of the Section.

We meet at Marston's Brewery Sports and Social Club for both winter get togethers with guest speakers, and as a starting point for our summer runs, all of which are well attended. We also join other Sections for runs and gatherings.

Our premier event is the Burton Parade, held on the second Sunday in May, which is very popular and up until Covid struck had to be limited to 100 entries to comply with fire regulations at the club – numbers have since fallen a little but we expect them to recover. Titch Allen was a regular at the Parade and particularly loved the buffet after the ride.

One previous event which we pioneered was the Curborough Training Day, at which members were given the opportunity to ride other machines. This was so successful it was taken over by headquarters and has been part of the national calendar.

We have an active committee comprising six to eight who meet to organise our events. Several members are very keen to organise runs, both local and further afield, ranging from 30 to over 200 miles.

Most of our members ride post-war or classic machines, and some own vintage and veteran examples which make an appearance at events which cater for them, such as the Parade.

Some of our runs are strictly for 25-year-old machines, although we never discourage riders of modern machines on other runs, in the hope that they will be converted to the joys of owning and riding older bikes.

Several times a year we hold what we call eating events, such as a Pie and Peas Run, Harvest Supper, Breakfast Run, and a Cheese Night. On most of these we are joined by wives and partners, which makes for a nice social event, including raffles to raise money for local charities.

During Covid we started our own website with regular newsletters etc, which is now ongoing together with a WhatsApp group which gives us good communication between members. We try to attend several local galas where we put on a display and try to encourage new members by talking to visitors, to promote the Club and ensure its future.

Insurance Matters

Riding your friend's bike – we all want to do it, but are we insured? – BOB CLARK on PJI's personal approach

insurance@vmcc.net

This month, we look at the question of insurance when you are riding a bike that belongs to someone else and isn't on your insurance policy. There are all sorts of situations where this can be desirable or necessary. A common one is when another member offers us a ride on their machine.

Years ago I remember watching an acquaintance looking closely at my CZ 175 in the lunch stop car park. We fell to talking and it turned out that he'd always wondered what the CZ singles were like to ride, so I said, "want to try it?" The upshot was that I rode his immaculate early 1950s twin back to the start, to find him already there with my scruffy old CZ and a big grin on his face!

But it might not be a simple 'have a go' scenario that sees you riding someone else's bike. You might want to test ride a machine you are thinking of buying, and sometimes there are sad occasions when a fellow member takes ill during a ride-out and someone's got to get their bike home.

Now in the old days you maybe had 'riding other bikes' on your policy, so you were insured if the policeman asked. Of course, if you crashed someone else's bike the principle was, 'he who bends it, mends it.' Until now, because through our partnership with Peter James Insurance (PJI) we have put in place something much better.

If you're over 25 and set up or renewed your policy after 1st December 2022, you've now got a rather special and unique add-on: 'member to member' cover. Subject to certain limits this means your PJI comprehensive policy covers you on other bikes. The borrowed bike must be:
- Insured for road use – it doesn't matter who the insurer is
- Owned by another VMCC member
- Over 20 years old
- Being ridden on the road – member-to-member cover doesn't include events like 1000 Bikes.

Back in the day, you could ride your mate's bike in shirtsleeves, sans helmet, and who knows what insurance. This is actually Colin Cade on his own BSA c1967.

Please remember this only works in both directions if the two of you have VMCC Motorcycle Insurance policies. If your VMCC mate has but you don't, their comprehensive policy will normally apply to your bike when they are riding it. But your non-VMCC policy – if it allows you to ride other bikes at all – will almost certainly only provide third party cover when you are riding theirs. And also remember: this policy is *only* available to VMCC members – it simply can't be bought by the general public or members of other clubs.

You should always think carefully and get multiple quotes when setting up or renewing insurance policies, but what have you possibly got to lose by asking Peter James Insurance for a quote? It's easy to do: email classics@peterjamesinsurance.co.uk or ring them between 9am and 5pm, Monday to Friday.

Safe riding, summer is on the way!

Buying a bike? Get a quote from VMCC Motorcycle Insurance — Call 0121 274 5355

Saved by the WELD

BOB MINTO on how his 1928 AJS was saved by some expert welding and machining

Above: Finished bike, beautifully repaired = one happy owner
Below: Ouch, that's nasty, and only 60 miles after completing the rebuild

In March 2020, just two weeks after lockdown, I bought a 1928 AJS 350 K4 in a European auction – it arrived literally a couple of day later from Holland in a crate.

On inspection it required a full strip down and reconditioning of pretty much everything. The bike had left the factory in 1928 bound for Austria, or so I'm led to believe, and spent the next 92 years flitting between Austria and Italy before ending up in the Netherlands.

While I was working on the mechanics of the bike I also enquired about getting her registered in the UK. The VMCC and all the lovely contacts within helped me get the info and certification I needed to satisfy the DVLA and needless to say the AJS was duly registered. It was all pretty seamless.

Broken Box

I'd never restored a bike this old before, and certainly not a flat tanker from 1928, so I was on a bit of a learning curve. There had been some evidence of shady workmanship attempted previously on the gearbox but the last thing I was expecting to see the rear end of the box to break away completely, just 60 miles after the rebuild.

Far left: Further evidence of the previous shady repair
Left: That's better, Val's machined replacement neatly welded on
Above: Better than new? Possibly

This was bad news as I clearly needed a new gearbox casing, but where would I find one for a 1928 AJS? I knew it wouldn't be an easy task and after a lot of searching did find a suitable box for sale in Australia, the drawbacks being that it was a complete box, not just the shell, and that the asking price was $1200 Australian.

Quite apart from the cost it would have mucked up the matching numbers currently on the bike. Buying that box would have been the easy option but it just didn't sit right with me, not after all the work returning the AJS to the UK, going through a full restoration and getting her registered with the DVLA.

Then a friend of mine introduced me to Val Roberts. Val is an excellent engineer and it was he who suggested cutting out the entire back end of the box and machining/welding in a complete new piece.

I loved the idea but not being an engineer was a little worried that it might not work. Still, I was clearly in the hands of an expert and to be honest it was the only option considering the damage to the box. Val duly machined a new section and his mate did a fantastic welding job attaching it to the existing gearbox shell. In fact, he did it so well that I think the box is now stronger than it was when it left the factory in Wolverhampton all those years ago.

I rebuilt the bike just in time for the Shuttleworth Sprint where the bike stood up very well and the box is now better than new. The most important thing for me was not to lose the matching frame/box/engine numbers and both these guys that carried out this specialist work enabled that to happen. I still have a matching numbers bike and have kept its history. I simply can't thank them enough.

Contact Val Roberts
(01651) 873812
http://davalmachining.co.uk

Complete box, ready to refit

All finished, ready for Shuttleworth

Buying Your First Classic

Handsome beast – pre-unit Triumph Bonneville is undoubtedly a classic

Buying Your First Classic

BSA B25 can make a good first classic bike

Should you buy a classic bike? OLIVER HULME is your guide

Why buy a classic bike? It's a good question – after all, modern bikes are invariably easier to ride and more reliable. They don't (as a rule) leak oil or lose their electrics, nor do they need much attention between services.

On the other hand, there are plenty of good reasons for buying a classic. They are great fun to ride, have character and are usually fixable at home by a competent mechanic. But the ultimate reason is yours, and yours alone, which is all that matters. It could be that you are returning to motorcycles after a long break, perhaps because life, jobs, families and cars got in the way. But often it's down to memories of halcyon days. As a classic dealer once said to me: "We are buying our own nostalgia."

Looking Back...

You might remember the fun of those blasts to the coast in summer or heading for the hills with nothing but a tent and a Party Four strapped on behind. Late night dashes through the city streets, on some mission that felt so important at the time. But you'll remember those winter rides too, when the wind cut through, icicles formed on your nose and the rain found its way through that battered wax-cotton jacket.

There were moments of perfection when the weather and road were just right, and times of heroic failure, of nursing an ancient Honda back home on one cylinder, or picking the gravel from fresh wounds, or hauling something out of the hedge you stuffed it into. Or the satisfaction of coaxing a bike back into life with the help of a couple of mates and a big hammer.

So that's nostalgia, but perhaps you already live a two-wheeled life, but the modern stuff doesn't do it for you any more and you feel the need to get back to basics. There's the challenge of finding just what you want, and the good news is that there's an old bike to suit just about everyone. It might be a stinky Greeves two-stroke, a throaty old Norton, the slightly unhinged howl of a DOHC Kawasaki or the sheer unadulterated class of a Ducati or Moto Guzzi. It could be a bike you owned when young (or lusted after because you couldn't afford it) – a candy purple Yamaha FS1E or a late '60s Triumph Bonneville, maybe an original Suzuki Katana.

Classics give a very different, and involving, riding experience. Beard not compulsory

A thing of beauty in your back garden – but will it fit your lifestyle?

Want to relive your sweet sixteens? 1970s sports mopeds are sought-after

Or maybe you're in your 20s or 30s, and just like the style and feel of old bikes. Modern bikes are a bit like an iPhone – they work perfectly, but don't need much interaction. A classic motorcycle on the other hand, demands some input and effort from the rider, and the result can be a far more satisfying ride which transcends the everyday. Ultimately, it's all about feeling alive.

A New, Old World

Many of the people I know who ride classic bikes tend to prefer the rough and ready to the soulless corporate offerings, and that extends to the dealers as well as the bikes. Traditional bike shops of blessed memory might have vanished from the high streets, but they're still on the outskirts, keeping going in industrial units that aren't quite big enough. These are the shops you'll start to frequent, the ones with hard working owners, old bikes lined up outside and mechanics with long hair and grease on their foreheads. A few of the major modern bike dealers do seem to care about classics, often the ones that are flourishing , often with a handful of '70s bikes tucked away in the corner of the showroom because the owner really doesn't want to part with them.

Forget the past for a moment, though. One big attraction of classic bikes is that they look so stylish, and it's a look that's more popular than ever. That's why so many modern manufacturers offer 'retro' motorcycles – I'm thinking a brand new Triumph Bonneville or Royal Enfield Interceptor. But park one of those 21st century recreations next to an original and it's obvious which is the better looking. The same goes when you start them up – they are good facsimiles, but not the real thing.

My own experience of classic British motorcycle ownership arrived when I bought a very ordinary BSA Starfire 250 and took

When these Triumphs were new, bike dealers were on the high street

Triumph twins are a popular choice among the British bikes

it to a major bike meeting. I parked up among a forest of new Harley-Davidsons, ZZeFR this, and GPxRR that before wandering off to grab coffee and a bun. When I returned the little BSA was surrounded by people discussing it, reminiscing about the bike they owned in the past, and wanting to know how much it cost, how hard was it to start and so on. Which motorcycle will turn heads? A fully-equipped new adventure bike might get a glance, but just watch the heads turn as a '50s AJS 350 rumbles past. The regular star of my local bike night is a 50cc Raleigh Runabout...

In fact, meeting people – the social side – is one of the more important aspects of classic ownership. There are clubs like the VMCC, bike nights and gatherings all year round, friendships to be made and information to be gleaned. If you need help, someone will have the answer. You might end up down a one marque rabbit hole or find a fascination for ex-military machinery. Solo riders will always find themselves meeting some kindred spirit along the way, shows are friendly and convivial affairs, while jumbles are a great way to lose yourself for a few hours.

Royal Enfield Continental was a factory made cafe racer

What is a Classic?

What then, to ride? I've had as much pleasure riding a 200cc Francis-Barnett two-stroke through leafy English lanes as I've had taking a 750 GPz Kawasaki on an A-road blast. They both have their moments, and their faults.

Speaking of Francis-Barnetts, can a pedestrian AMC commuter be considered a classic? Some say no, thinking a Falcon is too 'grey porridge' to be worthy of the name. If you call a Villiers-powered runabout 'classic' then surely a Honda CG125 or C50 stepthough qualifies too, just as much as a Vincent Black Shadow. In short, how do you define what a classic actually is?

When Titch Allen formed the Vintage Motorcycle Club (back in 1946), a 'vintage' bike was anything made prior to 1930, or as little as 16 years old. Later, the VMCC took on the 25-year guideline – anything 25 years old or more could be considered a classic, whether it's British, Japanese, European, whatever.

If you accept that, then there's plenty of scope. For some, a classic has to be British, and buying an old Brit bike is actually a good call. Spares availability is excellent and complete bikes are plentiful, so there's bound to be one that suits your style, size and ability. There's also a vast amount of knowledge about them, plus a forest of magazines, whole libraries full of books, owners' club experts and individual owners with encyclopaedic knowledge.

But things are changing. Now, anyone under 60 probably grew up on Japanese bikes, not British ones. As a result, there's rocketing interest in Japanese classics, which have their own magazines, experts and clubs too. And while the spares situation isn't quite as plentiful, and is complicated by more variants (especially imports) you can still get most things at a price. Italian bikes didn't change as frequently as Japanese models, which helps, and their ancillaries are often universal, which can be a boon. BMW flat-twin owners are among the best served of all when it comes to spares, and few would argue about an air-cooled BeeEmm's classic status.

Just for the Ride

Owning a classic motorcycle can change you as a person. Riding one, whether alone or with a group, can be transcendental when everything's going well. Of course, there will be challenges too, in fact, moments of incandescent rage, but that's all part of the territory. An old motorcycle will be simple enough to look after by yourself.

You'll get used to taking it apart in the winter and putting it back together again in the spring. It may not run any better afterwards, but you'll know more about it. And I find that doing things yourself and understanding how they work brings on a

A 1970s Japanese machine can offer a good compromise between character and practicality

Older bikes such as this Panther will need more adjusting to, if you're used to modern machines

feeling of calm. If a modern bike won't go (a rare occurrence, I'll grant you), where do you start? If the carburettor float bowl on your old BSA is overflowing, then you'll probably know from experience that the float is sticking, and what to do about it. You will break down, it's inevitable. But even this can be a blessing. The old boy mowing his lawn will come over as you scratch your head and offer to help. And then you haven't just satisfied yourself, but him too.

Kick starting (which applies to a shrinking proportion of old bikes now – most bikes less than 40 years old have push button starting) is becoming a lost art, though it's really just a case of getting to know the technique your bike needs.

Then there's the brakes. Drum brakes or discs from the 1970s will be nowhere near as good as you remembered or expected, while other road users will be able stop much more quickly than you can. No indicators? You'd better get used to hand signals. Pre-1975 British bikes have their gear change on the right, though Japanese and European classics are usually left foot. Although a right-foot shift might seem confusing at first, a little practice will stop you hitting the brake instead of the gears. Older British machines also have the changing sequence backwards, in a one-up-three-down arrangement, rather than one-down-three up. Except on Triumphs. Confused yet?

My First Classic(s)

I bought my Yamaha XS650 Special for £1000 in 1993 when it was 14 years old, and it is still in my shed after years of sterling service. But my first real classic buy was a 1969 BSA Starfire 250, bought at the VMCC jumble at Shepton Mallet five years ago. A running US import, the most complicated part of the purchase was getting it registered. The little BSA is lots of fun over short distances, but I don't tend to ride it far as the riding position doesn't suit me. The Starfire is famous for grenading in spectacular fashion, and this one did subsequently snap an exhaust valve, but fixing it was a breeze.

A year later I bought a splendidly dog-eared 1973 Triumph Bonneville on the phone (by accident, these things happen) from an HJ Pugh auction – I put in a silly bid which I didn't expect to win and then did. So I changed the oil and the high-rise bars, blatted around on it for three months with no trouble at all and then I rode it 1500 miles to the Shetlands and back. It performed faultlessly all the way, using less than a pint of oil, most of which dribbled from an incontinent primary drive. As I never fail to tell people, the Triumph had in a past life had a starring role as a getaway vehicle in an episode of The Sweeney.

You return from your first short ride and give the machine a close look over. Is there oil or petrol leaking from somewhere unexpected? Could well be. Are there unpleasant noises coming from anywhere? Do the lights still all work, and if they don't, does your local car accessory shop have 6v lightbulbs?

If something has gone wrong, consult the manual to see why it broke and decide you really should change the oil and tidy up the bodged together crimped-on wiring while you are about it. Check the battery is charging properly, and a couple of decent tyres might not go amiss.

This all sounds a bit like hard work, but that changes over time. Gradually, you'll gain confidence in the bike and your ability to fix it. The rides become longer and the satisfaction greater, and you'll discover skills you didn't know you had.

So if you want a challenge, but don't fancy taking up golf or running marathons, then a classic motorcycle is fabulous way of feeling alive. And with it comes great knowledge, new friendships and great comradeship, of the kind you might have forgotten existed. ∎

Top 10 Reasons to go Classic

Beware pattern parts...

You may meet a different type of motorcycle dealer...

Why you should buy a classic bike (and why, maybe, you shouldn't)

Why You Should
1: Character
2: Simplicity, which makes fault finding easier. Just listen for obvious strange noises, try and keep the oil inside and electricity from escaping.
3: Styling – and it's the real deal, not a retro.
4: Fixable at home. A moderately talented amateur mechanic can fix their bike at home, which is an obvious money saver.
5: Cheaper spares. Whether it's new, old stock, second-hand parts, or pattern stuff, spares are always cheaper than modern kit. A new rear tyre for my Bonneville cost £70-£80, against £130 for my 2019 Husqvarna 401... and those need replacing in pairs.
6: Depreciation is low or non-existent. All my classics are worth between £500 and £2500 more than I paid for them – the Husky is worth half what I paid for it. Whether this will continue in a world moving away from fossil fuels is open to debate.
7: Friendship. Owning a classic will make you friends – it's not just the camaraderie, but their help when things go wrong.
8: Cheaper insurance on a classic policy, though some providers won't accept NCD.
9: No MoT or tax. If the bike's over 40 years old, register it as historic and you won't need either.
10: Banish boredom. This will be a thing of the past, replaced with confusion, frustration and, eventually, satisfaction.

Why You Shouldn't
1: Brakes. Can be terrible by modern standards, whether early Japanese discs or British drums – they just aren't built for modern roads. Italian stuff is slightly better.
2: Electrics. Primitive and often held together with previous owner bodges.
3: Lights. Bad enough back in the day, now at glowworm standards. Fortunately, modern LED bulbs are a simple upgrade – buy them.
4: Maintenance. You can't just park up after a ride and expect it to be perfect next time – wipe it down and check for loose bolts and fluid leaks.
5: Pattern parts. Can be a bit iffy, especially rubber components. I'm on my third set of BSA gaiters, while factory ones I fitted 20 years ago to my Yamaha are perfect.
6: Dodgy geezers. It has to be said, there are chancers out there trying to get their hands on your money by selling you a duff bike. When buying, take an expert with you and don't be blinded by shiny chrome.
7: Idiosyncrasies. Esoteric features, sometimes unique to a particular model – see sludge traps, magdynos and fully enclosed brake discs.
8: Previous owners. An old bike will usually have had many previous owners, all with different attitudes to maintenance.
9: Restoration cost. This will be more than you could imagine – budget for three times your first estimate.
10: No MoT. Great for the owner, but the bike has also missed out on a dealer visit and once-over every year. Now you have to rely on the seller's honesty. See points 6 and 8.

Rule of Three

So what can you expect for a budget of £3000–£5000? Three typical bikes...

The Japanese Option: Yamaha RD250

The Yamaha RD250 is not a big bike and its centre of gravity is low, making for effortless handling. The seat height is nicely universal and will fit almost anybody. The footrests sit where you would like them, while the bars are slightly upswept, though this does stick you up in the wind. The seat is comfortable and narrow at the nose.

This is an air-cooled two-stroke, and it sounds like one, with that distinctive combination of tearing newspaper and a clattering bin full of beer cans at tickover, until throttle is applied, when the ripping/clattering becomes a howl.

At first, I felt the power take-up on this low miles US import was a little milder than expected, but like any two-stroke you need to find out where the power band is. Once I learnt to get past 5000rpm, this RD would rev to 8000 within the blink of an eye. It fair flies along once it gets rolling, flips in and out of corners, brakes when you need it to (though see below) and picks the power up instantly once hazards have been negotiated.

A little scuffed around the edges, but this two-stroke twin had plenty of go

Evocative - must have one picture

Yamaha is small, light and manageable

The Yamaha is not some over-stressed and fragile rev-hungry monster though. Thanks to the reed valves there is some torque, allowing you to keep things rolling at lower speeds, in high winds or on uphill stretches, and it will even pootle along at low revs if you so desire. US spec models had six-speed boxes, and all I can say is that there are plenty of ratios, all of which do their stuff and snick in and out unnoticed. Legal limit cruising is entirely possible, though it might be a bit comfier at speed with UK rather than US bars.

The RD excels on country roads and handling up to 60mph or so is great – it's low and light, doesn't weave or feel unstable, and you can fling it through bends without a problem. Anything faster might make you feel a bit more nervous until you set the suspension up for yourself. Despite being low, everything is well tucked in and you'll have to push it hard to ground anything.

Bits and pieces like switchgear and clocks are good for their era, but the lights and horn are pathetic. The RD250's drum brakes are of the hitting-a-brick-wall variety, especially if you are used to a disc. Treating an old motorcycle with a little sensitivity is no bad thing.

The RD is fast, stops, handles well and has a comfortable ride. You wouldn't have to worry about not getting where you wanted to go in a respectable time, and with decent reliability. It's probably a bit thirsty but what you get for your money is the kind of bike some lust over, which goes like stink, is reliable and is easy to look after. You could use it in modern traffic and that traffic will have trouble keeping up with you, not the other way round.

An unmolested RD250 is a fine motorcycle, a delight to ride, refined at low revs and a rip-snorting fun machine at the top end. In short, it's a magic carpet ride through time and will take you back to the days when nothing mattered but having fun.

Thanks to Somerset Classic Motorcycles for the loan of their glorious 10,000-mile RD250.

The British Option: BSA A65

The lines on a BSA Lightning A65 are clean. There's nothing sticking out anywhere, no jagged edges to catch yourself on, no expanse of metal requiring a tortured riding position. On this example – a Thunderbolt with a twin-carb Lightning head and a US tank but UK bars – the riding geometry was near perfect, and it was easy to paddle around.

Controls are minimal. No choke lever, and just two switches on the bars for the horn and dip switch, with the lights operated by a toggle switch on the headlight. After tickling both carbs, two kicks got things going – the first to get the fuel into the inlet tract, the second to bring the big twin into life with a satisfying whoompf.

Immediately apparent on the road were the lightness of the clutch and how slick the gearchange was. One down, then up all the way. The '60s suspension coped well with potholed roads and cornering was very much a case of point it, lean it in, give it a squirt and you're out the other side, looking for another decent curve to enjoy. The front brake was near perfect.

All British twins (Commandos apart) vibrate, don't they? The BSA was no exception, though it was very different to the other '60s and '70s twins I've ridden. There was nothing near to the rhythmic thumping of a Royal Enfield, or the blast of a Triumph. Instead, the Lightning spec engine was a buzzy thing. While swinging through bends or hacking through traffic this won't matter, but on a long ride it would become wearisome.

BSA in its element – twisty English B road on a summer's day

Twin-carb twin was well sorted, though the single-carb is more restful

BSAs tend to be cheaper than the equivalent Triumph or Norton

Power came in at around 5000rpm – a lot higher than the A65's contemporaries – so if you want to make progress the buzziness is amplified. The BSA felt as if it would be most at home on 100-mile blasts on our twistier A and B roads. For the high mileage rider, planning the single-carb Thunderbolt – a smoother and more civilised mount – would be a better choice.

On the plus side, a BSA A65 needs less maintenance than the equivalent Triumph to keep it on the road, especially on the top end. The much talked about issues with the timing side main bearing aren't as bad as some think. You can convert to a roller bearing, but given regular oil changes with good quality oil, anyone using an A65 today isn't likely to experience problems.

You can pick up a decent running A65 for less than £5000 and trawling the classifieds should pick up a roadworthy example for as little as £3500. That makes the A65 one of the cheaper big British twins you can lay your hands on, and well worth considering.

Thanks to Mike Ives Motorcycles for letting me play with his A65.

The Italian Option: Moto Guzzi V50

Welcome to a useable, everyday classic bike. When the Moto Guzzi V50 was introduced, testers considered the V-twin to be charming, though a little idiosyncratic on the road. The lack of a shock absorber on the shaft drive was said to cause the back wheel to lock up if you got the revs wrong while changing gear.

However, the 1983 model I rode didn't have any such issues. An Italian market import which arrived in the UK several years ago, the finish showed that it had been carefully looked after by a previous owner. Although badged as a V50 MkII, the bike was in V50 MkIII specification with cb points, a plastic front mudguard and front brake callipers on the rear of the fork legs. The engine made no nasty noises, and there was nothing in the way of the alleged driveline lash. Perhaps 1980s road testers just rode the V50 harder than me...

Easy to ride, easy to live with

Practical classic? Light, good on fuel, shaft drive, electric start...

Italian import V50 had kept its finish

Starting from cold produced the momentary lurch from side-to-side reaction common to some transverse twins, but this vanished once the bike warmed up. Some motorcycles feel just right, and the V50 gave the rider an instant feel of confidence that it was going to go exactly where you squirted it, even on back roads of dubious quality.

The front brake (operating one of the two front discs) was more than capable of slowing things down on its own, and a dab on the foot pedal (operating Guzzi's linked front/rear system) rapidly brought things to halt in a safe and controllable fashion. In fact, with brakes like these the V50 would be perfectly at home in modern traffic.

There were some typically Italian issues. The switchgear was something of a challenge as the designer apparently had shoved the buttons anywhere they would fit. The indicator button was mounted on top of the cluster and took a while to get used to, while the side stand was also uncomfortably short for me. I've often wondered if Italian side-stand designers are in cahoots with the manufacturers of indicator lenses and clutch levers – it's just a thought.

Still, not only are most parts readily available, but a V50 can be had for a very reasonable price, anything from £2500-£4000, and a bit of diligent searching will find you a road-worn runner with MoT for not much more than half that. In short, the V50 handled, would happily cruise at the legal limit, stopped almost as well as an ultra-modern 500, started at the push of a button, was light and easy to move about, and hauled me around without complaint. You would need to update a few components and keep it clean to stop it from rotting away, but for the everyman and everywoman, this is an everyday classic motorcycle.

Thanks to Classic Motorcycles Ltd of Northwich for the loan of the V50. ■

FOR SALE, WANTED & EXCHANGE

Now with FREE PICTURES in Bikes For Sale ads!
Details: See page 75

BIKES FOR SALE

AJS MODEL 16 1936. Coil ignition, good condition. Restored a few years ago – file with photos and some receipts. Original reg BER 912, V5 in my name. £7950. 01843 832899, Thanet area.

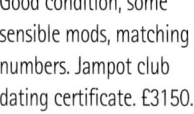
AJS M20 500cc 1953. Good condition, some sensible mods, matching numbers. Jampot club dating certificate. £3150. Also AJS M16 1953 tele-rigid, Martyn Bratley restored carb, £2900. Both dry stored and owned 15 years plus. John 01903 815497 W. Sussex.

ARIEL HUNTMASTER 1958. Superb example from private collection. 51,000 miles, matching numbers, original registration, buff logbook and V5C. Enclosed chaincase, stainless rack, 12V with indicators. Photos available, ready to ride, free delivery arranged. £6450. Phil 01723 372219 Yorkshire.

BMW-POWERED racing three-wheeler. 980cc twin graded as 1972. Vintage Morgan style chassis and bodywork but rear engined. Recent construction. Supercharged by Shorrocks 16psi boost. My age (85) forces very reluctant sale. Trailer. Malcolm Cookson, morganist2@gmail.com 01229 823279.

BMW R65LS 1983. Immaculate condition with a new camchain. Must be seen, it really is like new. £3750ono. Ill health forcing sale, selling on behalf of my brother. Call for details 07789 903590.

BSA C10L 1954 in good condition. Starts easily. Slow but sure. Incl. manuals and some history. Age and space force sale. £2700 FIRM. More info Peter 01438 743515.

BSA J11 1934, 500cc V-twin. New big-ends, gearbox rebuilt, all major components present, lots of remade items including smalls. Non-tank panel model, worthwhile easy project, no paperwork, £6000ono. g.walker940@ntlworld.com 01282 778957.

BSA M20. Running order, first reg 1947 but generally wartime spec. Widow's sale. £6000ono. Geoff 07779 294917 geoff.gat@gmail.com Philippa 07905 101861.

CAN-AM QUALIFIER look alike. Built from 1980 military bike, genuine '77 Qualifier tank, new ally rims and s/s spokes, new tyres, rewired, 6-speed, new Sebac shocks, many new and rare parts. T&T exempt V5C. 07833 700300, Suffolk.

EXCELSIOR U8 1961 150cc. Good condition, good wheels, easy starter. A joy to ride. Age and space force sale. £1600 FIRM. Peter 01438 743515.

HARLEY-DAVIDSON Road King Classic FLHCRI 1997. 1340cc EFI Evo engine. 3100m. Unmarked chrome & Vivid Black. Dressed with most options available at delivery time. £8000. Matching detachable sissy and King Tour Pack also available. Contact 07775 995560. Essex.

HONDA 400/4 1977. Frame powder coated, new exhaust pipes, rims, spoke, battery, indicator lights, cables, hydraulic pipes and piston. Carburetors reconditioned. Tank and side panels re-painted. Forks reconditioned etc. An outstanding example. £5850ono. taffbeck@talktalk.net

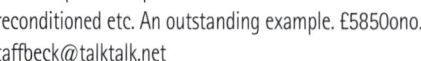

HONDA C70E 1986. MOT to end of Sept, taxed and in use. Starts and runs OK. Owned for 5 years. Haynes manual. Mostly original but cosmetically challenged. £1100ono. Call for more information 01935 478391 (Somerset).

HONDA C90 F reg. VGC, unrestored. Runs really well, 12k miles. Did charity run in 2010 John O' Groats to Land's End, local bike from new. £2000ono, poss px Pre-65 or Twinshock Trials bike. Lots of photos. Oxfordshire 07827 944857.

HONDA CB500/4 1972. Mike Hailwood Replica built with all new Davies Motorsport rear sets, yokes, fairing mounts, clip-ons, stainless spokes, alloy rims, modified hubs, alloy tank and wheels, handmade exhaust, real leather seat. Only displayed indoors, stunning. £6000 Ben 01208 816427.

Honda NTV650. V-twin, shaft drive. 61,000 miles but totally reliable. New oils and filter, brakes overhauled, seat re-covered professionally. New battery, good screen, everything works as it should. MOT Aug '23, on SORN. Ideal club run bike, no knee cracking kickstarter and no oil leaks. £699ono. Ride it home. North Norfolk 01366 348020.

JUNIOR SPRINT YAMAHA RS100 (1975). Frame up restoration with full engine and gearbox rebuild. Mods include flanged alloy wheels with s/s butted spokes, refurbished forks and new shocks, PVL ignition, Allspeed exhaust, Koso Rev counter. £2300ono. Andy 07833 592727.

LAMBRETTA Li125S 1967. Italian import. Home restoration completed 2017. Original frame, forks, engine, gearbox & bodywork. New locks, 12v electrics, cables, springs, exhaust, clutch and rubber. 17,500km. Starts easily & runs well. £3300. John Skinner 01502 724129 East Suffolk.

LUCY LOMAX Citrobm. Reluctant sale of fantastic vehicle used extensively at home and abroad. Modified and improved over the years, now powered by virtually new BMW R850. Low insurance, tax and MOT exempt. Unique removable hardtop. £10,895. 07956 652460 bodgerbish@outlook.com

NORTON CS1 1930. In race condition plus numerous spares. £12,000. Might split the spares. Email me at ajlewis@pandloss.com for details about the bike and the list of spares.

NORTON HI-RIDER 1974. Tank and panels repainted, belt primary, otherwise original. £15,000. 01539 741341 (Cumbria).

Buying a bike? Get a quote from VMCC Motorcycle Insurance Call 0121 274 5355

NORTON MODEL 50 1955. Starts and runs well. Reconditioned magneto and dynamo. Good solid bike. £4250. Alex 07776 145373 alexbaraona@ntlworld.com

ROYAL ENFIELD BULLET TRIALS 350 1951. I replaced clutch, speedo, chain, points, carb etc. Not restored, just  fettled it. Not road reg but the Enfield club say it's easy to do if anyone want to. Ill-health forces sale. Club valuation £3900 – I would like £3500. Semington Wiltshire. 07710 710036.

ROYAL ENFIELD CRUSADER SPORTS 1961 in mint condition. Alloy cylinder head and Omega piston. Valuable registration. For sale due to bereavement, £4750ono. More photos available. 01559 370563 or 07817 213130. penboyr@aol.com

TRIUMPH VETERAN 1912 hub clutch model. Very original, transferable reg, 3 owners last 74  years. Featured in Don Morley's Triumph motorcycle book. Pioneer registered with history. Good condition, runs well. £13,250. Nigel Hussey 01458 448124, luxvintagelife@aol.com (Somerset).

TRIUMPH BONNEVILLE T140V 1973. Matching numbers and showing only 15,400 miles. Tax & Mot exempt. Rides well & looks smart. Health reasons forces sale. £5750. 07754 524115 or email glenn@glennhardcastle.co.uk

TRIUMPH TIGER 100 1957. Pre-unit all-alloy engine, superb condition, extensive history file. Owned 8 years,  featured on TV. Rare model from private collection. Receipts, photos available, V5C. £8950. Phil 01723 372219 Yorkshire.

TRIUMPH TIGER 100 1957. Matching numbers, all-alloy motor. Stalled project as no space. Had engine running OK, part stripped. Complete apart from centre stand, speedo. Tank requires repair. Buff logbook, MOT 1971. £4750. Pete 07505 134645. (B'ham).

VELOCETTE THRUXTON replica, not used for some time and will need recommissioning. Early sand cast Thruxton cylinder head, Wellfin alloy barrel on MSS bottom end, Reg Orpin Summerton cam, TLS front brake. Including Velo spares. £6000. Cambridge 01223 892265.

VINCENT COMET special. 566cc engine, AMC gearbox & clutch, 1 3/8" GP, magneto & 12v dynamo. Vincent frame with Gilera single sided fork & wheel, Honda swinging arm & rear wheel. Award winning bike. £12,000. R Kettle. 07815 559507. enginecad@hotmail.com

YAMAHA RACING BIKES restored to original condition 95% original parts. Private collection, restored by myself. TZ350F TZ125G TD2 TR2 TD1C. Contact Mick on 01903 502679 or 07388 292888 or lee1066@talktalk.net.

YAMAHA XT600Z 1986 (electric/kick start). Total engine rebuild (everything). Almost mint Tenere model (big tank), all original, very rare. Red/White. £4500. Keith 07949 377310.

ZENITH JAP 680cc 1925. Lovely condition throughout. Original machine, matching  numbers. Last run 3 years ago. Genuine reason for sale. £28,000ovno. 01225 763919, 07906 444461. joan_groves@hotmail.co.uk

TRIUMPH TR6SS Pre-Unit 1962. Excellent mechanical, paint and tinware condition. Generally dry use only, 12-volt converted. Well maintained for 25 years. A pampered bike, gets what it wants when it wants. Garage kept. Offers around £9000. More pictures/info hornsby_jm@yahoo.co.uk

SPARES

AJS 1927 498cc head, c/w valves, alloy ex rocker and places, VGC £350. AJS 1930 350cc twin port head and barrel VGC £250. AJS 1924 350cc barrels sv, 2 types, £100 each. Joe Priestley 07964 822802.

AJS/MATCHLESS 1930s. Rigid rear stand £150, rear lift handle/stay perfect £45, 5 1/2" front hub and drum £60. Head stem and girder fork spindles, heavy weight. Brian 01474 705714 (Kent). At Shepton Mallet 25/3/23.

ARROW/LEADER pillion footrests £15 pair. Sunbeam S8 rider's footrest £25. Royal Enfield 125cc piston kit +030 £50. LE brake pedal £20. Ariel rider's footrest £25. Can email pictures, collect from LS25 1QG. 07517 111332 for more details.

BOX TRAILER for race/track day. Converted ex-BT, good condition. Takes 3 bikes and/or kit. Gas hob, sink and solar powered lights, TV. Two wheel chocks, ramp. No longer needed due to change of vehicle. £2250ono. laverdamann@manx.net for photos.

BSA A10/A7 timing covers set £75. Lightning tank with taps and cap £145. A7 crankcases £100. A10/A7 frame, no docs £500. BSA headlamp nacelle & fork shrouds NOS £100. Oil frame swingarm and spindle £60. Plus P&P. 01242 861164. 07971 631685.

BSA 1920s/30s 7" front brake plate incl. shoes. Speedo drive £100. Triumph 1920s ratchet gear lever £100. Brian 01474 705714 (Kent). At Shepton Mallet 25/3/23.

HELMET FRONT mudguards (x2). One diameter 29.5", width 4.5", depth at apex 4.5". The other, dia 28.5", width 5", depth at apex 4.5". Both in good useable condition, painted black. £50 each plus carriage. Paul Devitt paul.devitt01@icloud.com 01732 461532.

MZ SPARES, TS125, TS150, TS250 ETC. Alpha valves and guides (New) various. Can email pictures, collect from LS25 1QG. 07517 111332 for more details.

NORTON DOMINATOR oil filter new £10, centre stand return spring new £5, set pushrods s/h good condition £25, oil junction block good condition £10, AJS petrol tank panels, poor chrome but could be painted £15. Maldwyn Griffiths, 51 Poplars Close, Mardy, Abergavenny NP7 6LU.

TRIUMPH CUB top and bottom yokes £15. Petrol tank £20. Barrel £15. Royal Enfield casquette £25. Rear mudguard £10. Seat grab rail £5. Chrome air filter £10. AJS Model 16 puller £5. Yamaha FZR f/wheel £15. Plus postage. alanlevo@icloud.com

VINCENT GARAGE CLEAROUT. Forks, Knight mudguard, seat pan, Craven rack, pistons, sprockets, dynamo. Over 100 parts new and s/hand. £6000 the lot. Phone to view by appointment. Also new BSA Spitfire 8" hub £700 – fits Gold Star. 0115 9272 069.

WESLAKE NOS Dave Nourish 850cc conversion to suit Triumph or Westlake crankcases, complete with Carrillo rods, crankpin dia 1.7502/1.7497. Also Triumph Speed Twin NOS 1959 front forks complete with yokes, front wheel and brake. Ring Will 07929 270357.

CLOTHING, PUBLICATIONS, WORKSHOP

MV AGUSTA since 1945, by Ian Falloon; high quality large format 288 page hardback limited edition tome with over 720 photographs and illustrations, covering every MV since 1945. £45 (list £90), buyer collects (Dorset), will post (heavy) £10. 01935 815887.

RST JACKET and Trousers. Size Large, nearly new. Zip-in thermal lining. Retirement sale. £50 plus P&P. Ray 01935 422430 (Dorset).

THE COMPLETE BOOK OF DUCATI MOTORCYCLES – Every model since 1946 – second edition, by Ian Falloon; high-quality 280 page hardback book with over 530 photographs and illustrations. £24 (list £45), buyer collects (Dorset), will post (heavy) £10. 01935 815887.

Buying a bike? Get a quote from VMCC Motorcycle Insurance | Call 0121 274 5355

THE MOTORCYCLE 1950s 177 copies. Triumph Replacement Parts 1955 £10. Norton Maintenance Instructions 1930 £10. 'Bike' bound volume 1979 £8. Triumph Instruction Manual 1955 £10. Honda manual & handbook C100 and C110 £8. Bob Bunce 01525 872708 (Beds).

TWO-PIECE LEATHERS various sizes, good newish condition (free fitting! Tea and cake!) 07931 466650 (Herts).

WANTED

A CLASSIC motorcycle wanted by genuine club member, consider any bike in any condition. Good price paid, call David on 07983 301756.

A CLASSIC motorcycle wanted, consider any bike in any condition. Good price paid by true enthusiast, Tony 01704 601002.

AUTOCYCLE from a good home, wanted to go to a good home. Distance no object for the right machine. Phone Rex 07506 070057.

BSA ZB32 Alloy head and barrel for sprint bike project. 07841 902933.

CAMPAGNOLO disc pads, rear disc brake or any supplier, ally sprocket (on Hagon JAP sprinter). Also original Welbike for local museum, any leads welcome. Jerry 07931 466650.

CLASSIC MOTORCYCLE any size wanted by enthusiast, can be in any condition or incomplete. Cash waiting, phone 07811 189755.

BEADED EDGE tyres 28 x 2, new or used. Also any pedal gear for my 1903 and 1904 restoration projects. Call Andy on 07773 663403 or email andy@balgores.com

BSA C12 carburettor. I can clean it and sort it out to run. Possible other bits if you have a box full. Ring Steve Frost 01283 701458.

FRANCES BARNETT STAG. Blackburne engine or parts wanted for this 250cc engine – camshaft, cam followers and timing gear. Drawings or photos would help identify parts. Also Druid front forks for Stag. Alan 07748 766664.

GILERA 150 5v 'Arcore' ('70s) bike in very good original or mechanically restored condition to ride not show! I'm based in Worcestershire so would really prefer to view a bike in West or East Midlands. Private buyer, Andrew, 07813 845894.

HONDA C200 cylinder head. The 90cc ohv version. Must have usable valve seats but otherwise condition relatively unimportant. Richard von Mach. Tel. 07928 231104.

LUCAS M41 headlamp ring or complete headlamp to complete my 1921 N.U.T. restoration. Call Andy on 07773 663403 or email andy@balgores.com

NEW IMPERIAL 1912-1919 wanted by enthusiast, the earlier the better. Any genuine machine or box of bits considered. Andy Dean 01189 772178 andy@keephatch.net (Berks).

RON JERRARD rode Syd Lawton's 1954 350cc Manx; an ex Ivor Lloyd/Reid & Haysom 7R in the 1955 Junior Manx; a Jack Difazio Gold Star in the 1956 Senior Clubmans (2nd). Son searching for them. Email recycledreading@gmail.com

TRIUMPH PRE-UNIT parts, any amount. Also Ariel Colt parts or bike. 01473 217486, Ipswich, Suffolk. Best time, evenings.

VINTAGE SCOOTER wanted. Lambretta, Vespa, Dayton, Zundapp or any vintage scooter. 01257 271005 or email andrew185@btinternet.com

TRADE SMALLS

A O SERVICES. Sells the V reg 2a Dynamo Regulator both 6 and 12V in the one unit +/- earth (please specify). Made in Norfolk and with full after sales service £52 sent. Regulator rectifiers £38, 18D2/D1 electronic ignitions, advice on battery charging faults. Charge indicator BSM in 6V or 12V £22. Alternator wiring kit £38. Dynamo wiring kit £36. Unique Magneto timing unit, precisely finds timing point without dismantling, £37. Magneto Ignition Switch for twins. £25. Testing of regulator/rectifiers, send with £5 to 35 Griston Rd. Watton, Thetford, IP25 6DN www.aoservices.co.uk 01953 884681 Al Osborn.

ALL YOUR OIL AND LUBRICATION SUPPLIES. For classic and vintage motorcycles, motorcars, trucks, tractors, boats and workshop machinery. Mail Order service or collect by appointment. Service with a smile from fellow enthusiasts. THE VINTAGE OIL COMPANY – 01283 509562 – vintagebearing@aol.co.uk

BALL AND ROLLER BEARINGS. Obsolete bearings supplied, reconditioned or manufactured. The Vintage Bearing Company. 17 Studio One, Waterside Court, Burton-on-Trent DE14 2WQ – 01283 509562 – vintagebearing@aol.co.uk

BEMW. For competitive prices on restorations, repairs and spares. Spares for vintage/classic BMWs from 1935. CJ750s, copies of the 1938 BMW R71, from £6,750. LH/RH sidecars, plus OHV machines available. 2 Forman St, Derby DE1 1JQ, Tel/Fax: 01332 298523, www.bemw.co.uk After 7pm and weekends 01332 824334.

CLASSIC MOTORCYCLE REPAIRS, engine rebuilds and repairs, machining services and parts manufacture. General motorcycle repairs and maintenance undertaken, mechanical and electrical. Re-bushing of worn parts i.e. brake plates and bearing housing. Manufacture one-offs or batches. Full or part engine and gearbox rebuilds. Contact Michael (01233) 840323.

CLASSIC PAINTWORK RESTORATION SERVICES. Paintwork, lining, petrol tank repairs and restoration. Call Glenn 07904 244567 or 01858 575480, www.gddesign.co.uk for info.

CLUTCH PLATES RE-CORKED. Andy and Quae are pleased to announce they have taken over the business of re-corking clutches from Bob Metson who has retired. All types of clutches re-corked. Only natural cork used. Call 01559 371770. info@theclutchcorkcarvery.co.uk Facebook@ theclutchcorkcarvery Glyncoch, Tanglwst, Newcastle Emlyn, Carmarthenshire SA38 9NJ.

CONTROL CABLES AND DRIVE CABLES made to pattern or drawing for any motorcycle. Workshop services for unusual fittings. Small batches catered for. Loose parts available to order. Carrot Cycles Unit 2 Monks Way, Lincoln. www.carrotcycles.co.uk info@carrotcycles.co.uk 01522 528234.

LEATHER WORK for all new and old leather items remade or restored. Toolboxes, tool rolls, saddles Brooklands jackets etc. View images with Instagram gez_cater_bespoke_leatherwork 07403 625321 or email gezcater@yahoo.co.uk

PARALLEL ENGINEERING. Precision alignment of motorcycle frames and rolling chassis. Motorcycle servicing and maintenance. Fault finding. Engine, gearbox, primary drive, rebuilds and upgrades. Wheel building. Front suspension rebuilds. Complete rewiring. Norton Commando specialist. High standard of workmanship. West Midlands/Shropshire based. Contact Simon, 07794 637159 info@parallelengineering.co.uk

VINTAGE AND CLASSIC Motorcycles wanted. We are always looking to buy interesting vintage and classic British, German and American motorcycles. Easy transaction, prompt payment. International transport possible with Chas Mortimer. Enquire for a valuation of your bike(s). www.centurylimited.eu info@centurylimited.eu 0045 5363 8956.

VINTAGE GRIPS. Replica celluloid handlebar grips. 20 styles available (made to order). Email vintagegrips@outlook.com or call 07803 837183, 8am-8pm Monday-Saturday.

HOLIDAYS

BRITTANY BIKER BREAKS – bed and breakfast exclusively for motorcyclists, in small hamlet in rural Brittany 30 minutes from St Malo ferry. Delightful accommodation, home cooking and secure garaging & workshop for bikes. Guided tours arranged. Kim Rowland +33 (0)2 9945 29 53. brittanybikerbreaks@gmail.com www.brittanybikerbreaks.com

Classified Advertising Information

Max 40 words including all contact details – 'Bikes for Sale' ads can include one picture. All motorcycles, three-wheelers and spares must be over 25 years old. Two ads free per member per issue.

TRADE SMALLS & HOLIDAYS: For small-scale and part-time traders. Max 50 words £15, 100 words £30, invoiced per quarter (min £50).

SEND TO:
Email adverts@vmcc.net Post: VMCC, Allen House, Wetmore Road, Burton upon Trent, Staffs DE 14 1TR. Please quote your membership number and if your ad is hand written please write it clearly.

Multi-bike policies – VMCC Motorcycle Insurance   Call 0121 274 5355

MEN OF KENT VELO DAY
with Kent & Sussex Velo club
Hamstreet Victory Hall, Hamstreet TN26 2NJ on
1st May 2023, 9am onward
(Hamstreet is a small village just south of Ashford, Kent).
Hoping this year to have tea, coffee and burgers, all proceeds to the Air Ambulance charity.
Tables available for small donation if you wish to sell anything.

Enquries to veloseckent@gmail.com
Richard Woolnough 01303 862515

SOMERSET SECTION CHEDDAR WEEKEND

15th/16th April 2023.
Two days of motor cycling in Somerset – Social Run Saturday, 57th Annual Road Safety Run Sunday.
www.VMCCsomerset.co.uk
cheddartrial@hotmail.com
Or S.A.E. Dave Boon 39 Welsford Ave, Wells BA5 2HX

SURREY & SUSSEX SECTION

2 Stroke Tiddlers Run
Wednesday 22nd March
2 stroke bikes up to 250cc.
Chris Brown
01342 834744 or 07752 301750
Email:- guvbrown@btinternet.com

Nigel Pepper Memorial Run
Friday 7th April
All VMCC eligible bikes welcome.
Tulip route cards, approximately 80 miles
Lunch-stop at a pub where food is available
Sharon Pepper
01403 268952
Email:- shazzapep@yahoo.co.uk

Girder Fork Weekend
Saturday 8th – Sunday 9th July
All Girder Fork Bikes Welcome
Camping available
Route cards provided
Stay over until the Tuesday and join our Annual BBQ
Andy Belenkin
01273 509097 or 07703 192921
Email:- andy.belenkin@gmail.com

COME TO COUPES MOTO LEGENDE
The VMCC is pleased to announce that we have rebooted our relationship with this flagship event for classic bikes.

It takes place annually at the Circuit Dijon Prenois, just south west of Dijon – it's a track-based parade and reliability test for all pre-1993 motorcycles. The VMCC will have its own designated trackside garage and we'll be taking two of our circuit machines – the Bailey Rudge 250 and Velocette KSS 350.

Several members have already registered and will bring some beautiful machines. Why not come too? You could:
- Bring your own pre-1993 motorcycle
- Ride one of the Club's machines (if available)
- Spectate

Whichever way, you'll be part of one of Europe's biggest classic motorcycle events.

Contact:
martin@vmcc.net before 7th March for entry forms and prices. Event entry deadline is 14th March, so don't waste time!

Coupes Moto Legende is BIG – don't let it pass you by!
www.coupes-moto-legende.fr

THE TAVERNERS
present
FOUNDERS DAY

SUNDAY 23rd July 2023

THIS YEAR'S THEME
100 years of BMW and 120 years of J.A.P

Ken Fox will be bringing his wall of death along again with free entry

FOR AUTOJUMBLE STALLS PLEASE DOWNLOAD THE FORM FROM
(available late February) http://www.foundersday.co.uk/founders-day/
CONTACT STEVE HALL 07443 933418 or 01162393198

MASSIVE MOTORCYCLE AUTOJUMBLE
STANFORD HALL

NEAR LUTTERWORTH, LEICESTERSHIRE LE17 6DH

Arena Events • Motorcycle Displays • Beer Tent
ADMISSION: 9.00am Adults £10.00   Children U16 Free

Free Entry to
The Wall Of Death
Included in your Entry Fee

100 years of BMW

120 years of J.A.P

www.thetaverners.co.uk

Diary of 1000 Rides

Over 1300 rides and events listed – open to all VMCC members

THE VINTAGE & Classic MOTOR CYCLE CLUB

Photo: Mario Costa-Sal

SPRING RIDES
MARCH – APRIL – MAY

Over 400 runs, rides and socials listed

Photo: Chris Moreton

SPRING

MARCH

1st March — **Surrey and Sussex, Wrinkly Run 10.30am**
Venue TBA Brian Robins 07901 183181
surreysussexvmcc@gmail.com

1st March — **West Kent Mid week run 10.30am**
Village hall car park, Ide Hill on B2042.
Ron Wright 07761 005995 Betron.wright@gmail.com

1st March — **Gwent, Baffle Haus Coffee Morning 11am**
Baffle Haus Cafe, The Cedars, Goyytre NP4 0AD.
Richard Williams 01873 840483
markhillier61@icloud.com

2nd March — **West Wiltshire, Winter Wandering 12 noon**
Quarrymans Arms, Box SN13 8HN.
Colin Smith 07778 281332
colin.smith1951@btinternet.com

2nd March — **Oxford, Thursday Run 10am**
H Café, Dorchester on Thames OX10 7LY.
Roger Cope 01844 237888

4th March — **Dorset March Hare Run 11am**
Marsh & Ham C/P, Blandford DT11 7AW.
Bernard Jones 01258 472554
secretary@dorsetvmcc.co.uk

4th March — **East Sussex Run to Brede Pumping Station 10am**
Brian's Barn, Brownbread Street. Section secretary
07434 280380 secretary@eastsussexvmcc.co.uk

5th March — **Isle of Wight March Winds breakfast run 9am**
Carisbrooke Nunnery car park, Whitcombe Rd.
Newport PO30 1YS. Ron Wallis 01983 752861
ron.wallis10@gmail.com

5th March — **Banbury March Hare Run 9.30am**
Horsefair. P. Brooks 01926 813855

5th March — **West Kent Gutless Wonder Run 10.30am**
Eynsford layby on A225 south of railway bridge at
Eynsford. Ron Wright 07761 005995
Betron.wright@gmail.com

5th March — **Worcestershire Breakfast Meet 10am**
Lakeside Cafe, Moorlands DY11 7XN.
Richard Caddick 01299 403334

5th March — **Northampton Pre-Pioneer Run 11am**
Tove short stay car park, Towcester NN12 6LD.
Ian Townsend 07527 434783
iantownsend@enterprisecontrol.co.uk

5th March — **West South Wales St Davids Day Run 10.30am**
Penblewin car park just off A40 roundabout Narberth.
Derrick Mason 07817 447069

7th March — **Herefordshire & Mid Wales Brunch ride-in 11am**
The Bean Box Café, Bridge Street, Hay-on-Wye,
HR3 5DE. Gary Jones 07870 389317 jgjones@sky.com

8th March — **North East Lunch Meeting 12 noon**
Harewood Arms, Harewood.
Steve Rowley 07704 374773 rowley_s2@sky.com

8th March — **South Lincs and Peterborough March Wrinkly Run 10.30am**
Venue TBA Gary Sleeman 01733 770241 gary.sleeman1@gmail.com

8th March — **Chiltern Coffee Morning 11am**
Full Moon Pub, HP5 2UH. P. Barfield 01442 824143
chilternvmcc@hotmail.com

9th March — **Essex Club night and Auction 7.30pm**
Venue postcode CM3 8RG. Dave Iszard 07543 901340
daveandnicki@sky.com

9th March — **Herefordshire & Mid Wales Tesco to the Moon 9.30am**
Tesco café, Belmont HR2 7XS. Geoff McGladdery
07588 559698 geoffmac@globalnet.co.uk

9th March — **Isle of Man Club Night 8pm**
Vagabonds Rugby Club. Gary Corlett 07624 496672

9th March — **North Staffs Club Night & section AGM 8pm**
Moorville Hall Hotel. Ian Pettifor 07760 346003
contact@northstaffsvmcc.com

9th March — **North Cotswold Thursday Pub Meet 12 noon**
Norton Grange, nr Evesham.
Chris Delaney 07966 395032 chrisdelaney650@gmail.com

11th March — **Notts and Derby Saturday Morning Coffee Run**
Griffins Head Car Park, Moor Rd, Papplewick NG15 8EN.
Graham Bower 07745 888938
nottsandderbyvintageclub@outlook.com

11th March — **South Dorset Social Breakfast Meet 9.30am**
The Three Compasses, Charminster DT2 9QT.
Martin Figg 07896 507278 figg.martin@gmail.com

12th March — **Dartmoor Club Run – Out in the Sticks 10am**
Bovey Tracey, Town Centre Car park, TQ13 9S.
Roy Turner 07702 908 425

12th March — **Cornwall, West Cornwall Run 10.30am**
Chiverton Arms, Chiverton Cross, Blackwater TR4 8HS.
Clive Pascoe 07428 653921

12th March — **Cotswold Winter Wandering 12 noon**
Butchers Arms, Sheepscombe, Stroud GL6 7RH.
Peter Kent 01452 812113, 01452 610375

12th March — **Goodwood Winter Wobble 10.30am**
The Forge, Reynolds Lane, Slindon,
West Sussex BN18 0QT. Dave Johnson 01243 582074
goodwoodvmcc@aol.com

12th March — **Essex Cobwebs Run 9.30am**
Writtle green car park, Writtle, Chelmsford CM1 3DT.
Paul Fletcher 07719 463620

12th March — **Notts and Derby Sunday Lunch Meet 12 noon**
Yondermann Café, A623 Wardlow Mires SK17 8RW.
Graham Bower 07745 888938
nottsandderbyvintageclub@outlook.com

12th March — **Somerset Spring Run 10am**
Nether Stowey Church Centre, Nether Stowey TA5 1LJ.
Kevin Hellier 01278 732010

13th March — **Essex Cobwebs Run 9.30am**
Writtle Green car park CM1 3DT.
Paul Fletcher 07719 463620

13th March — **North Cotswold Club Night 8pm**
College Arms, Lower Quinton. Chris Delaney
07966 395032 chrisdelaney650@gmail.com

13th March — **Worcestershire AGM 7.30pm**
The Bell, Lower Broadheath WR2 6QG.
John Porter 01386 553329

15th March — **Chiltern Breakfast ride in 10am**
London Gliding Club restaurant LU6 2JP. P.
Barfield 01442824143 chilternvmcc@hotmail.com

15th March — **West Wiltshire Green Lane Run time TBA**
Venue TBA. Keith Johnston 07836 376107 keith.johnston55@hotmail.co.uk

15th March — **Berkshire Mid-Week Lunch 12 noon**
Venue TBA. Malcolm White 01344 642866
info@berkshire-vmcc.org.uk

15th March	**Chiltern Pub Night 8pm-ish** Full Moon, Cholesbury Lane, Hawridge HP5 2UH. P. Barfield 01442 824143 chilternvmcc@hotmail.com
16th March	**Oxford Thursday Run 10am** Milletts OX13 5HB. Vince Ellis 01235 526333
16th March	**Bedfordshire Midweek lunch 12 noon** Jordans Mill, Holme Mills, Langford Road, Broom SG18 9JY. Richard Chambers 07905 203823
16th March	**West Wiltshire Wandering 12 noon** The Bell Inn, Yatton Keynall, SN14 7BG. Colin Smith 07778 281332 colin.smith1951@btinternet.com
16th March	**Worcestershire Breakfast meeting 10am** The Nest, Ledbury HR8 2PZ. Richard Caddick 01299 403334
18th March	**Dorset Breakfast Meet 10am** Thorngrove Garden Centre, Common Mead Lane, Gillingham, SP8 4RE. Paul Wirdnam 07775 923206 secretary@dorsetvmcc.co.uk
19th March	**South Dorset Club Run 10.30am** The Three Compasses, Charminster DT2 9QT. Martin Figg 07896 507278 figg.martin@gmail.com
19th March	**Taverners Sporting Trial 10am** Rileys railway, Marefield, 1.5m off B6047, north of A47. Mark McEvoy 07973 142440 mmcevoy@infoteknix.co.uk
19th March	**Dorset Spring Run 11am** Wardon Hill Trading Post DT2 9PW. Bernard Jones 01258 472554 secretary@dorsetvmcc.co.uk
19th March	**West Kent Social Run 10.30am** Kemsing High Street car park TN15 6NB. Ron Wright 07781 005995 Betron.wright@gmail.com
19th March	**Banbury Breakfast Run 8pm** Brackley Market Place. D. Carr 07521 651749
19th March	**Isle of Man Section Trial 1.30pm** Ballagaraghyn, Jurby. Shaun Seal 07624 485133
19th March	**Northampton Mad March Hare 10.30am** Milligans Cafe A6, Finedon NN9 5HX. John Bulmer 07850 909340 patnjohnbulmer@ntlworld.com
19th March	**Men of Kent Spring Jaunt 10.30am** Headcorn Aerodrome, Shenley Road, Headcorn near Ashford TN27 9HX. Richard Barsby 07989 352990 richardbarsby61@tiscali.co.uk
19th March	**South Cotswold Sunday Lunchtime Meet 12 noon** The Wild Carrot at Chevenage House GL8 8XW. Jeremy Retford 07831 314884 jeremyretford@btinternet.com
19th March	**Notts and Derby Sunday Afternoon Run 1pm** Ripley Market Pace DE5 3BR. Gordon Milburn 07800 826733 nottsandderbyvintageclub@outlook.com
19th March	**North Cotswold March Hare Run 10am** The Square, Chipping Campden. Chris Delaney 07966 395032 chrisdelaney650@gmail.com
21st March	**Isle of Wight Cold Knees Lunch Run 11.30am** Hare and Hounds car park, Downend, Arreton PO30 2NU Ron Wallis 01983 752861 ron.wallis10@gmail.com
22nd March	**Essex Mid week Run 9.30am** Venue TBA. Dave Iszard 07543 901340 daveandnicki@sky.com
22nd March	**Herefordshire & Mid Wales Breakfast meet 10am** The Mulberry Cage, Radway Bridge Garden Centre HR1 3RX. Geoff McGladdery 07588 559698 geoffmac@globalnet.co.uk
23rd March	**Essex Mid week Run 9.30am** Venue TBA. Dave Bradley 07808 294139
23rd March	**North Cotswold Wrinkly Lunch 12 noon** Studley. Chris Delaney 07966 395032 chrisdelaney650@gmail.com
23rd March	**Flat Tank Club night 7.30pm** Huntsman Inn, Falfield. Charles Wright 01452 790296
23rd March	**South Dorset Club Night 8pm** The Three Compasses, Charminster DT2 9QT. Martin Figg 07896 507278 figg.martin@gmail.com
24th March	**Bristol Skittles Night 7pm** Mangotsfield Football Club BS16 9EN. Alan Jones 0117 9570376
25th March	**Men of Kent Classic Bike Jumble 9am** Village hall, Dunkirk, near Canterbury/Faversham ME 13 9LF. Colin Townsend 07789 606686 redcherrycam@hotmail.co.uk
25th March	**Somerset Autojumble 9.30am** Bath and West Showground, Shepton Mallet, BA4 6QN. Dave Atterbury 01297 32853
25th March	**North Birmingham Paul's Spring Run 10am** Venue TBA or see www.vmcc-nbs.co.uk Paul Raybould 01902 676396 NorthBirminghamVMCC@outlook.com
25th March	**Herefordshire & Mid Wales Trail ride 1 10am** Hundred House car park LD1 5RY. NW of Builth Wells on A481. Paul Farley 01874 610303 palmag@btinternet.com
25th March	**Notts and Derby Saturday Morning Coffee Run 10am** Ripley Market Place, DE5 3BR. Graham Bower 07745 888938 nottsandderbyvintageclub@outlook.com
26th March	**Clyde Valley Blue Haze Day 10.30am** Broadlees Golf, Anderson Drive, Chapelton ML10 6GH. Willie Malone 07756 031113 williamgmalone@gmail.com
26th March	**Flat Tank Dinner and Prizegiving 12 noon** George Inn, Cambridge. Charles Wright 01452 790296 charles.l.wright@aol.com
26th March	**Cornwall, Mid Cornwall Run 10.30am** Mid Cornwall Services, Victoria, Saint Austell PL26 8UF. Peter Lee 01209 212276
26th March	**North East Annual Auction 1.30pm** Coronation Hall, Boroughbridge. Steve Rowley 07704 374773 rowley_s2@sky.com
26th March	**Worcestershire Breakfast with VJMC 10am** Salwey Arms, Woofferton SY8 4AL. Richard Caddick 01299 403334
26th March	**Central Scottish Great Spring Autojumble 10am** Forfar Auction Mart, 48 John St, Forfar DD8 3EZ. Arthur 07951 873416 arthur.vintagent@gmail.com
26th March	**East Lancs Gordon's Run 11am** Lay-by near Petre Garage Langho, Whalley Road BB6 8AB. David Prismall 01706 217572 davidprismall@hotmail.com
26th March	**Herefordshire & Mid Wales Breakfast ride-in 10am** Hill Barn Bungalow, Aymestrey, Hereford HR6 9SR. Pete Howells 01886 853293

26th March	**Bedfordshire Breakfast Meet 10am** Jordans Mill, Holme Mills, Langford Road, Broom SG18 9JY, Richard Chambers 07905 203823
26th March	**Stonehenge Winter Wandering 12 noon** Home. Lionel Butler 01725 510760
26th March	**Lakeland Brown Cow ride-in 11am** Brown Cow Inn, Waberthwaite, (on A595) nr Bootle LA19 5YJ. John Silcock 01229 861264
26th March	**Dartmoor Breakfast meet 10am** The Jolly Roger, St John's Lane, Bovey Tracey TQ13 9FF. Derek French 07747 032659
26th March	**South Lincs and Peterborough Daffodil Run 10.30am** Venue TBA. Gary Sleeman 01733 770241 gary.sleeman1@gmail.com
26th March	**West South Wales Sunday Ride Inn 10.30am** A local cafe in West South Wales area. Angelo Conti 01267 281394
26th March	**Ironmasters Mad March Hare Run 10.30am** Cricket Pitch Lay-by, Shifnal. Colin Bryan 01785 841257
27th March	**Northumbrian Club Night 8pm** Birtley Golf Club, Birtley Ln, Birtley DH3 2LR. Pete Bagnall 07968 646357 petebagnall44@hotmail.com
28th March	**West Wiltshire Coffee Morning 10am** The Ship Inn Cafe, Luckington, SN14 6PA. Kevin Phillips 07952 173693 starfield181@gmail.com
28th March	**Goodwood Noggin 'n' Natter 8pm** The Red Lion, London Road, Ashington RH20 3DD. Dave Johnson 01243 582074 goodwoodvmcc@aol.com
29th March	**East Sussex Richard's Wrinkly Run 10.30am** Brians Barn TN33 9NX. Section secretary 07434 280380 secretaty@eastsussexvmcc.co.uk
30th March	**Oxford Thursday Run 10am** Turnpike Pub, Yarnton OX5 1PJ. Phil Stock 01865 460235
30th March	**Worcestershire Black Country Run 9.30am** Cob House, Wichenford, WR6 6YE. Steve King 01384 396201

APRIL

1st April	**Isle of Wight Vintage and Classic Motorcycle show 8am** The Winter Gardens, Pier Street, Ventnor PO38 1SZ. Ron Wallis 01983 752861 ron.wallis10@gmail.com
1st April	**Cotswold Felix Burke Weekend Social Run 10am** Andoversford Village Hall, Crossfields, Andoversford GL54 4LQ. Ken Hill 07587 180345 ken@haresear.co.uk
2nd April	**Blackpool & District Hoghton Tower Sprint 10am** Lay-by on A6 adjacent to Barton Hall entrance, Broughton. Terry A Robinson 07960 116769 terry.robinson6@btinternet.com
2nd April	**Glasgow Pip Squeak Run 10.30am** Kilmarnock, car park near BP station on Western Road KA3 1TX. Gordon Mowat 07931 561898 rustynuts@talktalk.net
2nd April	**Goodwood Norman Broadbridge Run 10.30am** Tangmere Military Aviation Museum, Gamecock Terrace, Tangmere, PO20 2ES. John Taylor 01903 892314 goodwoodvmcc@aol.com
2nd April	**Dorset Blandford Run 11am** Corn Exchange, Blandford DT11 7AG. Peter Miller 01258 721356 secretary@dorsetvmcc.co.uk
2nd April	**North West Brian's Easter Bunny Run 10am** Details TBA. Angie Graham 07773 555819 angiegraham2012@yahoo.co.uk
2nd April	**Essex Early Easter Run 9.30am** Billericay, Lake Meadows Park. Dave Bradley 07808 294139
2nd April	**East Yorkshire Spring Run 10.30am** Pig in the Willow Cafe, East Cottingwith YO42 4TQ. Glen Bradley 07496 932866 gbradley8@gmail.com
2nd April	**Banbury April Fools' Run 9.30am** Horsefair. O. Turner 07831 777790
2nd April	**Isle of Man Road Run 2pm** Venue TBA. Gary Corlett 07624 496672
2nd April	**South Wales Spring Run 7.30pm** Llanharry Workingmen's Club, Elm Road, Llanharry CF72 9HR. Bob James 01443 227439
2nd April	**Warwickshire Spring Run** Venue TBA. Barry Heath 07786 718867 b4heath@yahoo.co.uk
2nd April	**West Kent Girder fork run 10.30am** Eynsford layby on A225 south of railway bridge, Eynsford. Ron Wright 07761 005995 Betron.wright@gmail.com
2nd April	**Cotswold Felix Burke Memorial Road Trial 10am** Andoversford Village Hall, Crossfields, Andoversford GL54 4LQ. Ken Hill 07587 180345 ken@haresear.co.uk
2nd April	**North Staffs Oatcake Run 10.30am** Bradnop Village Hall. John Broadhurst 01538 385122
5th April	**Surrey and Sussex Wrinkly Run 10.30am** Venue TBA. Brian Robins 07901 183181 surreysussexvmcc@gmail.com
5th April	**West Kent Mid week Run 10.30am** Polhill lay by on A224 Halstead at the top of Polhill. Ron Wright 07761 005995 Betron.wright@gmail.com
5th April	**North Birmingham Club Night 8pm** The Round Oak Inn, Ounsdale Road, Wombourne WV5 8BU. David Spencer 07975 629810 NorthBirminghamVMCC@outlook.com
5th April	**Gwent Baffle Haus Coffee Morning 11am** Baffle Haus Cafe, The Cedars, Goyytre NP4 0AD. Richard Williams 01873 840483 markhillier61@icloud.com
5th April	**Cotswold Section Run 7pm** Lower Lode, Forthampton, GL19 4RE. Graham Rowcliffe 07515 288414 01684 293224 grahamrowcliffe58@outlook.com
5th April	**Essex Small and/or Old 9.30am** Billericay further details to come. George Smith 07504 736960
6th April	**Dartmoor Early Evening Run 6.30pm** Opposite Royal Seven Stars Hotel, The Plains, Totnes TQ9 5DD. Mike Burton 07790 459795
6th April	**North Cotswold Thursday Pub Meet 12 noon** The Mill Inn, Withington. Chris Delaney 07966 395032 chrisdelaney650@gmail.com
6th April	**Herefordshire & Mid Wales Shropshire & Long Mynd 9.30am** OK Diner Leominster, HR6 0DQ. Geoff McGladdery 07588 559698 geoffmac@globalnet.co.uk
6th April	**West Wiltshire April Mid Week Run 10am** Silbury Hill car park, A4 near Beckhampton. Peter Fielding 07952 173693 starfield181@gmail.com

6th April	**Blackpool & District Wray Classic Bike Night 4.30pm** St Michael's Village Hall, Blackpool Rd, St Michael's on Wyre PR3 0UA. Terry A Robinson 07960 116769 terry.robinson6@btinternet.com
7th April	**Ipswich & Suffolk Good Friday Run 10.30am** Woodbridge car park on Station Road near lights. Trevor Dickings 01473 798653
7th April	**Herefordshire & Mid Wales Cwmpas Ride 12 noon** Choose your own start. John Munday 01982 551091 jcmunday@btinternet.com
7th April	**Dorset Hot X Bun Run 11am** Recreation Ground, Okeford Fitzpaine, DT11 0PL. Paul Wirdnam 07775 923206 secretary@dorsetvmcc.co.uk
7th April	**Worcestershire Good Friday Run 9.30am** The Cob House, Wichenford WR6 6YE. Bob Arnold 01905 353189
7th April	**Surrey and Sussex Nigel Pepper Memorial Run 11am** Southern Counties Historic Preservation Trust Centre, Copthorne RH10 3HZ. Sharon Pepper 01403 268952 shazzapep@yahoo.co.uk
8th April	**South Dorset Social Breakfast Meet 9.30am** The Three Compasses, Charminster DT2 9QT. Martin Figg 07896 507278 figg.martin@gmail.com
9th April	**Herefordshire & Mid Wales The Dams Run 10am** Cattle Shed Café, Penrhos Court, Lyonshall, Kington HR5 3LH. Rob Woodford 07847 098597
9th April	**Cornwall Girder fork/flat tanker Run 10.30am** St Erth. George Pengelley 01209 214521
9th April	**Essex Early Easter Run 9.30am** Tesco car park, Maldon CM9 4LE. Dave Iszard 07543 901340 daveandnicki@sky.com
10th April	**Chiltern Low Power Run 10.30am** Full Moon, Cholesbury Lane, Hawridge HP5 2UH. P Barfield 01442 824143 chilternvmcc@hotmail.com
10th April	**Men of Kent Ashford Classic Bike Show 10am** Ashford Cattle Market, Monument Way, Willesborough TN24 0HB. Richard Woolnough 01303 862515 woolnough@mchenry.plus.com
10th April	**North Cotswold Club Night 8pm** College Arms, Lower Quinton. Chris Delaney 07966 395032 chrisdelaney650@gmail.com
11th April	**Surrey and Sussex Evening Run 6.30pm** Copthorne Social Club, Copthorne, Crawley RH10 3RE. Brian Robins 07901 183181 surreysussexvmcc@gmail.com
11th April	**Herefordshire & Mid Wales Brunch ride-in 11am** Honey Café, Bronllys, Brecon, Powys LD3 0LH. Gary Jones 07870 389317
11th April	**Taverners Wrinkly Run 10am** Apple Trees, 1 Bradgate Close, Mountsorrel Leicester LE12 7DZ. Roger Monk 01509 412662
11th April	**Ipswich & Suffolk Evening ride 6.30pm** Ipswich School, Sports Centre, Rushmere St Andrews. Trevor Dickings 01473 798653
11th April	**South Cotswold Tuesday Evening Pub Meet 6.30pm** The Salutation at Ham GL13 9QH. Jeremy Retford 07831 314884 jeremyretford@btinternet.com
12th April	**North East Lunch Meeting 12 noon** Harewood Arms, Harewood. Steve Rowley 07704 374773 rowley_s2@sky.com
12th April	**Northampton Mid week Run 10am** Royal Oak Blisworth NN7 3BU. Trevor Pinfold 01604 859215 trevorpinfold168@btinternet.com
12th April	**Warwickshire Club Night 8pm** Kenilworth Rugby Club, Glasshouse lane, Kenilworth CV8 2AJ. Barry heath 07786 718867 b4heath@yahoo.co.uk
12th April	**King's Lynn Ride-a-Bike Night 7pm** Make your own way. Club Secretary 01842 811077 malcolmrolph@talktalk.net
12th April	**West Wiltshire Green Lane Run** Venue TBA. Keith Johnston 07836 376107 keith.johnston55@hotmail.co.uk
12th April	**South Lincs and Peterborough April Wrinkly Run 10.30am** Venue TBA. Gary Sleeman 01733770241 gary.sleeman1@gmail.com
12th April	**Berkshire Mid-Week Lunch 12 noon** Venue TBA. Malcolm White 01344 642866 info@berkshire-vmcc.org.uk
12th April	**Cotswold Section Run 7pm** Lower Lode, Forthampton GL19 4RE. Graham Rowcliffe 07515 288414 01684 293224 grahamrowcliffe58@outlook.com
12th April	**Chiltern Midweek Run 10.30am** Full Moon, Cholesbury Lane, Hawridge HP5 2UH. P. Barfield 01442 824143 chilternvmcc@hotmail.com
13th April	**Herefordshire & Mid Wales Trail ride 2 10am** Regent House Filling Station, Clyro HR3 5SB. Paul Farley 01874 610303 palmag@btinternet.com
13th April	**Oxford Thursday Run 10am** Turnpike Pub, Yarnton OX5 1PJ. Jim Maine 01993 882759
13th April	**Worcestershire Breakfast meeting 10am** Hayley's Kitchen, Hartlebury DY11 7XZ. Richard Caddick 01299 403334
13th April	**South Hants Day Run 10.30am** Portchester Castle, Church Ln, Portchester, Fareham PO16 9QW. Clive Brown 01329 841290
13th April	**North Cotswold Wrinkly Run 10am** Ellendon Farm Shop. Chris Delaney 07966 395032 chrisdelaney650@gmail.com
15th April	**Dorset Breakfast Meet 10am** Thorngrove Garden Centre, Common Mead Lane, Gillingham SP8 4RE. Paul Wirdnam 07775 923206 secretary@dorsetvmcc.co.uk
15th April	**Somerset Cheddar Weekend 10am** Cheddar Football Club, Cheddar BS27 3RL. Dave Boon 01749 672672
15th April	**Allen House Castle Coombe Track Session 9am** Castle Coombe Race Circuit, Chippenham SN14 7EY. Annie Durrant 01283 540557 events@vmcc.net
16th April	**Allen House Gordon Prime Memorial Run 10am** Carew Cheriton Control Tower Airfield, Carew SA70 8SX. Jim Codd 07773 504561 jimcodd33@gmail.com
16th April	**Mid Lincs Bluestone Heath Run 10am** Horncastle cattle market, The Wong LN9 6EB. Peter Gunnee/S. Parker 01652 657169 p.gunnee@talktalk.net
16th April	**Devon Easter Run 11am** Riverside Caravan Park, South Molton, EX36 3HQ. John Young 07847 53725 jebyoung@hotmail.com

16th April	**Cyclemotor Welsh Run 10.30am** Castle Street Car Park, Abergavenny NP7 5EE. Philippa Wheeler 01873 858344
16th April	**South Cotswold Sunday Lunchtime Café Meet 12 noon** Old Station Cafe, Tintern NP16 7NX. Jeremy Retford 07831 314884 jeremyretford@btinternet.com
16th April	**Reivers Pedal and Pop Run 9am** Kirkley Cafe, Ponteland NE20 0AJ. Mike Laidler 01670 715537
16th April	**South Dorset Club Run 10.30am** The Three Compasses, Charminster DT2 9QT. Martin Figg 07896 507278 figg.martin@gmail.com
16th April	**North Staffs All Wind & Water (mills) Run 11am** Crown Street Car Park, Stone. Ted Foreman 07999 463022
16th April	**Cheshire and North Wales First run of the season 11.15 am** Public car park in Corwen LL21 0DN. secretary@candnw.vmcc.net Neil Shirley 01352 713204 chairman@candnw.vmcc.net
16th April	**Isle of Man Section Trial 1.30pm** Arassey Plantation. Shaun Seal 07624 485133
16th April	**East Lancs Jubilee Run 11am** East Lancs Railway car park, Rawtenstall. Bill Leach 01706 225727
16th April	**Bedfordshire Spring Run 10am** Jordans Mill, Holme Mills, Langford Road, Biggleswade SG18 9JX. Bryan Marsh 07309 731191 bryan.marsh@btinternet.com
16th April	**West South Wales Pre-31 and Girder fork run 10am** Carew Cheriton Control Tower Museum. Jim Codd 01834 813173 07773 504561
16th April	**King's Lynn Frank and Ida Allen Memorial Run 10am** Hubbles Café, Fendick's Fishery and Camping Site Methwold Road, Whittington PE33 9GP. Dick Fendick 01366 728852 malcolmrolph@talktalk.net
16th April	**Northampton Hugh's Run 10.30am** Pure Triumph, Wellingborough NN8 1LD. Hugh Gallagher 01933 419800 hughie_gallagher@btinternet.com
16th April	**Stonehenge Spring Run 11am** Breamore Countryside Museum, Upper Street, Fordingbridge SP6 2DB. Lionel Butler 01725 510760
16th April	**Taverners Sporting Trial 10am** Lount. Mark McEvoy 07973 142440 mmcevoy@infoteknix.co.uk
16th April	**North Birmingham Long Mynd Run 10am** Venue TBA, see www.vmcc-nbs.co.uk Ron Higgins 01746 764188 NorthBirminghamVMCC@outlook.com
16th April	**Dartmoor Lunch at Louis 10.30am** Meet at Tesco car park, Lee Mill Industrial Estate, Central Ave, Ivybridge PL21 9PE. Derry Bowman 01752 785026
17th April	**North Cotswold Sunday Run 10am** Venue TBA. Chris Delaney 07966 395032 chrisdelaney650@gmail.com
18th April	**Ipswich & Suffolk Evening ride 6.30pm** Ipswich School, Sports Centre, Rushmere St Andrews. Trevor Dickings 01473 798653
18th April	**South Cotswold Tuesday Evening Pub Meet 6.30pm** The Old Fox at Coaley GL11 5EG. Jeremy Retford 07831 314884 jeremyretford@btinternet.com
18th April	**Blackpool & District Dave Winter's Long Run 9.30am** St Michael's Village Hall, Blackpool Rd, St Michael's on Wyre, Preston PR3 0UA. Terry A. Robinson 07960 116769 terry.robinson6@btinternet.com
18th April	**Isle of Wight April Showers Lunch Run 11.30am** Hare and Hounds car park, Downend, Arreton PO30 2NU. Ron Wallis 01983 752861 ron.wallis10@gmail.com
19th April	**Cotswold Section Run 6.30pm** White Hart, Broad Oak, Newnham, GL14 1JB. Graham Rowcliffe 07515 288414 / 01594 516319 grahamrowcliffe58@outlook.com
19th April	**Chiltern Breakfast ride in 10am** London Gliding club resturant LU62JP. P. Barfield 01442 824143 chilternvmcc@hotmail.com
19th April	**Men of Kent Fish and Chip run 7pm** Village Hall, Dunkirk, near Canterbury/Faversham, Kent ME13 9LF. Frank Mitchell 07837 918 087 richarsbarsby61@tiscali.co.uk
19th April	**Chiltern Pub Night 8pm-ish** Full Moon, Cholesbury Lane, Hawridge HP52UH. P. Barfield 01442 824143 chilternvmcc@hotmail.com
20th April	**Flat Tank Silver Fox Run 11am** Silver Fox Cafe, Broadoak A48. Charles Wright 01452 790296
20th April	**South Hants Day Run 10.30pm** The Square, Wickham, Fareham PO17 5JT. Ian Harrop 07932 484209
20th April	**West Wiltshire Winter Wandering 12 noon** The Beaufort Arms, Hawkesbury Upton, GL9 1AU. Colin Smith 07778 281332 colin.smith1951@btinternet.com
20th April	**Bedfordshire Midweek Run 10.15am** Shefford Town Memorial Hall, Hitchin Road, Shefford SG17 5JA. Don Mckeand 01525 720629
20th April	**Notts and Derby Evening Run 7.30pm** Griffins Head Car Park, Moor Rd, Papplewick, Nottingham NG15 8EN. Graham Bower 07745 888938 nottsandderbyvintageclub@outlook.com
21st April	**East Sussex Bill Bailey Run 9.30am** Chalet Cafe, Cowfold. Section secretary 07434 280380 secretary@eastsussexvmcc.co.uk
22nd April	**Somerset 39th Twin Dragon Run 9am** Cadbury Garden Centre, Congresbury. Phil Ham 01278 671626
22nd April	**Allen House International Classic Motorcycle Show 9am** Stafford. Gary Sleeman gary@vmcc.net
23rd April	**North Cotswold Super Sausage Café Run 10am** Halford. Chris Delaney 07966 395032 chrisdelaney650@gmail.com
23rd April	**North East Spring Run 10.30am** Venue TBA. Nigel Hutchinson 07977 333629
23rd April	**Northampton Jim's Jaunt 10am** Hunsbury Hill car park, Northampton NN4 9UE. Richard Stone 01604 768069 richardstone47@hotmail.co.uk
23rd April	**Cotswold Summer Wandering 12 noon** Royal Spring Inn, Vention Lane, Lower Lydbrook GL17 9RL. 01594 860492 Peter Kent 01452 610375

23rd April	**Blackpool & District Crook O' Lune – Woody's Run 9.30am** Ferry Cafe, Knott End. Terry A. Robinson 07960 116769 terry.robinson6@btinternet.com
23rd April	**Anglian John Abrahams Memorial Run 10.30am** Bottisham Airfield Museum, Newmarket Road Bottisham Martyn Blunt 07880 026257 martynblunt@hotmail.co.uk
23rd April	**Northumbrian Barry Stevens Memorial Motorbike Show 11am** Path Head Water Mill, Summerhill, Blaydon on Tyne NE21 4SO. Pete Bagnall 07968 646357 petebagnall44@hotmail.com
23rd April	**Surrey and Sussex Sunday Social Run 11am** Venue TBA. Brian Robins 07901 183181 surreysussexvmcc@gmail.com
23rd April	**Ironmasters Fools Gold Run 10.30am** Priorslee Lake Jnt4 M54. Phil Nation 01952 691020
23rd April	**Dorset Bluebell Run 11am** Recreation Ground, Okeford Fitzpaine, DT11 0PL. Paul Wirdnam 07775 923206 secretary@dorsetvmcc.co.uk
23rd April	**Banbury Grey Porridge & Girder Fork Run 9.30am** Horsefair. R. Philpot 01295 256982
23rd April	**Gwent Reservoir Run 10am** Abergavenny Bus Station. Mark Hillier 07870 535933 markhillier61@icloud.com
23rd April	**Cornwall Freey Run 10.30am** Ladock. Chas Mills 01637 872660
23rd April	**Isle of Man Road Run 2pm** Venue TBA. Gary Corlett 07624 496672
23rd April	**Dartmoor Breakfast meet 10am** The Jolly Roger, St John's Lane, Bovey Tracey TQ13 9FF. Derek French 07747 032659
23rd April	**Herefordshire & Mid Wales Three Wheels on my Wagon 9.30am** Bromyard Market Square HR7 4BP. Richard Caddick 07588 559698 r.j.k.caddick@talktalk.net
23rd April	**King's Lynn St George's Day Run 10am** Matteshall, Norfolk NR20 3QP. Andy Culyer 07961 853774 culyer@btopenworld.com
23rd April	**West Kent Members' Memorial Run 10.30am** Teston Country Park off B2163 south of Teston level crossing. Ron Wright 07761 005995 betron.wright@gmail.com
23rd April	**Norwich and District Blakeney Run 10am** Acacia, Queen Street, Spooner Row NR189JU. Richard Mack 07860 208045 newimpboy@gmail.com
23rd April	**West Wiltshire St Georges Day Run 10am** Fox & Hounds Car Park, Acton Turville. Brian Newbury 07952 173693 starfield181@gmail.com
23rd April	**East Lancs Basil's Run 10.30am** East Lancs Railway car park, Rawtenstall. Gary Pye 01254 775633
23rd April	**Stonehenge Spring Nifty Run 11am** Breamore Countryside Museum, Upper Street, Fordingbridge SP6 2DB David Benn
23rd April	**Worcestershire Three Wheeler Run 9.30am** Market Square, Bromyard HR7 4BP Richard Caddick 01299 403334
23rd April	**Taverners Tulip Run 10am** 19 Hall Close, Glen Parva, Leicester LE2 9HZ. Kev Ellard 07378 371349 ellardshome@aol.com
23rd April	**South Lincs and Peterborough April Showers Run 10.30am** Venue TBA. Gary Sleeman 01733 770241 gary.sleeman1@gmail.com
25th April	**Herefordshire & Mid Wales Breakfast meet 10am** Golden Valley café, Pontrilas, Hereford HR2 0BA. Terry Pickering 07850 602222
25th April	**Ipswich & Suffolk Evening ride 6.30pm** Ipswich School, Sports Centre, Rushmere St Andrews. Trevor Dickings 01473 798653
25th April	**Devon Evening Pub Meet 6.30pm** Red Lion, East Street, Chulmleigh, EX18 7DD. Nick Smiles 07711 444686 nickesmiles@googlemail.com
25th April	**Goodwood Noggin 'n' Natter 8pm** The Red Lion, London Road, Ashington, West Sussex, RH20 3DD. Dave Johnson 01243 582074 goodwoodvmcc@aol.com
25th April	**Surrey and Sussex Evening Run 6.30pm** Venue TBA. Brian Robins 07901 183181 surreysussexvmcc@gmail.com
25th April	**West Wiltshire Coffee Morning 10am** Crowns Cafe, REME Museum, Lynham, SN15 4PT. Kevin Phillips 07952 173693 starfield181@gmail.com
25th April	**South Cotswold Tuesday Evening Pub Meet 6.30pm** Beaufort Arms, Hawksbury Upton GL9 1AU. Jeremy Retford 07831 314884 jeremyretford@btinternet.com
26th April	**Cotswold Section Run 6.30pm** Carpenters Arms, Miserden GL6 7JA. 02385 821283 Graham Rowcliffe 07515 288414 grahamrowcliffe58@outlook.com
26th April	**Men of Kent Bike Night Meeting 8pm** The Carpenters Arms, Coldred Hill, Coldred CT15 5 AL. Richard Barsby 07989 352990 richardbarsby61@tiscali.co.uk
26th April	**Reivers Shake Down Run 10am** Nelson's Cafe, Swarland NE65 9BQ. Dave Spencer 07719 599278
26th April	**North East Meet and Eat 7pm** Sun Inn Norwood Harrogate HG3 1SZ. Steve Rowley 07704 374773 rowley_s2@sky.com
26th April	**Cyclemotor Southern Saunter 10.30am** Honeystreet Mill Cafe, Honeystreet Village SN9 5PS. Dave Benn 07870 258257
26th April	**South Wales Wednesday evening ride out 7pm** Home. Bill Phelps 029 2089 0255 webadmin@southwalessectionvmcc.co.uk
27th April	**Bristol Lunchtime meet 12 noon** Beaufort Arms Hawksbury Upton GL19 1AU. Alan Burton 07774 923721
27th April	**North Cotswold Wrinkly Run 10am** Bretforton. Chris Delaney 07966 395032 chrisdelaney650@gmail.com
27th April	**Notts and Derby Evening Run 7pm** Ripley Market Place DE5 3BR. Pete Latham 07964 980752 nottsandderbyvintageclub@outlook.com
27th April	**South Hants Day Run 10.30am** The Square, Wickham, Fareham PO17 5JT. Dave Bettridge 02380 464822

27th April	**Oxford Thursday Run 10am** Milletts Farm. Roy Farrell 01367 710338
27th April	**South Dorset Club Night 8pm** The three Compasses, Charminster DT2 9QT. Martin Figg 07896 507278 figg.martin@gmail.com
27th April	**Worcestershire Breakfast Meet 9.30am** Watering Hole, Aymestrey HR6 9SR. Richard Caddick 01299 403334
29th April	**Northumbrian C2C Run 8am** Tynemouth Priory Car Park, Tynemouth, North Shields NE30 4DB. Andreas Schrocksnadel 07855 323697 oatb@aol.com
29th April	**Chiltern Spring Run 10.30am** Full Moon, Cholesbury Lane, Hawridge HP52UH. P. Barfield 01442 824143 chilternvmcc@hotmail.com
30th April	**Gwent Founders Relay Rally 9am** ATS Euromaster, Abergavenny. Mark Hillier 07870 535933 markhillier61@icloud.com
30th April	**West South Wales Commemorative Run 10.30am** Withybush Airfield, Haverfordwest SA62 4BN. Dave Evans 01437 731576. Derrick Mason 07817 447069
30th April	**East Sussex Snow-Mann Test Day 9.30am** Bo-Peep Hill, Bo-Peep Lane. Section secretary 07434 280380 secretaty@eastsussexvmcc.co.uk
30th April	**Somerset Relay Rally 9am** Burcott Mill, Burcott, BA5 1NJ. Mike Chipperfield 01749 679371
30th April	**Norwich and District Founders Relay Rally 9.30am** Wymondham Market Place. Nick Farthing 07703511754 nick_farthing@talk21.com
30th April	**Blackpool & District Relay Rally – Wrea Green 10am** Bryning Lane, Wrea Green, Preston PR4 2WJ. Terry A Robinson 07960 116769 terry.robinson6@btinternet.com
30th April	**Pennine Founders Relay Rally 10.30am** Hollingworth Lake Visitors Centre, Littleborough, Rochdale. Geoff Green 07817 178287 secretary@penninevmcc.org.uk
30th April	**South Wales Founders Relay Rally 10am** Rob Jones 01685 877212 robejones2@gmail.com
30th April	**Cheshire and North Wales Founder's Relay Rally 9.30am** Bunbury Water Mill, Bowe's Gate Rd., Tarporley, CW6 9PY. secretary@candnw.vmcc.net Neil Shirley 01352 713204 chairman@candnw.vmcc.net
30th April	**Allen House Founders Relay Rally** Checkpoints across the country. Angie Graham 07773 555819 angiegraham2012@yahoo.co.uk
30th April	**East Lancs Relay Rally 9.30am** Bancroft Mill, Gillians Lane, Barnoldswick BB18 5QR. Graham Daniels 07952 348339 grahamdaniels9@hotmail.com
30th April	**Cheshire Cats Relay Rally 10am** J&S Accessories, Chester Rd, Northwich CW8 2HB. Bernie Horrigan 07747 859831 horriganbernard@gmail.com
30th April	**Herefordshire & Mid Wales Founders Relay Rally 9am** Hotspur café, Shobdon airfield, Leominster, HR6 9ND. Steve Allen steve@vmcc.net 07588 559698
30th April	**Lakeland Alston Cafe ride-in 11am** The Station Cafe, Alston Station, Cumbria, CA9 3HN. Edward Stephenson 07932 544789 lakeland.vmcc@gmail.com
30th April	**Northumbrian Ride-in to Alston Railway Station 11am** Railway Station, Station Rd, Alston CA9 3JB. Pete Bagnall 07968 646357 petebagnall44@hotmail.com
30th April	**Isle of Wight Cross the Solent Run 9am** Wightlink Ferry Terminal, Fishbourne, PO33. Ron Wallis 01983 752861 ron.wallis10@gmail.com
30th April	**Berkshire Calleva Gallop 10.30am** Calleva Arms, Little London Road, Silchester RG7 2PH. Malcolm White 01344 642866 info@berkshire-vmcc.org.uk
30th April	**North East Section Meeting 2pm** Coronation Hall, Boroughbridge. Steve Rowley 07704 374773 rowley_s2@sky.com
30th April	**Cheshire and North Wales Founder's Relay Rally 9am** Bunbury Water Mill, Bowe's Gate Rd., Tarporley CW6 9PY. Neil Shirley 01352 713204 chairman@candnw.vmcc.net
30th April	**Surrey and Sussex Founders Relay Rally 9am** SCHVPT, East Hill Lane, Effingham Road, Copthorne RH10 3HZ. Brian Robins 07901 183181 surreysussexvmcc@gmail.com
30th April	**Wakefield and West Yorkshire Founders Relay Rally 9am** Squires Café, Newthorpe, nr Sherburn in Elmet LS25 5LX. Alistair Durie and Neil Lewis 07483 862303 neil.r.lewis@btinternet.com
30th April	**Banbury Founders Relay Rally** M. Phipps

MAY

1st May	**South Cotswold Summer riding quest** Your home. Jeremy Retford 07831 314884 jeremyretford@btinternet.com
1st May	**Men of Kent Velocette Owners Club open morning 10am** Hamstreet Village Hall, B2067, Hamstreet TN26 2NJ. Richard Woolnough 01303 862515 woolnough@mchenry.plus.com
2nd May	**North Birmingham Mike's Mid-Weeks Run 10am** Venue TBA. www.vmcc-nbs.co.uk/ Mike Cutler 07885 785972 NorthBirminghamVMCC@outlook.com
2nd May	**Ipswich & Suffolk Evening ride 6.30pm** Ipswich School Sports Centre, Rushmere St Andrews. Trevor Dickings 01473 798653
3rd May	**Wakefield and West Yorkshire Scissett Coffee Morning 10am** Mustang Café, Scissett, HD8 9HU. Alistair Durie and Neil Lewis 07483 862303 neil.r.lewis@btinternet.com
3rd May	**Cotswold Section Run 6.30pm** Colesbourne Arms, Colesbourne, GL53 9NP. 01242 870376 Graham Rowcliffe 07515 288414 grahamrowcliffe58@outlook.com
3rd May	**Gwent Baffle Haus Coffee Morning 11am** Baffle Haus Cafe, The Cedars, Goyytre Pontypool NP4 0AD. Richard Williams 01873 840483 markhillier61@icloud.com
3rd May	**Surrey and Sussex Wrinkly Run 10.30am** Venue TBA. Brian Robins 07901 183181 surreysussexvmcc@gmail.com
3rd May	**East Sussex Paul's Wrinkly Run 10.30am** Boship roundabout. Section secretary 07434 280380 secretary@eastsussexvmcc.co.uk

3rd May	**West Kent Mid-week run 10.30am** Village Hall car park, Hever. Ron Wright 07761 005995 betron.wright@gmail.com
3rd May	**Chiltern Evening Run 7pm** Full Moon Cholesbury Lane, Hawridge HP5 2UH. P. Barfield 01442 824143 chilternvmcc@hotmail.com
3rd May	**North Birmingham Club Night 8pm** Round Oak Inn, Ounsdale Road, Wombourne WV5 8BU. David Spencer 07975 629810 NorthBirminghamVMCC@outlook.com
4th May	**South Hants Day Run 10.30am** Basingwell Street Car Park, Bishop's Waltham SO32 1PA. Dave Tanner 01329 827262
4th May	**Worcestershire Gospel Pass and Llangors 10am** Oakchurch HR4 7NH. Richard Caddick 01299 403334
4th May	**West Wiltshire May Mid-week Run 10am** Venue TBA. Keith Johnstone 07952 173693 starfield181@gmail.com
4th May	**Blackpool & District Wray Classic Bike night 5pm** St Michael's Village Hall, Blackpool Rd, St Michael's on Wyre PR3 0UA. Terry A. Robinson 07960 116769 terry.robinson6@btinternet.com
4th May	**Essex Bluebell Long Weekend 10am** Museum of Power, Langford near Maldon CM9 6QA. what three words: consults. clinic. partner. Lesley Willmore 07971 266167
6th May	**Notts and Derby Saturday Morning Coffee Run 10am** Griffins Head Car Park, Moor Rd, Papplewick NG15 8EN. Graham Bower 07745 888938 nottsandderbyvintageclub@outlook.com
6th May	**Dorset Hedgerow Run 11am** Station Road C/P, Sturminster Newton, DT10 1BN. Dave Bramley 07771 871864 secretary@dorsetvmcc.co.uk
7th May	**Northampton Penny Farthing Run 10.30am** Venue TBA. Chris Towell 07860 719363 chris@cltowellandson.co.uk
7th May	**King's Lynn Run to Somewhere 10am** West Norfolk area, venue TBA. Andy Hunn 01366 328869 Club Secretary - malcolmrolph@talktalk.net
7th May	**East Yorkshire The Edmond's Run 10.30am** New Inn Farm, Ruston Parva, Driffield YO25 4DG. Nichola Clark 07488 236993 nichola. clark5@yahoo.co.uk
7th May	**Northumbrian Rookhope Ryde 10am** Wylam Riverside Car Park, Main Road, Wylam NE41 8HR. Pete Bagnall 07968 646357 petebagnall44@hotmail.com
7th May	**Cotswold Summer Wandering 12 noon** Farmers Arms, Birtsmorton, nr Malvern WR13 6AP. 01684 833308 Peter Kent 01452 610375
7th May	**South Wales Seaside run 11am** Venue TBA. Howard Jayne 02920 868203 howard.jayne@talktalk.net
7th May	**Banbury Coronation Run** Horsefair. D. Osenton 01295 811621
7th May	**Lakeland Whitehaven Ride-in 10.30am** Food Glorious Food, Dave Millings Motorcycles, Preston St, Whitehaven CA28 9DL. Dave Glynn
7th May	**Isle of Wight Mayfly Breakfast Run 9am** Carisbrooke Nunnery car park, Whitcombe Road, Newport PO30 1YS. Ron Wallis 01983 752861 ron.wallis10@gmail.com
7th May	**North West Holmeswood Run 10am** Don Fraser car park, Holmeswood Rd, Rufford, Holmeswood L40 1TX. Angie Graham 07773 555819 angiegraham2012@yahoo.co.uk
8th May	**North Cotswold Club Night 8pm** College Arms, Lower Quinton. Chris Delaney 07966 395032 chrisdelaney650@gmail.com
9th May	**Surrey and Sussex Evening Run 6.30pm** Venue TBA. Brian Robins 07901 183181
9th May	**Ipswich & Suffolk Evening ride 6.30pm** Ipswich School Sports Centre, Rushmere St Andrews. Trevor Dickings 01473 798653
9th May	**South Cotswold Tuesday Evening Pub Meet 6.30pm** The Fleece Inn, Hillesley GL12 7RD. Jeremy Retford 07831 314884 jeremyretford@btinternet.com
9th May	**Herefordshire & Mid Wales Brunch ride-in 11am** Riverbank Café, Tregaron SY25 6QS (on A485). Gary Jones 07870 389317
10th May	**Norwich and District Ranworth Broad 12 noon** C J Ball & Son, Woodlands, Salhouse Rd, Norwich NR7 9AB. John Pearson 07712 552501 jppearson7@gmail.com
10th May	**King's Lynn Ride-a-Bike Night 7pm** Make your own way. Club Secretary 01842 811077 malcolmrolph@talktalk.net
10th May	**Cotswold Section Run 6.30pm** Village Inn, Twyning Green, Twyning GL20 6DF. 01684 293500 Graham Rowcliffe 07515 288414 grahamrowcliffe58@outlook.com
10th May	**South Lincs and Peterborough May Wrinkly Run 10.30am** Venue TBA. Gary Sleeman 01733 770241 gary.sleeman1@gmail.com
10th May	**Dorset Mystery Summer Ride Out 6pm** Halsey Arms, Pulham, DT2 7DZ. Paul Wirdnam 07775 923206 secretary@dorsetvmcc.co.uk
10th May	**Essex Club night ride-in 6.30pm** Venue TBA. Dave Iszard 07543 901340 daveandnicki@sky.com
10th May	**Chiltern Midweek Run 10.30am** Full Moon, Cholesbury Lane, Hawridge HP52UH. P. Barfield 01442 824143 chilternvmcc@hotmail.com
10th May	**West Wiltshire Green Lane Run** Venue TBA. Keith Johnston 07836 376107 keith.johnston55@hotmail.co.uk
10th May	**Warwickshire Club night 7.30pm** Kenilworth Rugby Club, Glasshouse lane, Kenilworth CV8 2AJ. Barry heath 07786 718867 b4heath@yahoo.co.uk
10th May	**Northampton Midweek run 10am** Royal Oak, Blisworth NN7 3BU. Trevor Pinfold 01604 859215 trevorpinfold168@btinternet.com
10th May	**North East Lunch Meeting 12 noon** Harewood Arms, Harewood. Steve Rowley 07704 374773 rowley_s2@sky.com
10th May	**King's Lynn Ride a Bike Night 7pm** Venue TBA, make your own way. Club Secretary 01842 811077 malcolmrolph@talktalk.net

10th May	**Berkshire Mid-Week Run 10.30am** Venue TBA. Malcolm White 01344 642866 info@berkshire-vmcc.org.uk
11th May	**Taverners Evening Run 7.30pm** Bulls Head, Hinckley Road, Leicester LE9 9JE. Roger Monk 01509 412662
11th May	**North Cotswold Wrinkly Run 10am** Evesham. Chris Delaney 07966 395032 chrisdelaney650@gmail.com
11th May	**Blackpool & District Steve King Memorial Run 9.30am** Butty Hut, A6 Ashmead, New Holly Garage, Preston Lancaster Rd PR3 0BL. Terry A. Robinson 07960 116769 terry.robinson6@btinternet.com
11th May	**Oxford Thursday Run 10am** H Café, Dorchester on Thames OX10 7LY. Pete Ryman 01235 200367
11th May	**Dartmoor Early Evening Run 6pm** Opposite Royal Seven Stars Hotel, The Plains, Totnes TQ9 5DD. Derek French 07747 032659
11th May	**South Hants Day Run 10.30am** The Square, Wickham, Fareham PO17 5JT. Colin Shepley 07972 173940
12th May	**Goodwood Friday Run 10.30am** Venue TBA. Dave Johnson 01243 582074 goodwoodvmcc@aol.com
13th May	**Worcestershire Shropshire Hill Climbs revisited 9.30am** The Squirrel, Foldgate Lane, Ludlow SY8 1LS. Jonathan Parkes 07985 622775
13th May	**Herefordshire & Mid Wales Trail ride 3 10am** Venue TBA. Tony Fones 07588 559698 geoffmac@globalnet.co.uk
13th May	**Allen House MCN Festival 9am** Peterborough. Gary Sleeman gary@vmcc.net
13th May	**Norwich and District Camping Weekend 10am** Waveney Valley Holiday Park, Airstation Lane, Rushall, Diss IP21 4QF. Stephen Lee 07768 088740 strathearnhouse@btinternet.com
13th May	**Lakeland Metal Bridge Rally 10.30am** Metal Bridge Inn, Metal Bridge, near Carlisle CA6 4HD. Geoff Brazendale 01228 549445
13th May	**South Dorset Social Breakfast Meet 9.30am** The Three Compasses, Charminster DT2 9QT. Martin Figg 07896 507278 figg.martin@gmail.com
13th May	**Cotswold Signpost Rally 10am** Quenington Village Hall, Quenington, Cirencester GL7 5BS. Tim Cannock 07721 755549 tim.c.cannock@gmail.com
13th May	**Somerset Ruth's Day Out 10am** Pitney Playing Fields, Pitney. Ruth Pope 01458 251174
14th May	**Herefordshire & Mid Wales In search of the Green Man 10am** Snack Van, B&Q Hereford HR4 9SH. Steve Sumner 07494 713969 nvqsteve@yahoo.co.uk
14th May	**Northampton Bobs Earls Barton Run 10.30am** Billing Garden Village NN3 9EX. Bob Wyman 07711 322933 rjw5500@gmail.com
14th May	**Pennine North Lancashire Run 10.30am** The Comrades Club, Manchester Rd., Shaw, Oldham OL2 8SB. Geoff Green 07817 178287 secretary@penninevmcc.org.uk
14th May	**Blackpool & District Coronation Revival** Butty Hut, A6 Ashmead, New Holly Garage, Lancaster Rd, Preston PR3 0BL. Terry A. Robinson 07960 116769 terry.robinson6@btinternet.com
14th May	**North Cotswold Tidderls 10am** Venue TBA. Chris Delaney 07966 395032 chrisdelaney650@gmail.com
14th May	**Devon Exmoor Run 11am** Quince Honey Farm, South Molton, EX36 3AD. Nick Smiles 07711 444686 nickesmiles@googlemail.com
14th May	**West South Wales Teify Run 10.30am** Glyncoch, Tanglwst, Newcastle Emlyn Carm's SA38 9NJ. Andy & Quae 01559 371770
14th May	**South Dorset Club Run 10am** Weymouth Pavillion car park DT4 8ED. Rod Hann 01935 872528 rodhann@hotmail.co.uk
14th May	**Isle of Man Road Run 2pm** Venue TBA. Gary Corlett 07624 496672
14th May	**Taverners Spring Has Sprung Run 10.30am** McDonalds, Thurmaston, Leicester LE4 8GP. Kev Ellard 07378 371349 ellardshome@aol.com
14th May	**West Kent Godwin Oast House Run 10.30am** West Malling High Street car park. Ron Wright 07761 005995 betron.wright@gmail.com
14th May	**Stirling Castle Tiddlers Tootle 9am** Asmill Caraven Site, Doune, Stirling. FK16 6AA. Don Riley 01698 854390 jjleddy2@gmail.com
14th May	**North East Wetherby Run 10.30am** Wetherby Brewery, York Road Industrial estate LS22 7SU. Graham Wilson 07772 724078 gericwilson@ntlworld.com
14th May	**Clyde Valley Tiddler's Tootle 10.30am** Ashmill Caravan Park, Doune . Don Riley 01698 854390 mdriley@btinternet.com
14th May	**Surrey and Sussex Sunday Social Run 11am** Venue TBA. Brian Robins 07901 183181 surreysussexvmcc@gmail.com
14th May	**South Hants The Raleigh Run 10.30am** The Hinton Arms Petersfield Road, Cheriton, Alresford SO24 0NH. Dave Tanner 07710 592438
14th May	**North Staffs Leafy Lanes Run 11am** Clifford Arms, Great Haywood. Neil Hodgson 07931 412354
14th May	**Bedfordshire Roger and Arthur King Memorial Run 10am** Shefford Town Memorial Hall, Hitchin Road, Shefford SG17 5JA. Will Curry 01582 882122
14th May	**King's Lynn Windmill Run 10am** Butter Cross, Swaffham, Norfolk. Club Secretary 01842 811077 malcolmrolph@talktalk.net
14th May	**Banbury Mayfly Run 9.30am** Horsefair. G. Campbell 01295 678109

14th May	**Cornwall Dartmoor Run 10am** Morrisons Supermarket car park Priory Rd, Bodmin PL31 2ST. Bernard Hand 01840 211276
15th May	**South Dorset Club Run 10am** Bagwell Farm campsite DT3 4EA (3 miles east of Weymouth). Rod Hann 01935 872528 rodhann@hotmail.co.uk
16th May	**Ipswich & Suffolk Evening ride 6.30pm** Ipswich School, Sports Centre, Rushmere St Andrews. Trevor Dickings 01473 798653
16th May	**Taverners Wrinkly Run 10am** Apple Trees, Bradgate Close, Mountsorrel, Leicester LE12 7DZ. Roger Monk 01509 412662
16th May	**South Dorset Weymouth Week 10am** Bagwell Farm campsite DT3 4EA (3 miles east of Weymouth). Rod Hann 01935 872528 rodhann@hotmail.co.uk
16th May	**Isle of Wight Joys of Spring Lunch Run 11.30am** Hare and Hounds car park, Downend, Arreton PO30 2NU. Ron Wallis 01983 752861 ron.wallis10@gmail.com
16th May	**Surrey and Sussex Fish 'n Chip Run 6.30pm** The Motorcycle Workshop, London Road, Bolney RH17 5PY. Tim Penn 01444 232035 tpenn@tpenn.plus.com
16th May	**South Cotswold Tuesday Evening Pub Meet 6.30pm** The Railway Inn at Cam GL11 5NS. Jeremy Retford 07831 314884 jeremyretford@btinternet.com
16th May	**Taverners Wrinkly Run 10am** Apple Trees, Bradgate Close, Mountsorrel, Leicester LE12 7DZ. Roger Monk 01509 412662
17th May	**East Sussex Secretary's Saunter 10.30am** Brian's Barn, Brownbread St, Ashburnham TN33 9NX. Section secretary 07434 280380 secretaty@eastsussexvmcc.co.uk
17th May	**Essex Evening Run 6.30pm** Venue TBA. Dave Iszard 07543 901340 daveandnicki@sky.com
17th May	**Wakefield and West Yorkshire Scissett Coffee Morning 10am** Mustang Café, Scissett, HD8 9HU. Alistair Durie and Neil Lewis 07483 862303 neil.r.lewis@btinternet.com
17th May	**Chiltern Pub Night 8pm-ish** Full Moon, Cholesbury Lane, Hawridge HP5 2UH. P. Barfield 01442 824143 chilternvmcc@hotmail.com
17th May	**Cotswold Section Run 6.30pm** Red Hart Inn, Blaisdon, GL17 0AH. 01452 830477 Graham Rowcliffe 07515 288414 grahamrowcliffe58@outlook.com
17th May	**North West Alan Johnson Evening Run** Mere Brow Village Hall PR4 6JX. Angie Graham 07773 555819 angiegraham2012@yahoo.co.uk
17th May	**South Dorset Weymouth Week 10am** Bagwell Farm campsite DT3 4EA (3 miles east of Weymouth). Rod Hann 01935 872528 rodhann@hotmail.co.uk
17th May	**Reivers Rob's Out and About Run 10am** Moorhouse Farm Shop, Stannington NE61 6DX. Rob Dalkin 07703 892706
17th May	**Essex Evening Run 6.30pm** Venue TBA. Dave Iszard 07543 901340 daveandnicki@sky.com
17th May	**Bedfordshire Visit to Velo Club 7pm** Rose and Crown, High Street, Ridgmont MK43 0TY. Brent Fielder 07754 146605
17th May	**Bristol Lunchtime meet 12 noon** Chew Valley Lake Cafe, Walley Lane BS40 8XS. Alan Burton 07774 923721
17th May	**Chiltern Breakfast ride-in 10am** London Gliding club resturant LU62JP. P. Barfield 01442 824143 chilternvmcc@hotmail.com
18th May	**Bedfordshire Mid-week Run 10.15am** Shefford Town Memorial Hall, Hitchin Road, Shefford SG17 5JA. Don McKeand 01525 720629
18th May	**South Hants Day Run 10.30am** The Square, Wickham, Fareham PO17 5JT. Ian Harrop 07932 484209
18th May	**West Wiltshire Wandering 12 noon** The Waggon & Horses, Beckhampton SN8 1QJ. Colin Smith 07778 281332 colin.smith1951@btinternet.com
18th May	**Somerset Evening Meet 7pm** Ell's, (Rose and Crown), Huish Episcopi, nr Langport. James Ward 01458 251999
18th May	**South Dorset Weymouth Week 10am** Bagwell Farm campsite DT3 4EA (3 miles east of Weymouth). Rod Hann 01935 872528 rodhann@hotmail.co.uk
18th May	**North Cotswold Thursday Pub Meet 12 noon** The Snowshill Arms, Snowshill. Chris Delaney 07966 395032 chrisdelaney650@gmail.com
18th May	**Worcestershire Willy's Welsh Wander 9.30am** Cob House, Wichenford, WR6 6YE. Bill Danks 01562 67103
18th May	**Notts and Derby Barrie's Chip Shop Run 7pm** Ripley Market Place DE5 3BR. Graham Bower 07745 888938 nottsandderbyvintageclub@outlook.com
19th May	**South Dorset Weymouth Week 10am** Bagwell Farm campsite DT3 4EA (3 miles east of Weymouth). Rod Hann 01935 872528 rodhann@hotmail.co.uk
20th May	**Dorset Breakfast Meet 10am** Thorngrove Garden Centre, Common Mead Lane, Gillingham, SP8 4RE. Paul Wirdnam 07775 923206 secretary@dorsetvmcc.co.uk
20th May	**South Durham Quaker Social Run 10am** Manfield. Brian Smith 01325 286623
20th May	**Isle of Man Section Trial 1.30pm** Bim's Field. Shaun Seal 07624 485133
20th May	**Blackpool & District Central Lancs Girder Fork Run 10am** A6 layby nr entrance to Barton Hall, Broughton. Terry A. Robinson 07960 116769 terry.robinson6@btinternet.com
20th May	**Central Lancashire Flat Tank & Girder Fork Run 10.30am** Goosnargh Village Hall, Church Lane, Goosnargh PR3 2BH. Scott Hodges 07813 608891 hyper_products@hotmail.com
21st May	**North Birmingham The Three Lakes Run 10am** Venue TBA. www.vmcc-nbs.co.uk Peter Gray 07929 611546 NorthBirminghamVMCC@outlook.com

21st May	**Blackpool & District Ghost Bikes Meet 10am** Ghost Bikes, Unit 1a, Fishwick Park, Mercer St, Preston PR1 4LQ. Terry A. Robinson 07960 116769 terry.robinson6@btinternet.com
21st May	**Notts and Derby Robin Hood Run 10.30am** Horse and Groom, Main Street Linby NG15 8AE. Bruce Phillips 07442 168932 nottsandderbyvintageclub@outlook.com
21st May	**Mid Lincs Pre-'40s Run 10am** Wickenby Airfield, Langworth, Lincoln, LN3 5AX. Peter Gunnee/S. Parker 01652 657169 p.gunnee@talktalk.net
21st May	**Worcestershire Peter's Three Lakes Run 10am** Venue TBA. Peter Gray 01384 397421
21st May	**Cyclemotor Nasty Run 10.30am** Rising Sun PH, Halls Green Weston SG4 7DR. Chris Sawyer 07950 903794
21st May	**East Lancs Ghost Bikes Run 10.30am** Layby near Petre Garage Langho, Whalley Road BB6 8AB. David Prismall 01706 217572 davidprismall@hotmail.com
21st May	**Lakeland Dent Cafe ride-in 11am** Dent Heritage Centre, Dent LA10 5QJ. Colin Steer 01768 7074536
21st May	**Ironmasters Tiddlers Tour 10.30am** Bradford Arms on A5, past Weston Park. Alan Richardson 01785 841257
21st May	**Warwickshire Simon's Morning Coffee Run** Venue TBA. Barry Heath 07786 718867 b4heath@yahoo.co.uk
21st May	**Flat Tank Chairperson's Run 11am** Vine Villa, B4215, Highleadon, Gloucester. Charles Wright 01452 790296
21st May	**Anglian Houghton Mill Run 10.30am** Dobbies Garden Centre, Huntingdon PE28 2AA. Martyn Blunt 07880 026257 martynblunt@hotmail.co.uk
21st May	**South Lincs and Peterborough Out West Run 10.30am** Venue TBA. Gary Sleeman 01733770241 gary.sleeman1@gmail.com
21st May	**Bristol Ray Cordy Memorial Run 9.30am** Wishing Well, Wapley Road Codrington, Bristol BS37 6RY. John Beddis 01454 886506.
21st May	**North Cotswold Girder/rigid Run 10am** Touchdown Café, Wellesbourne. Chris Delaney 07966 395032 chrisdelaney650@gmail.com
21st May	**Norwich and District Caston Caper 10am** Postbox Bungalow, Northacre, Attleborough NR17 1DG. Peter Thacker 0195 3488575 maggie.thacker@btinternet.com
21st May	**Anglian Houghton Mill Run 10.30am** Dobbies Garden Centre, Huntingdon PE28 2AA. Martyn Blunt 07880 026257 martynblunt@hotmail.co.uk
21st May	**Cheshire and North Wales Not the Colwyn Bay Rally 1pm** Bunbury Water Mill, Mill Lane, Bowe's Gate Rd, Tarporley CW6 9PY. Neil Shirley 01352 713204 chairman@candnw.vmcc.net
21st May	**South Cotswold Sunday Lunchtime Café Meet 12 noon** The Old Prison Café, Northleach GL54 3JH. Jeremy Retford 07831 314884 jeremyretford@btinternet.com
21st May	**Berkshire Section Run 10.30am** Venue TBA. Malcolm White 01344 642866 info@berkshire-vmcc.org.uk
21st May	**Northampton Girder Fork Run 10.30am** Sywell Aerodrome NN6 0BN. Peter Tomkins 07917 407400 peter_james_tomkins@yahoo.co.uk
21st May	**Dartmoor Mystery Tour 10.30am** Opposite Royal Seven Stars Hotel, The Plains, Totnes TQ9 5DD. Contact TBA
21st May	**Gwent Cross Boarders Run 10am** Abergavenny Bus Station. Mark Hillier 07870 535933 markhillier61@icloud.com
21st May	**South Durham Quaker Run 10am** Cricket Club, Middleton St George. David Porteous 07706 992855 david.porteous3@gmail.com
21st May	**Herefordshire & Mid Wales The Seaside Run 10am** The Yellow Snack Van, A44 near Llandegley LD1 5UF. Rob Woodford 07847 098597
21st May	**West South Wales Black Mountain Road event 10.30am** Venue TBA. Morgan Thomas 07790 451182
23rd May	**Goodwood Noggin 'n' Natter 8pm** The Red Lion, London Road, Ashington RH20 3DD. Dave Johnson 01243 582074 goodwoodvmcc@aol.com
23rd May	**Taverners John Thompson Run 7.30pm** Waitrose, Granite Way, Mountsorrel LE12 7TZ. Roger Monk 01509 412662
23rd May	**Surrey and Sussex Evening Run 6.30pm** Venue TBA. Brian Robins 07901 183181 surreysussexvmcc@gmail.com
23rd May	**South Cotswold Tuesday Evening Pub Meet 6.30pm** The Bell Inn, Frampton on Severn GL2 7EP. Jeremy Retford 07831 314884 jeremyretford@btinternet.com
23rd May	**Ipswich & Suffolk Evening ride 6.30pm** Ipswich School, Sports Centre, Rushmere St Andrews. Trevor Dickings 01473 798653
23rd May	**Devon Evening Pub Meet 6.30pm** Mount Pleasant Inn, Nomansland EX16 8NN. John Young 07847 53725 jebyoung@hotmail.com
24th May	**Herefordshire & Mid Wales Breakfast meet 10am** The Nest, Little Verzons Farm, Hereford Rd, Ledbury HR8 2PZ. Geoff McGladdery 07588 559698 geoffmac@globalnet.co.uk
24th May	**Cotswold Section Run 6.30pm** Farmers Arms, Guiting Power, GL54 5TZ. 01451 850358 Graham Rowcliffe 07515 288414 grahamrowcliffe58@outlook.com
24th May	**East Sussex Fish & Chip run 7pm sharp** Brian's Barn, Brownbread St, Ashburnham TN33 9NX. Section secretary 07434 280380 secretaty@eastsussexvmcc.co.uk
24th May	**Men of Kent Bike night 8pm** The Shipwrights Arms, Hollowshore, Faversham ME13 7TU. Frank Mitchell 07837 918087 richardbarsby61@tiscali.co.uk

25th May	**East Yorkshire Goathland Camping Weekend** Abbots House Farm, Goathland YO22 5NH. Alan Barker 07887 592400 lindaandalanbarker@hotmail.co.uk
25th May	**South Dorset Club Night 8pm** The Three Compasses, Charminster DT2 9QT. Martin Figg 07896 507278 figg.martin@gmail.com
25th May	**Worcestershire Breakfast Meet 9.30am** Athena Tavern, Ludlow SY8 1RZ. Richard Caddick 01299 403334
25th May	**Notts and Derby Evening Run 7.30pm** Layby A6, 1 mile south of Whatstandwell. Mike Worthy 07979 642680 nottsandderbyvintageclub@outlook.com
25th May	**South Hants Day Run 10.30am** B2177 Southwick Rd/James Callaghan Drive, Portsmouth PO6 3RU. Dave Bettridge 02380 464822
25th May	**Bristol Lunchtime Meet 12 noon** George Inn, Gurney Slade, Radstock BA3 4TQ. Stuart Edwards 07369 249011
25th May	**Blackpool & District Run to Haverthwaite Railway 9.30am** Butty Hut, A6 Ashmead, New Holly Garage, Lancaster Rd, Preston PR3 0BL. Terry A. Robinson 07960 116769 terry.robinson6@btinternet.com
25th May	**North Cotswold Wrinkly Run 10am** Norton Lindsey. Chris Delaney 07966 395032 chrisdelaney650@gmail.com
25th May	**Oxford Thursday Run 10am** H Café, Dorchester on Thames OX10 7LY. David Webster 01865 452232
25th May	**Taverners Evening Run 7.30pm** Malt Shovel pub, Barkby, Leicester LE7 3QG. Roger Monk 01509 412662
27th May	**Allen House Coupes de Legendes 9am** Dijon. Coupes Moto Légende +33 (0)1 60 39 69 69 coupesml@lva.fr www.coupes-moto-legende.fr
27th May	**Lakeland Back Green Rally 1pm (27th) and 10am (28th)** Back Green, Hesket Newmarket CA7 8JG. Paul Richardson 016974 78037
27th May	**Notts and Derby Meet The Neighbours Run 2pm** Motus Commercials, A52 Mackworth, DE22 4NB. Mick Leach 01283 815487 nottsandderbyvintageclub@outlook.com
27th May	**Allen House Welsh Classic M/C Festival Anglesey 9am** Trac Yns Mon Anglesey Circuit, A4080, Ty Croes LL63 5TF. Classic Bike Track Days 07971 424472 info@classicbiketrackdays.com
28th May	**North Cotswold Bluebell Run 10am** Venue TBA. Chris Delaney 07966 395032 chrisdelaney650@gmail.com
28th May	**Dorset GIANTS Run 10.30am** Spire Hill Farm, Sturminster Newton DT10 2SG. Paul Miles 07774 921600 secretary@dorsetvmcc.co.uk
28th May	**East Lancs Cravendale Run 10.30am** Layby near Petre Garage Langho, Whalley Road BB6 8AB. Graham Bretherton 01722 716076
28th May	**South Hants Ted Craven Run 10.30am** Hill Park Memorial Working Men's Club, Highlands Rd, Fareham PO15 6JD. Dave Tanner 07710 592438
28th May	**Somerset All Day Breakfast Run 8am** Spaxton Village Hall, Spaxton TA5 1BT. Phil Ham 01278 671626
28th May	**Isle of Wight Underpowered Wobble Pt1 2pm** Chessell Pottery barns, Brook Road, Yarmouth PO41 0UE. Andrew Eason 07507 338633 andrew.eason1@btinternet.com
28th May	**Bedfordshire Breakfast Meet 10am** Danish Camp Riverside Visitor Centre, Chapel Lane Willington MK44 3QG. Richard Chambers 07905 203823
28th May	**North East Coronation Run 10.30am** Coronation Hall, Boroughbridge. Keith Hudson 07835 995059
28th May	**Essex Club Ride 9.30am** Venue TBA. Dave Iszard 07543 901340 daveandnicki@sky.com
28th May	**Dartmoor Breakfast meet 10am** The Jolly Roger, St John's Lane, Bovey Tracey TQ13 9FF. Derek French 07747 032659
28th May	**Cornwall Historic Vehicle Run 10.30am** Chiverton Arms, Chiverton Cross, Blackwater TR4 8HS. Steve Brighton 07767 203464
28th May	**Banbury Whitsun Run 9.30am** Horsefair. F. Dumbleton 01327 260680
28th May	**Northampton Ewan's Run 10am** Abthorpe service station A43 NN12 6TQ. Ewan Mackenzie 01908 564215 ewdor@me.com
29th May	**Chiltern Girder Fork Run 10.30am** Full Moon, Cholesbury Lane, Hawridge HP5 2UH. P. Barfield 01442 824143 chilternvmcc@hotmail.com
30th May	**West Wiltshire Coffee Morning 10am** Black Shed Cafe, Patch Bridge, Slimbridge GL2 7BP. Kevin Phillips 07952 173693 starfield181@gmail.com
30th May	**Ipswich & Suffolk Evening Ride 6.30pm** Ipswich School, Sports Centre, Rushmere St Andrews. Trevor Dickings 01473 798653
30th May	**East Lancs Ernie's Bowland Run 7pm** Victoria Hotel, St John's Street, Great Harwood BB6 7EP. Graham Daniels 07952 348339 grahamdaniels9@hotmail.com
30th May	**South Cotswold Tuesday Evening Pub Meet 6.30pm** The Lamb, Eastcombe GL6 7DN. Jeremy Retford 07831 314884 jeremyretford@btinternet.com
31st May	**Cotswold Section Run 6.30pm** Yew Tree, Chaceley Stock, GL18 1JS. 01452 780333 Graham Rowcliffe 07515 288414 grahamrowcliffe58@outlook.com
31st May	**Wakefield and West Yorkshire Scissett Coffee Morning 10am** Mustang Café, Scissett, HD8 9HU. Alistair Durie and Neil Lewis 07483 862303 neil.r.lewis@btinternet.com
31st May	**East Sussex Dave's morning slug run 10.30am** Brian's Barn, Brownbread Street, Ashburnham TN33 9NX. Section secretary 07434 280380 secretary@eastsussexvmcc.co.uk
31st May	**South Wales Wednesday evening ride-out 7pm** Your home. Bill Phelps 02920 890255 webadmin@southwalessectionvmcc.co.uk
31st May	**Reivers Teesdale Special, Follow the Leader 10am** Venue TBA. Denny Chappell 07719 599278

SUMMER RIDES
JUNE – JULY – AUGUST

Over 500 runs, rides and socials listed

Photo: Richard Woodcock

SUMMER

JUNE

1st June   **Men of Kent Sittingbourne Touring Week 12 noon**
Sharsted Sports Club, Faversham Road,
Newnham ME9 0LG. Alan Wibberley 07776 202843
arwibberley@aol.com

1st June   **North Staffs Kate's Evening Run 7.15pm**
Moorville Hall hotel. Kate Wain 07561 530136

1st June   **Somerset Club Night and short run 6.30pm**
Cossington Village Hall,
Cossington TA7 8LH Bryan Pope 01458 251174

1st June   **West Wiltshire Mid-Week Run 10am**
Silbury Hill Car Park, A4 near Beckhampton.
Des Guppy 07952 173693
starfield181@gmail.com

1st June   **South Hants Evening Run 7.30pm**
High St, Droxford, Southampton SO32 3PA.
Andy Collett 07584 663991

1st June   **Blackpool & District Wray Classic Bike night 5pm**
St Michael's Village Hall, Blackpool Rd, St Michael's on Wyre, Preston PR3 0UA. Terry A. Robinson 07960116769
terry.robinson6@btinternet.com

2nd June   **Northumbrian The 2nd Hadrian Rally 10am**
Boe Rigg, Charlton, Northumberland, NE48 1PE. Dave Harrision 07737 755286 harra1954@talktalk.net

2nd June   **West South Wales Welsh/Irish Rally 10am**
Nant-y-Ffin motel/hotel, Llandissilio,
Cylnderwen SA66 7SU. Les Thomas 01834 908056

3rd June   **Chiltern Summer Run 10.30am**
Full Moon, Cholesbury Lane, Hawridge HP52UH. P. Barfield 01442 824143
chilternvmcc@hotmail.com

4th June   **Men of Kent 67th Sittingbourne Run 10am**
Sharsted Sports Club, Faversham Road,
Newnham ME9 0LG. Alan Wibberley 07776 202843
arwibberley@aol.com

4th June   **Warwickshire Kenilworth Run Time TBA**
Hatton layby on A4177 52.300584749368966,
-1.640432239196066. Barry Heath 07786 718867
b4heath@yahoo.co.uk

4th June   **North Cotswold Past Members Run 10am**
Venue TBA. Chris Delaney 07966 395032
chrisdelaney650@gmail.com

4th June   **Isle of Wight Beat the Grockles Breakfast Run 9am**
Carisbrooke Nunnery car park, Whitcombe road,
Newport PO30 1YS. Ron Wallis 01983 752861
ron.wallis10@gmail.com

4th June   **North Staffs Oldest & Slowest 11am**
Leek Market Place. Mike Walker 07757 648889

4th June   **Norwich and District Round Norfolk Challenge 8am**
Seething Control Tower, Toad Lane,
Seething NR35 2EQ.what3words: beginning.film.marbles
Steve Hallam, Richard Mack,
Peter Thacker 07732 364524, 01953 603773,
01953 488575 shallam89@gmail.com

4th June   **Wakefield and West Yorkshire Emley Moor Run Around 10.30am**
Brooklands Nurseries, Scholes, New Mill, Holmfirth HD9 1UJ. Neil Lewis 07483 862303 neil.r.lewis@btinternet.com

4th June   **Cyclemotor Stony Stratford Classic Car & Bike Show**
Stony Stratford Market Place.
Malcolm Tappin 01494 672459 tappin@globalnet.co.uk

4th June   **Cheshire and North Wales Llangollen Gathering 10am**
Llangollen Motor Museum, Pentrefelin,
Llangollen LL20 8EE. secretary@candnw.vmcc.net
Neil Shirley 01352 713204 chairman@candnw.vmcc.net

4th June   **Cornwall Land's End Run Time TBA**
Bodmin and Wenford Railway General Station,
Harleigh Rd, Bodmin PL31 1AQ.
Roger Hore 07767 415564 or 01208 73571

4th June   **Lakeland Ride-In 11am**
Marina View Café, Marine Road, Maryport, CA15 8AY.
Eddie Stephenson 07932 544789

4th June   **Anglian Fenland Gallop 10.30am**
Chatteris, location TBA. Martyn Blunt 07880 026257
martynblunt@hotmail.co.uk

4th June   **North Birmingham South Staffordshire Ride 10am**
Venue TBA. www.vmcc-nbs.co.uk
Trevor Shakespeare 07790 185100
NorthBirminghamVMCC@outlook.com

4th June   **Dorset Jeff Clew Memorial Run 10.30am**
Shillingstone Railway, Station Rd, Shillingstone,
DT11 0SA. Rod Hann 01935 872528
secretary@dorsetvmcc.co.uk

4th June   **West Kent Social Run 10.30am**
Wrotham Hill car park, off A20 roundabout.
Ron Wright 07761 005995 betron.wright@gmail.com

5th June   **Northampton Wales Week**
Venue TBA. 01604 768069
richardstone47@hotmail.co.uk

5th June   **Reivers Rally 10am**
Alnwick Rugby Club, Greensfield, Willowburn Avenue,
Alnwick NE66 1BE. Howard Perrin 07981 700179

5th June   **Men of Kent Club Night 8pm**
Sharsted Sports Club, Faversham Road,
Newnham ME9 0NB. Frank Mitchell 07837 918087
richardbarsby61@tiscali.co.uk

5th June   **Cotswold Touring Week 10am**
Apple Orchard Campsite, Adsett, Westbury on Severn GL14 1PH. 01452 760618 Jenny Hart 01684 276610

6th June   **Herefordshire & Mid Wales Brunch ride-in 11am**
Owls Nest Café ,Lower Road, Llandovery SA20 0DJ.
Gary Jones 07870 389317 jgjones@sky.com

6th June   **Ipswich & Suffolk Evening ride 6.30pm**
Ipswich School, Sports Centre,
Rushmere St Andrews. Trevor Dickings 01473 798653

7th June   **North Birmingham Club Night 8pm**
The Round Oak Inn, Ounsdale Road, Wombourne,
WV5 8BU. David Spencer 07975 629810
NorthBirminghamVMCC@outlook.com

7th June   **King's Lynn Inter-Section Meet 12 noon**
The Five Miles from Anywhere PH,
Upware, nr Ely. Club Secretary 01842 811077
malcolmrolph@talktalk.net

7th June	**East Sussex Jerry's Bantam Run 10.30am** Brian's Barn, Brownbread Street, Ashburnham TN33 9NX. East Sussex 07434 280380 secretary@eastsussexvmcc.co.uk
7th June	**North East Stutton Evening Run 7pm** Hare & Hounds, Stutton, Tadcaster. Graham Wilson 07772 724078
7th June	**Gwent Baffle Hause Coffee Morning 11am.** Baffle Haus Cafe, The Cedars, Goyytre, Pontypool NP4 0AD. Richard Williams 01873 840483 markhillier61@icloud.com
7th June	**Surrey and Sussex Wrinkly Run 10am** Venue TBA. Brian Robins 07901 183181 surreysussexvmcc@gmail.com
7th June	**Lakeland Wray Cafe Ride-in 11am** Bridge House Tearooms, Main Street, Wray LA2 8QP. Colin Brunt 07990 880068
7th June	**South Dorset Club Run Time TBA** The Three Compasses, Charminster DT2 9QT. Rod Hann 01935 872528 rodhann@hotmail.co.uk
7th June	**Cotswold Section Run 6pm** Campsite, Apple Orchard, GL14 1PH. 01452760618 Graham Rowcliffe 07515 288414 grahamrowcliffe58@outlook.com
7th June	**Chiltern Evening Run 7pm** Full Moon, Cholesbury Lane, Hawridge HP5 2UH. P. Barfield 01442 824143 chilternvmcc@hotmail.com
7th June	**West Kent Mid week run 10.30am** Kemsing High Street car park. Ron Wright 07761 005995 betron.wright@gmail.com
7th June	**Worcestershire Baffle Haus with Gwent 11am** Baffle Haus, Pontypool NP4 0AD. Richard Caddick 01299 403334
8th June	**Oxford Thursday Run 10am** Milletts Farm OX13 5HB. Roger Laban 01993 704482
8th June	**Taverners Evening Run 7.30pm** Wistow, Kibworth Road, Leicester LE8 0QF. Roger Monk 01509 412662
8th June	**Dartmoor Early Evening Run 6pm** Opposite Royal Seven Stars Hotel, The Plains, Totnes TQ9 5DD. Roy Turner 07702 908425
8th June	**North Cotswold Picnic Run 10am** Venue TBA. Chris Delaney 07966 395032 chrisdelaney650@gmail.com
8th June	**North Staffs Early Summer Run 7pm** Leek Market Place. Richard Bills 07588 707701
8th June	**South Hants Evening Run 7.30pm** Churchillian Cark, Portsdown Hill Rd, Cosham, Portsmouth PO6 3LS. Russell Daysh 01329 311331
9th June	**Goodwood Friday Run 10.30am** Venue TBA. Dave Johnson 01243 582074 goodwoodvmcc@aol.com
9th June	**Flat Tank and Cotswold Weekend 3.30pm** Apple Orchard Campsite, Adsett Lane Westbury on Severn GL14 1PF. Dennis Beale, Robert Rendell 07969 62333 denbeale@gmail.com
10th June	**Taverners BBQ Trial 2pm** Vickers Farm, Marefield, nr Tilton LE7 9LE. Pete Monk 07826 683600 pmonk83@yahoo.com
10th June	**South Dorset Social Breakfast Meet 9.30am** The Three Compasses, Charminster DT2 9QT. Martin Figg 07896 507278 figg.martin@gmail.com
10th June	**Cotswold Cotswold/Flat Tank Weekend** Apple Orchard Campsite, Adsett, Westbury on Severn GL14 1PH. 01452 760618 Jenny Hart 01684 276610
10th June	**Notts and Derby Limestone Peak Run 2.30pm** Layby A515, 1 mile north of Ashbourne. Clive Russell 01335 390369 nottsandderbyvintageclub@outlook.com
11th June	**Dorset Howard's Dorset Dawdle 11am** Coffee House, Kings Stag DT10 2AY. Howard Smedley 01258 821532 secretary@dorsetvmcc.co.uk
11th June	**South Cotswold John Oliver Elver Run 10am** Stonehouse Car Park, Stonehouse GL10 2NG. Dave Carroll or Jeremy Retford, Jeremy 07831 314884, Dave dodursley@tiscali.co.uk
11th June	**Dartmoor East Devon Run 10am** The Royal Seven Stars Hotel, The Plains, Totnes TQ9 5DD. Derek French 07747 032659
11th June	**Somerset Girder Fork and Rigid Frame Run 10am** Sweets Cafe, Westhay BS28 4UE. Mike Chipperfield 01749 679371
11th June	**Cyclemotor The Postcombe Run 10.30am** Englands Rose PH, Postcombe OX9 7DP. Malcolm Tappin 01494 672459 tappin@globalnet.co.uk
11th June	**North Staffs Day Trip to Wales (possibly) 10.30am** Crown Street car park, Stone. Ian Pettifor 07760 346003 ianpettifor631@btinternet.com
11th June	**Banbury Observation Run 9.30am** Horsefair. D. Jebbit 01295 750538
11th June	**Cornwall West Devon Borders Run 10.30am** Strawberry Fields Farm Shop, Lifton PL16 0DH. Dave Beachem 07871 158212
11th June	**Pennine Four Counties Run 10.30am** The Comrades Club, Manchester Rd., Shaw, Oldham OL2 8SB. Geoff Green 07817 178287 secretary@penninevmcc.org.uk
11th June	**Reivers The Bamburgh Run 10am** Etal Village, TD12 4TN. Simon Hadden 07843 774731
11th June	**Devon West Devon Borders Run 10.30am** Strawberry Fields Farm Shop, Lifton, PL16 0DH. John Young 07847 753725 jebyoung@hotmail.com
11th June	**Norwich and District, Deopham Green 10am** Walnut Tree Farm, Stalland Lane, Deopham NR18 9DN. Phil Pheonix 07786 668786 phoenix627@btinternet.com
11th June	**Worcestershire Grand Tour of Scotland** Venue/time TBA. Richard Caddick 01299 403334
11th June	**Lakeland Tea and Scones ride-in 2pm** Boltongate Village Hall, (nr Ireby) CA7 1DA. John Bell 01697 371657
12th June	**Surrey and Sussex Long Distance Event 10am** Copthorne Social Club, Copthorne, Crawley RH10 3RE. Brian Robins 07901 183181 surreysussexvmcc@gmail.com

12th June	**North Cotswold Club Night 8pm** College Arms, Lower Quinton. Chris Delaney 07966 395032 chrisdelaney650@gmail.com
13th June	**North Birmingham Flight of Fantasy Run 10am** Venue TBA. www.vmcc-nbs.co.uk Julian Edwards 01562 883224 NorthBirminghamVMCC@outlook.com
13th June	**Surrey and Sussex Evening Run 6.30pm** Venue TBA. Brian Robins 07901 183181 surreysussexvmcc@gmail.com
13th June	**Ipswich & Suffolk Evening ride 6.30pm** Ipswich School, Sports Centre, Rushmere St Andrews. Trevor Dickings 01473 798653
13th June	**South Cotswold Tuesday Evening Pub Meet 6.30pm** The Crown and Sceptre, Horns Rd, Stroud GL5 1EG. Jeremy Retford 07831314884 jeremyretford@btinternet.com
14th June	**Essex Club night 7.30pm** The Bell, Woodham Ferrers. Dave Iszard 07543 901340 daveandnicki@sky.com
14th June	**Berkshire Mid-Week Run 10.30am** Malcolm White 01344 642866 info@berkshire-vmcc.org.uk
14th June	**Essex Club Run 7.30pm** Venue/ride leader TBA. Dave Iszard 07543901340 daveandnicki@sky.com
14th June	**South Lincs and Peterborough Wrinkly Run 10.30am** Venue TBA. Gary Sleeman 01733 770241 gary.sleeman1@gmail.com
14th June	**Wakefield and West Yorkshire Scissett Coffee Morning 10am** Mustang Café, Scissett, HD8 9HU. Alistair Durie and Neil Lewis 07483 862303 neil.r.lewis@btinternet.com
14th June	**Northampton Mid-week run 10am** Royal Oak, Blisworth NN7 3BU. Trevor Pinfold 01604 859215 trevorpinfold168@btinternet.com
14th June	**Cotswold Section Run 6.30pm** Severn Bore, Minsterworth GL2 8JX. 01452 750318 Graham Rowcliffe 07515 288414 grahamrowcliffe58@outlook.com
14th June	**Dorset Fish and Chip Run 6pm** Halsey Arms, Pulham, DT2 7DZ. Paul Miles 07774 921600 pauledwinmiles@me.com
14th June	**North East Lunch Meeting 12 noon** Harewood Arms, Harewood. Steve Rowley 07704 374773 rowley_s2@sky.com
14th June	**Kings Lynn Ride-a-Bike Night 7pm meet up** Make your own way. Club Secretary 01842 811077 malcolmrolph@talktalk.net
14th June	**Chiltern Mid-week Run 10.30am** Full Moon, Cholesbury Lane, Hawridge HP5 2UH. P. Barfield 01442 824143 chilternvmcc@hotmail.com
14th June	**West Wiltshire Green Lane Run** Venue/time TBA. Keith Johnston 07836 376107 keith.johnston55@hotmail.co.uk
15th June	**Herefordshire & Mid Wales Trail ride 4 10am** Regent House Filling Station, Clyro HR3 5SB. Paul Farley 01874 610303 palmag@btinternet.com
15th June	**West Wiltshire Wandering 12 noon** The Hatchet Inn, Lower Chute, SP11 9DX. Colin Smith 07778 281332 colin.smith1951@btinternet.com
15th June	**Somerset Evening Meet 7pm** Lamb Inn, Spaxton. Phil Ham 01278 671626
15th June	**Notts and Derby Old and Slow Run 7.30pm** Ripley Market Place DE5 3BR. Jim Bradley 0115 932 9049 nottsandderbyvintageclub@outlook.com
15th June	**Bedfordshire Mid-week Run 10.15am** Shefford Town Memorial Hall, Hitchin Road, Shefford SG17 5JA. Don Mckeand 01525 720629
15th June	**South Hants Evening Run 7.30pm** Southwick Rd/James Callaghan Drive, Portsmouth PO6 3RU. Maurice Hayman 01329 282058
15th June	**North Staffs Longnor Chippy Run 6.30pm** Leek Market Place Richard Bills 07588 707701
17th June	**North East Scottish Girder Fork Run 10.30am** Clatt Village Hall, Aberdeenshire. Tony Mortishire 07887 740396 mortishire@btinternet.com
17th June	**Dorset Breakfast Meet 10am** Thorngrove Garden Centre, Common Mead Lane, Gillingham, SP8 4RE. Paul Wirdnam 07775 923206 secretary@dorsetvmcc.co.uk
17th June	**Clyde Valley Rock n Roll run 10.30am** Overton Farm Shop, Crossford, Carluke, ML8 5QF. Tim Ryan 07714 505386 timryan750@gmail.com
17th June	**Lakeland Ride-in to Barrow Dock Museum 11am** Dock Museum, North Road, Barrow-in-Furness, LA14 2PW. John Silcock 01229 861264
18th June	**Kings Lynn Early Birds Run 7am** The Clubhouse, NSSC Hovell's Lane, Northwold IP26 5LX. Dick Fendick 01366 728852 malcolmrolph@talktalk.net
18th June	**Isle of Man Road Run 2pm** QB Car Park. Gary Corlett 07624 496672
18th June	**South Dorset Club Run 10.30am** The Three Compasses, Charminster DT2 9QT. Martin Figg 07896 507278 figg.martin@gmail.com
18th June	**North East High Trees Run 10.30am** High Trees Garden Centre, Horsforth LS18 5HZ. Graham Wilson 07772 724078
18th June	**Mid Lincs Humber Bridge Run 10am** Humber Bridge Car park, (South Bank) DN18 5BD. Peter Gunnee 01652 657169 p.gunnee@talktalk.net
18th June	**Worcestershire Open Day 9.30am** Cob House, Wichenford, WR6 6YE. Richard Caddick 01299 403334
18th June	**North Cotswold The Long Run 9am** Venue TBA. Chris Delaney 07966 395032 chrisdelaney650@gmail.com
18th June	**Allen House Banbury Run 8am** British Motor Museum, Gaydon CV35 0BJ. Annie Durrant 07484 647046 banbury@vmcc.net
18th June	**West Kent Pre-'30s Run 10.30am** Eynsford layby on A225 south of the railway bridge. Ron Wright 07761 005995 betron.wright@gmail.com

19th June	**Herefordshire & Mid Wales** **Herefordshire & Beyond 9.30am** Green Dragon Hotel, Broad St, Hereford HR4 9BG. Terry Pickering 07850 602222 terry@sthereford.co.uk
20th June	**Herefordshire & Mid Wales** **Herefordshire & Beyond Day 2 9.30am** Green Dragon Hotel, Broad St, Hereford HR4 9BG. Terry Pickering 07850 602222 terry@sthereford.co.uk
20th June	**Gwent Ride a Bike Night 6.30pm** Abergavenny Bus Station. Mark Hillier 07870 535933 markhillier61@icloud.com
20th June	**East Lancs Shortest Night Run 7pm** Victoria Hotel, St John's Street, Great Harwood BB6 7EP. David Prismall 01706 217572 davidprismall@hotmail.com
20th June	**South Lincs and Peterborough Evening** **Fish and Chips Run 6.45pm** Venue TBA. Gary Sleeman 01733 770241 gary.sleeman1@gmail.com
20th June	**Ipswich & Suffolk Evening ride 6.30pm** Ipswich School Sports Centre, Rushmere St Andrews. Trevor Dickings 01473 798653
20th June	**Isle of Wight June Bug Lunch Run 11.30am** Hare and Hounds car park, Downend, Arreton PO30 2NU. Ron Wallis 01983 752861 ron.wallis10@gmail.com
20th June	**Blackpool & District Midsummer's Day Run 9am** Butty Hut, A6 Ashmead, New Holly Garage, Lancaster Rd, Preston PR3 0BL. Terry A. Robinson 07960116769 terry.robinson6@btinternet.com
20th June	**South Cotswold Tuesday Evening Pub Meet 6.30pm** The Rose and Crown, Nympsfield GL10 3TU. Jeremy Retford 07831 314884 jeremyretford@btinternet.com
21st June	**Essex Evening Club Run 6.30pm** Venue TBA. Dave Iszard 07543 901340 daveandnicki@sky.com
21st June	**Chiltern Breakfast ride-in 10am** London Gliding club restaurant LU62JP. P.Barfield 01442 824143 chilternvmcc@hotmail.com
21st June	**Herefordshire & Mid Wales Breakfast meet 10am** The New Strand, Church Road, Eardisley HR3 6PW. Geoff McGladdery 07588 559698 geoffmac@globalnet.co.uk
21st June	**North East President's social run 11am** Sun Inn, Norwood, Harrogate HG3 1SZ. Steve Rowley 07704 374773 rowley_s2@sky.com
21st June	**Chiltern Pub Night 6pm onwards** The Plough, Cadsden. P. Barfield 01442 824143 chilternvmcc@hotmail.com
21st June	**Dorset Mid-Week Run 2pm** Wardon Hill Trading Post DT2 9PW. Rod Hann 01935 872528 secretary@dorsetvmcc.co.uk
21st June	**Herefordshire & Mid Wales Herefordshire & Beyond** **Day 3 9.30am for 10am** The Green Dragon Hotel, 44-46 Broad St, Hereford HR4 9BG Terry Pickering 07850 602222 terry@sthereford.co.uk
21st June	**Cotswold Section Run 6.30pm** Yew Tree, Chaceley Stock GL18 1JS. 01452 780333 Graham Rowcliffe 07515 288414 grahamrowcliffe58@outlook.com
21st June	**Bristol Evening Run 7pm** Wishing Well, Wapley Road, Codrington, Bristol BS37 6RY. Mike Drake, Mike Fay, 07967 64164, 07974 650631
21st June	**Wakefield and West Yorkshire** **Sneaky Peak Run 9.30am** Mustang Café, Scissett, HD8 9HU. Rob Hudson 07801 548750 neil.r.lewis@btinternet.com
21st June	**East Sussex Evening run to the Star 7pm** Brian's Barn, Brownbread Street. Section secretary 07434 280380 secretary@eastsussexvmcc.co.uk
21st June	**Men of Kent Frank's Mid-Summers Day Run 10.30am** Car Park, Taylors Hill, Chilham, Canterbury CT4 8BZ . Frank Mitchell 07837 918087 richardbarsby61@tiscali.co.uk
21st June	**Devon Evening Pub Meet 6.30pm** The Exeter Inn, Chittlehamholt EX37 9NS. Nick Smiles 07711 444686 nickesmiles@googlemail.com
21st June	**West South Wales Mid-summer evening** **fish & chip run 7pm prompt** Coppet Hall car park SA69 9AJ nr Saundersfoot. Les & Shirley 01834 908056
22nd June	**South Dorset Club Night 7.30pm** The Three Compasses, Charminster DT2 9QT. Martin Figg 07896 507278 figg.martin@gmail.com
22nd June	**North Staffs Longest Day Run 7pm** Leek Market Place. Ian Pettifor 07760 346003 contact@northstaffsvmcc.com
22nd June	**Oxford Thursday Run 10am** H Café, Dorchester on Thames OX10 7LY. Rob Harris 01865 730109
22nd June	**South Durham Ride to Club Night 6pm** Cricket Club, Middleton St George, Darlington DL2 1JQ. Brian Smith and Steve Hodgson 01325 286623
22nd June	**South Hants Day Run 10.30am** Basingwell Street Car Park, Bishop's Waltham SO32 1PA. Dave Bettridge 02380 464822
22nd June	**North Cotswold Wrinkly Run 10am** Venue TBA. Chris Delaney 07966 395032 chrisdelaney650@gmail.com
22nd June	**Notts and Derby Evening Run 7pm (note earlier time)** The Triangle, Belper Mill Junction, DE56 1BJ. Graham Franks 07932 954603
22nd June	**Isle of Man Road Run 7.30pm** St Johns. Gary Corlett 07624 496672
22nd June	**Herefordshire & Mid Wales Herefordshire & Beyond** **Day 4 9.30am** Green Dragon Hotel, Broad St, Hereford HR4 9BG. Terry Pickering 07850 602222 terry@sthereford.co.uk
23rd June	**Lakeland Arnside Chippy Gathering 6.30pm** Arnside Chippy, The Promenade, Arnside, Carnforth LA5 0HF. Robert Lemon 01524 761581
23rd June	**Allen House ABR Festival 9am** Wragley Hall. Gary Sleeman gary@vmcc.net
23rd June	**Herefordshire & Mid Wales Herefordshire & Beyond** **Day 5 9.30am** Green Dragon Hotel, Broad St, Hereford HR4 9BG. Terry Pickering 07850 602222 terry@sthereford.co.uk

24th June	**North Birmingham Girder Fork Run, joint with Worcestershire 10am** Rowberries Nursery, Chaddesley Corbett. Martyn Round 0121 5501547 NorthBirminghamVMCC@outlook.com
24th June	**South Durham Walworth Concours and Social Run 1pm** Chequers PH, Dalton on Tees. David Headon 01325 720183
24th June	**Notts and Derby Saturday Coffee Run 10am** Griffins Head Car Park, Moor Rd, Papplewick, Nottingham NG15 8EN. Graham Bower 07745 888938 nottsandderbyvintageclub@outlook.com
24th June	**Worcestershire Girder Fork Run with NBS 10am** Rowberries Garden Centre DY10 4QN. Richard Caddick 01299 403334
24th June	**Chiltern Hills Run 10.30am departure** Full Moon, Cholesbury Lane, Hawridge HP5 2UH. P. Barfield 01442 824143 chilternvmcc@hotmail.com
24th June	**Blackpool & District Southport Auto Centre Show 9.30am** A6 Layby adj entrance to Barton Hall, Broughton. Terry A. Robinson 07960 116769 terry.robinson6@btinternet.com
24th June	**Reivers The Mansize Run 9am** Jan's Kitchen, Ponteland, NE20 9BD. Mike Coxon 07919 666818
25th June	**Berkshire Section Run 10.30am** Venue TBA. Malcolm White 01344 642866 info@berkshire-vmcc.org.uk
25th June	**East Yorkshire Th'Ouse & Th'Umber 10.30am** Ernie B's Cafe, Market Weighton Road, Hole on Spalding Moor YO43 4ED. Tony Dean 07860 474439 tony@deansouthwood.karoo.co.uk
25th June	**Herefordshire & Mid Wales Herefordshire on the Edge 2023 10am** Two start/finish points: Traveller's Rest HR9 7QJ (outskirts of Ross-on-Wye) and The Lion Hotel, Leintwardine SY7 0JZ. Geoff McGladdery 07588 559698 geoffmac@globalnet.co.uk
25th June	**Wakefield and West Yorkshire Horbury Show Around 10.30am** Carr Lodge Park, WF4 6NG Alistair Durie and Neil Lewis 07483 862303 neil.r.lewis@btinternet.com
25th June	**Blackpool & District/Central Lancs Section Bowland Fells Run 9.30am** Butty Hut A6, Ashmead, New Holly Garage, Lancaster Rd, Preston PR3 0BL. Terry A. Robinson 07960 116769 terry.robinson6@btinternet.com
25th June	**North Staffs Hills & Hollows Run 11am** Moorville Hall hotel. Danny Miles 01782 322510
25th June	**North West Longest Day Blue Haze Run 10am** Mere Brow Village Hall PR4 6JX. Angie Graham 07773 555819 angiegraham2012@yahoo.co.uk
25th June	**West South Wales Pembrokeshire Run. 10.30am** Withybush airfield, Fishguard Rd A40 SA62 4BN. Dave Evans 01437 731576
25th June	**Northampton Breakfast Run 8.30am** Sixfields stadium car park NN5 5QA. Dave Mead 01327 342570 david.r.mead@btinternet.com
25th June	**Banbury Not the Grand Day Out 9.30am** Horsefair. A. Yeomans 01295 261698
25th June	**Dorset Somerset Levels Run 10.30am.** Virginia Ash, Henstridge, BA8 0PL. Andy Grew 01935 595096 secretary@dorsetvmcc.co.uk
25th June	**Norwich and District The Middy 10am** High Barn, Shipdham Road, Carbrooke Norfolk IP25 6SY. Steve Hallam 07732 364524 shallam89@gmail.com
25th June	**Isle of Wight Robin's North Island Saunter 9am** Yarmouth Ferry terminal. Ron Wallis 01983 752861 ron.wallis10@gmail.com
25th June	**Surrey and Sussex Sunday Social Run 11am** Venue TBA. Brian Robins 07901 183181 surreysussexvmcc@gmail.com
25th June	**Ironmasters Roads-a-Roaming 10.30am** Redhill cafe layby, A5. Alan Richardson 01785 841257
25th June	**Northumbrian Breakfast Meet 9.30am** Hadrian Hotel, Front St, Hexham NE46 4EE. Tom Houchen 07968 646357 petebagnall44@hotmail.com
25th June	**South Lincs and Peterborough Longest Day Run 10.30am** Venue TBA. Gary Sleeman 01733 770241 gary.sleeman1@gmail.com
25th June	**Gwent Girder Fork Run 10am** Abergavenny Bus Station. John Sharman 01874 730753 markhillier61@icloud.com
25th June	**Bedfordshire Breakfast Meet 10am** Flitvale Garden Centre, Flitwick Road, Westoning MK45 5AA. Richard Chambers 07905 203823
25th June	**Lakeland St Bees ride-in 11am** Beach Café, St Bees, CA27 0ES. Bob Mayow 01946 822580
25th June	**North Cotswold Severn Valley Run 9am** Venue TBA. Chris Delaney 07966 395032 chrisdelaney650@gmail.com
25th June	**Cyclemotor Bikes in Beds 10am** The Dukes PH, High St, Woodford, Kettering NN14 4HE. Hugh Gallagher 01933 419800, 07805 247033
25th June	**Essex Breakfast Run 8.30am** Venue TBA. Dave Iszard 07543901340 daveandnicki@sky.com
25th June	**Northampton Bikes in Beds 10.30am** The Dukes Arms, Woodford NN14 4HE. Hugh Gallagher 01933 419800 hughie_gallagher@btinternet.com
27th June	**South Cotswold Tuesday Evening Pub Meet 6.30pm** The Thames Head Inn GL7 6NZ. Jeremy Retford 07831 314884 jeremyretford@btinternet.com
27th June	**Taverners Wrinkly Run 10am** Apple Trees, Bradgate Close, Mountsorrel, Leicester LE12 7DZ. Roger Monk 01509 412662
27th June	**West Wiltshire Coffee Morning 10am** AV 8 Cafe, Cotswold Airport, GL7 6BA. Kevin Phillips 07952 173693 starfield181@gmail.com
27th June	**Ipswich & Suffolk Evening ride 6.30pm** Ipswich School Sports Centre, Rushmere St Andrews. Trevor Dickings 01473 798653
27th June	**Surrey and Sussex Evening Run 6.30pm** Venue TBA. Brian Robins 07901 183181 surreysussexvmcc@gmail.com

27th June	**Goodwood Noggin 'n' Natter 8pm** The Red Lion, London Road, Ashington RH20 3DD. Dave Johnson 01243 582074 goodwoodvmcc@aol.com
28th June	**South Wales Wednesday evening ride out 7pm** Your home. Bill Phelps 02920 890255 webadmin@southwalessectionvmcc.co.uk
28th June	**Wakefield and West Yorkshire Scissett Coffee Morning 10am** Mustang Café, Scissett, HD8 9HU. Alistair Durie and Neil Lewis 07483 862303 neil.r.lewis@btinternet.com
28th June	**Cotswold Section Run 6.30pm** Carpenters Arms, Miserden, GL6 7JA. 01285 821283 Graham Rowcliffe 07515 288414 grahamrowcliffe58@outlook.com
28th June	**Cyclemotor Box Hill Run 10.30am** Surrey Oaks PH, Parkgate, Newdigate RH5 5DZ. Vic Hurst 02392 179548
28th June	**South Durham Evening Social Run 6.30pm** Cricket Club Middleton St George. Brian Smith 01325 286623
28th June	**East Sussex Dave's Girder Fork run 10.30am** Brian's Barn, Brownbread Street, Ashburnham TN33 9NX. Section secretary 07434 280380 secretary@eastsussexvmcc.co.uk
29th June	**Taverners Evening Run 7.30pm** County Hall, Glenfield Road Leicester LE3 8RA. Roger Monk 01509 412662
29th June	**Bristol Breakfast Run to Kemble Airfield** 9.30am or make your own way there. Destination AV8 Cafe, Kemble Airfield, Cirencester, GL7 6BA. Stuart Edwards 07369 249011
29th June	**Worcestershire Highest and Sea Level Ride 9.30 am** Cob House, Wichenford, WR6 6YE. Richard Caddick 01299 403334
29th June	**Taverners Evening Run 7.30pm** County Hall, Glenfield Road, Leicester LE3 8RA. Roger Monk 01509 412662
29th June	**South Durham Evening Excursion 6pm** Cricket Club Middleton St George Nigel Clark 07706 992855 david.porteous3@gmail.com
29th June	**North Cotswold Thursday Pub Meet 12 noon** The Old Bulls Head, Inkberrow. Chris Delaney 07966 395032 chrisdelaney650@gmail.com
29th June	**Notts and Derby Evening Run 7.30pm** Ripley Market Place DE5 3BR. Gordon Milburn 07800 826733 nottsandderbyvintageclub@outlook.com
29th June	**South Hants Day Run 10.30am** Basingwell Street Car Park, Bishop's Waltham SO32 1PA
30th June	**West South Wales Camping w/end 10am** Tirdail Nantgaredig SA32 7NH Carm's. Chris & Eirios Thomas 07974 373987
30th June	**Men of Kent Camping Weekend 12 noon** Hatchers Farm, The Street, Preston nr Canterbury CT3 1ED. Frank Mitchell 07837 918087 richardbarsby61@tiscali.co.uk

JULY

1st July	**Blackpool & District Wrea Green Field Day 9am** Village Green, Wrea Green, Preston. Terry A Robinson 07960 116769 terry.robinson6@btinternet.com
1st July	**Worcestershire Brewery visit 2pm** Heightington Brewery DY12 2XY. Richard Caddick 01299 403334
2nd July	**Lakeland Orton Scar Café ride-in 11am** Orton Scar Café, Orton, nr Tebay, CA10 3RQ. Eric Stephenson 01900 824898
2nd July	**Dorset Chairman's Challenge Run 10.30am** Thorngrove Garden Centre, Gillingham SP8 4RE. Paul Miles 07774 921600 secretary@dorsetvmcc.co.uk
2nd July	**Cornwall Antony Barfield's Run 10.30am** ATS Helston Clodgey Ln, Helston TR13 8PJ. Antony Barfield 07856 067433
2nd July	**Taverners Sunday Tiddler Run 10am** Buttercup Tearoom, Tilton Road, Leicester LE7 9FE. Don West 07485 075208 donwest123@yahoo.co.uk
2nd July	**Bedfordshire Albert Brown Run 9am** Wilden Village Hall MK44 2PB. 07754 146605 brentfielder@btinternet.com (preferred)
2nd July	**Isle of Wight Morning Sun Breakfast Run 9am** Carisbrooke Nunnery car park, Whitcombe Road, Newport PO30 1YS. Ron Wallis 01983 752861 ron.wallis10@gmail.com
2nd July	**East Lancs Ribblesdale Run 10.30am** Layby near Petre Garage, Langho, Whalley Road BB6 8AB. John Ashurst 07888712414
2nd July	**North Staffs Out and About with Tony 11am** Leek Marketplace.
2nd July	**North East Sun Run 10.30am** Sun Inn, Norwood, Harrogate HG3 1SZ. Steve Rowley 07704 374773 rowley_s2@sky.com
2nd July	**Wakefield and West Yorkshire Ray's Run Around 10.30am** Redbeck Café, Doncaster Road, Crofton, Wakefield WF4 1RR. Ray Bradley and Neil Lewis 07483 862303 neil.r.lewis@btinternet.com
2nd July	**West Kent Girder fork run 10.30am** Meopham station car park off A227, DA13 0HL. Ron Wright 07761 005995 betron.wright@gmail.com
2nd July	**Northampton Sunshine run 10am** Super Sausage Café, A5. Richard Stone 01604 768069 richardstone47@hotmail.co.uk
2nd July	**North Cotswold Breakfast Run 9am** Venue TBA. Chris Delaney 07966 395032 chrisdelaney650@gmail.com
3rd July	**East Sussex Evening run to The Flying Horse 7pm** Brian's Barn, Brownbread Street, Ashburnham TN33 9NX. Section secretary 07434 280380 secretary@eastsussexvmcc.co.uk
4th July	**Ipswich & Suffolk Evening ride 6.30pm** Ipswich School Sports Centre, Rushmere St Andrews. Trevor Dickings 01473 798653
4th July	**Herefordshire & Mid Wales Ride to Yeovilton Air Museum 7.30am** Tesco café, Belmont, Hereford, HR2 7XS. Terry Pickering 07850 602222 terry@sthereford.co.uk
4th July	**Blackpool & District Bike night 7pm** Stalmine Village Hall, Smithy Ln, Stalmine FY6 0LE. Terry A. Robinson 07960 116769 terry.robinson6@btinternet.com

5th July	**Gwent Baffle Haus Coffe Morning 11am** Baffle Haus Cafe, The Cedars, Goyytre, Pontypool, NP4 0AD. Richard Williams 01873 840483 markhillier61@icloud.com
5th July	**Essex Mid-week Run 9.30am** Venue TBA. Dave Iszard 07543 901340 daveandnicki@sky.com
5th July	**East Sussex Dave's two-stroke run 10am** Brian's Barn, Brownbread Street, Ashburnham TN33 9NX. Section secretary 07434 280380 secretary@eastsussexvmcc.co.uk
5th July	**Warwickshire Chairman's Social 7pm** Blue Lias Inn, Stockton Rd, Stockton, Southam CV47 8LD. Barry Heath 07786 718867 b4heath@yahoo.co.uk
5th July	**Surrey and Sussex Wrinkly Run 10am** Venue TBA. Brian Robins 07901 183181 surreysussexvmcc@gmail.com
5th July	**West Kent Mid-week run 10.30am** Village Hall car park, Ide Hill on B2042. Ron Wright 07761 005995 betron.wright@gmail.com
5th July	**Norwich and District Blue Sky Café 12 noon** CJ Ball M/Cycles, Salhouse Road, Norwich NR7 9AB. John Pearson 07712 552501 jppearson7@gmail.com
5th July	**Mid Lincs Midweek Run 10am** Humber Bridge Car Park (south bank) DN18 5BD. Peter Gunnee/D. Booth 01652 657169 p.gunnee@talktalk.net
5th July	**Cotswold Section Run 6.30pm** Gloucester Old Spot, Piffs Elms, GL51 9SY. 01242 680321 Graham Rowcliffe 07515 288414 grahamrowcliffe58@outlook.com
5th July	**Chiltern Evening Run 7pm** Full Moon, Cholesbury Lane, Hawridge HP5 2UH. P. Barfield 01442 824143 chilternvmcc@hotmail.com
5th July	**Bristol Evening meet 8pm** White Horse, The Green, Biddeston, Chippenham SN14 7DG. Stuart Edwards 07369 249011
6th July	**West Wiltshire Mid-Week Run 10am** Red Lion Car Park, Lacock. Reg Cox 07952 173693 starfield181@gmail.com
6th July	**Worcestershire Llangollen Museum Tour 9am** Rose and Crown, Tenbury WR15 8HA. Richard Caddick 01299 403334
6th July	**Oxford Thursday Run 10am** Turnpike Pub, Yarnton OX5 1PJ. Ed Walters 01865 863939
6th July	**Dartmoor Early Evening Run 6pm** Opposite Royal Seven Stars Hotel, The Plains, Totnes TQ9 5DD. Alan Langmaid 01803 863296
6th July	**North Staffs Classic Bike & Car Meet 7pm** Moorville Hall Hotel. Ian Pettifor 07760 346003 ianpettifor631@btinternet.com
7th July	**South Hants Evening Run 7.30pm** Car Park next to The Churchillian, Portsdown Hill Rd, Cosham PO6 3LS. Dave Tanner 01329 827262
7th July	**Northumbrian 44th Northumbrian Gathering 10am** Highburn House Country Holiday Park, Wooler, Northumberland, NE71 6EE. Rachael Houchin 07739 963049 NorthumbrianGathering@gmail.com
7th July	**Goodwood Friday Run 10.30am** Venue TBA. Dave Johnson 01243 582074 goodwoodvmcc@aol.com
7th July	**Surrey and Sussex Girder Fork Weekend 10.30am** Southern Counties Historic Preservation Trust Centre, Copthorne RH10 3HZ. (Map Ref. TQ 328406). Brian Robins 07901 183181 surreysussexvmcc@gmail.com
8th July	**Lakeland Seaton Classic bike show ride-in 10am** Seaton Village Hall, nr Workington, CA14 1PL. Dave Glynn 07851 148545
8th July	**Dartmoor Powderham Historic Vehicle Gathering 10am** Powderham Castle Estate, Kenton nr Exeter EX6 8JG. Mike Burton 07790 459795
8th July	**South Dorset Social Breakfast Meet 9.30am** The Three Compasses, Charminster DT2 9QT. Martin Figg 07896 507278 figg.martin@gmail.com
8th July	**King's Lynn Veteran and Vintage Weekend 10am** Fendick's Fishery and Camping Site, Methwold Road, Whittington PE33 9GP. Simon and Brian Robinson 01842 810307 malcolmrolph@talktalk.net
8th July	**Blackpool & District Pilling Vintage Weekend 9.30am** Pilling Village Hall, Taylor's Ln, Pilling PR3 6AB. Terry A. Robinson 07960 116769 terry.robinson6@btinternet.com
9th July	**Banbury Summer Run 9.30am** Horsefair. P. Knapton 07973 633184
9th July	**Devon Ron Ley Memorial Run 11am** Jonesy's Cafe, Winkleigh, EX19 8EZ. Nick Smiles 07711 444686 nickesmiles@googlemail.com
9th July	**South Hants George Hodges Run 10.30am** The Milburys, Beauworth, Alresford SO24 0PB. Dave Tanner 07710 592438
9th July	**Isle of Man Road Run 2pm** Venue TBA. Gary Corlett 07624 496672
9th July	**North Cotswold Shadders Run 9am** Venue TBA. Chris Delaney 07966 395032 chrisdelaney650@gmail.com
9th July	**King's Lynn Run to Somewhere 10am** West Norfolk area, details TBA. Andy Hunn 01366 328869 Club Secretary malcolmrolph@talktalk.net
9th July	**East Yorkshire The Derwent Amble 10.30am** Pig in the Willow cafe, East Cottingwith YO42 4TQ. Brian Springett 07889 799028 bspringett1954@gmail.com
9th July	**Warwickshire Pailton Steam and Bikes 11am** Fairfield Lake and Smite Brook Railway, Warwickshire. Barry Heath 07786 718867 b4heath@yahoo.co.uk
9th July	**West Wiltshire White Horse Navigational Scatter Trial 9.30am** 3 Magpies, Sells Green SN12 6RN. Peter Fielding 01225 763567 starfield181@gmail.com
9th July	**Worcestershire Midday Meet 12 noon** Bavenhill Engineering, Much Marcle HR8 2LJ. Richard Caddick 01299 403334
9th July	**Herefordshire & Mid Wales How many Bridges? 9am** Hereford Leisure centre café, Holmer Rd, Hereford HR4 9UD. Mike Smith 07785 368635
10th July	**North Cotswold Club Night 8pm** College Arms, Lower Quinton. Chris Delaney 07966 395032 chrisdelaney650@gmail.com

10th July	**South Durham Sunset Run 6pm** Middlesbough Motor Club, Coulby Newham. Howard Duddles 01642 822707
10th July	**South Wales Bring a bike night 7pm** Outside the Mughal Emperor, A48 Stalling Down CF71 7DT. Howard Jayne 02920 868203 howard.jayne@talktalk.net
11th July	**Ipswich & Suffolk Evening ride 6.30pm** Ipswich School, Sports Centre, Rushmere St Andrews. Trevor Dickings 01473 798653
11th July	**Herefordshire & Mid Wales Brunch ride-in 11am** Owl's Nest, Lower Road, Llandovery SA20 0DJ. Gary Jones 07870 389317 jgjones@sky.com
11th July	**West Kent Social Run Time TBA** Polhill layby at top of Polhill on A224. Ron Wright 07761 005995 betron.wright@gmail.com
11th July	**Surrey and Sussex Section BBQ 3.30pm** Southern Counties Historic Preservation Trust Centre, Copthorne RH10 3HZ. (Map Ref. TQ 328406). Brian Robins 07901 183181 surreysussexvmcc@gmail.com
11th July	**South Cotswold Tuesday Evening Pub Meet 6.30pm** The Foston's Ash 'Polo Pub' near Cranham GL6 7ES. Jeremy Retford 07831 314884 jeremyretford@btinternet.com
12th July	**Berkshire Mid-Week Run 10.30am** Venue TBA. Malcolm White 01344 642866 info@berkshire-vmcc.org.uk
12th July	**Lakeland Brown Cow ride-in 11am** Brown Cow Inn, Waberthwaite, (on A595) LA19 5YJ. John Silcock 01229 861264
12th July	**Wakefield and West Yorkshire Scissett Coffee Morning 10am** Mustang Café, Scissett, HD8 9HU. Alistair Durie and Neil Lewis 07483 862303 neil.r.lewis@btinternet.com
12th July	**Chiltern Midweek Run 10.30am** Full Moon, Cholesbury Lane, Hawridge HP5 2UH. P. Barfield 01442 824143 chilternvmcc@hotmail.com
12th July	**South Lincs and Peterborough Wrinkly Run 10.30am** Venue TBA. Gary Sleeman 01733 770241 gary.sleeman1@gmail.com
12th July	**Northampton Midweek run 10am** Royal Oak Blisworth NN7 3BU. Trevor Pinfold 01604 859215 trevorpinfold168@btinternet.com
12th July	**King's Lynn Ride-a-Bike Night 7pm prompt** Make your own way. Club Secretary 01842 811077 malcolmrolph@talktalk.net
12th July	**South Durham Evening Social Run 6pm** Cricket Club Middleton St George. Brian Smith 01325 286623
12th July	**North East Lunch Meeting 12 noon** Harewood Arms, Harewood Steve Rowley 07704 374773 rowley_s2@sky.com
13th July	**North Cotswold Wrinkly Run 10am** Venue TBA. Chris Delaney 07966 395032 chrisdelaney650@gmail.com
13th July	**South Hants Day Run 10.30am** The Square, Wickham, Fareham PO17 5JT. Terry Mead 01329 609566
13th July	**Blackpool & District Caton – Bullbeck Run 10am** Knott End Ferry Cafe, Ramsay Ct, Knott End on Sea FY6 0EA. Terry A Robinson 07960 116769 terry.robinson6@btinternet.com
13th July	**Cotswold Section Run 6.30pm** Royal Exchange, Hartpury, GL19 3BW. 01452 700273 Graham Rowcliffe 07515 288414 grahamrowcliffe58@outlook.com
13th July	**Northampton Alan's Evening Amble 10.30am** Queen Eleanor Wootton NN4 7JJ. Alan Berkshire 01604 831584 alberk75@outlook.com
13th July	**Cheshire and North Wales Machine Night 6.30pm** The Tap PH, Eastham Ferry, Wirral, CH62 0AU. secretary@candnw.vmcc.net Neil Shirley 01352 713204 chairman@candnw.vmcc.net
13th July	**Taverners Evening Run 7.30pm** Bulls Head pub, Hinckley Road Leicester LE9 9JE. Sam Page 07984 566400 stp751@hotmail.com
14th July	**Pennine Alston Run 9.30am** The Comrades Club, Manchester Rd., Shaw, Oldham OL2 8SB. Geoff Green 07817 178287 secretary@penninevmcc.org.uk
15th July	**Bristol Frenchay Flower Show 12.30pm** Frenchay Common, Beckspool Road, Bristol. BS16 1NB. Alan Freke 07775 859683
15th July	**Allen House Suzuki Live Cadwell Park 9am** Cadwell Park Circuit, Louth LN11 9SE. Classic Bike Track Days 07971 424472 info@classicbiketrackdays.com
15th July	**North Birmingham Barrie's Run 10am** Venue TBA, www.vmcc-nbs.co.uk Barrie Jones 01299 878375 NorthBirminghamVMCC@outlook.com
15th July	**Dorset Breakfast Meet 10am** Thorngrove Garden Centre, Common Mead Lane, Gillingham SP8 4RE. Paul Wirdnam 07775 923206 secretary@dorsetvmcc.co.uk
15th July	**Herefordshire & Mid Wales Trail ride 5** Venue TBA. Andy Spanjers 07557 442342
16th July	**South Durham Chairman's Run 10am** Cricket Club Middleton St George. Paul Feldon 01325 380293
16th July	**Dorset Young Ryan's Express 10.30am** Culverhayes C/P, Sherborne DT9 3NJ. Ryan Jeffrey 07495 010278 secretary@dorsetvmcc.co.uk
16th July	**Lakeland Westmorland Run 10am** Holme Social Club car park, Holme, nr Carnforth LA6 1QZ. Trevor Woodend 01524 782036
16th July	**East Lancs Wray Run 10.30am** Ribchester Arms, Blackburn Road, Ribchester PR3 3ZQ. Graham Bretherton 01722 716076
16th July	**North Cotswold, Cotswold Way Run 10am** Venue TBA. Chris Delaney 07966 395032 chrisdelaney650@gmail.com
16th July	**South Wales Roof of Wales run 11am** Caerphilly Mountain Snack Bar, Mountain Road, Caerphilly CF83 1JA. Howard Jayne 02920 868203 howard.jayne@talktalk.net
16th July	**North Staffs Ironbridge Run 11am** Crown Street car park, Stone. Alf Tilley 07739 802605

16th July	**Bristol Clubman's Run 10am** The Wishing Well, Wapley Road, Codrington, Bristol BS37 6RY. Frank Cropp 01225 708743
16th July	**West South Wales Gwili run & transport show 10am** Gwili railway, Bronwydd station SA33 6HT Carm's. Angelo Conti 01267 281394
16th July	**Cornwall Wheels Classic Vehicle Show 10am** Royal Cornwall Showground Wadebridge PL27 7JE. Roger Hore 07767 415564 or 01208 73571
16th July	**Surrey and Sussex Sunday Social Run 11am** Venue TBA. Brian Robins 07901 183181 surreysussexvmcc@gmail.com
16th July	**Somerset Veteran, Vintage and Anniversary Run 10am** TIG Leasing Garage, Chewton Mendip BA3 4PJ. Colin Bentham 01761 241516
16th July	**Worcestershire Pete's Special Run 9.30am** Market Square, Bromyard HR7 4BP. Pete Howells 01886 853293
16th July	**Cyclemotor Greenway Run 10.30am** Stratton Arms PH, Turweston NN13 5JX. Mark 01908 563464 or Clive 01327 706939
16th July	**Blackpool & District Dunsop Bridge Run + Leighton Hall Motorcycle Sprint 10am** Butty Hut, A6 Ashmead, New Holly Garage, Lancaster Rd, Preston PR3 0BL. Terry A. Robinson 07960 116769 terry.robinson6@btinternet.com
16th July	**South Dorset Club Run 10.30am** The Three Compasses, Charminster DT2 9QT. Martin Figg 07896 507278 figg.martin@gmail.com
16th July	**Herefordshire & Mid Wales Cafe racer ride 10am** Dom's Bike Stop, Stoke Prior Rd, Leominster HR6 0QJ. Mick White 07756 093802 mickw175@gmail.com
16th July	**Norwich and District The Hero 10am** High Barn, Shipdham Road, Carbrooke IP25 6SY. Steven Hallam 07732 364524 shallam89@gmail.com
16th July	**South Cotswold Sunday Lunchtime Café Meet 12 noon** Dragonfly Café, Lower Moor Nature Reserve Oaksey SN16 9TW. Jeremy Retford 07831 314884 jeremyretford@btinternet.com
16th July	**Clyde Valley Sound of Singles 10.30am** Big Red Barn, Elsrickle, Biggar, ML12 6QZ. Tim Ryan 07714 505386 timryan750@gmail.com
16th July	**Notts and Derby Sunday Run 10.30am** Layby A6 south of Whatstandwell. Ralph Taylor 01773 856592 nottsandderbyvintageclub@outlook.com
17th July	**Touring Breckland Touring Week 9.30am** Fendicks Fishery, Methwold Road, Whittington, Norfolk. Paul Fletcher 01245 321573 paul@fes1hq.plus.com
18th July	**South Cotswold Tuesday Evening Pub Meet 6.30pm** The Plough at Charfield GL12 8SR. Jeremy Retford 07831 314884 jeremyretford@btinternet.com
18th July	**Isle of Wight Hot and Sweaty Lunch Run 11.30am** Hare and Hounds car park, Downend, Arreton PO30 2NU. Ron Wallis 01983 752861 ron.wallis10@gmail.com
18th July	**Surrey and Sussex Evening Run 6.30pm** Venue TBA. Brian Robins 07901 183181 surreysussexvmcc@gmail.com
18th July	**Ipswich & Suffolk Evening ride 6.30pm** Ipswich School Sports Centre, Rushmere St Andrews. Trevor Dickings 01473 798653
19th July	**East Sussex Richard's Wrinkly Run 10.30am** Brian's Barn, Brownbread Street, Ashburnham TN33 9NX. Section secretary 07434 280380 secretary@eastsussexvmcc.co.uk
19th July	**Chiltern Breakfast ride-in 10am** London Gliding club resturant LU6 2JP. P. Barfield 01442 824143 chilternvmcc@hotmail.com
19th July	**West Wiltshire Green Lane Run 9am** Venue TBA. Keith Johnstone 07836 376107 keith.johnston55@hotmail.co.uk
19th July	**Essex Mid week Run 9.30am** Venue TBA. Dave Iszard 07543 901340 daveandnicki@sky.com
19th July	**Dorset Mid-Week Run 2pm** Wardon Hill Trading Post, DT2 9PW. Andy Grew 01935 593096 secretary@dorsetvmcc.co.uk
19th July	**North East Wetherby Evening Run 7pm** Harewood Arms, Follifoot. Paul Rogers 01943 879575
19th July	**South Hants Evening Run 7.30pm** Southwick Rd and James Callaghan Drive, Portsmouth PO6 3RU. Dave Tanner 01329 827262
19th July	**Lakeland Filling Station Café 11am** Filling Station Café, Keswick, CA12 5PR. David Weeks 01768 772315
19th July	**Wakefield and West Yorkshire Treasurer's Run Around 10.30am** National Mining Museum, Caphouse Colliery, New Rd, Overton WF4 4RH. Rob Whalley and Neil Lewis 07770 822424 neil.r.lewis@btinternet.com
19th July	**West South Wales Mid week fish & chip run 7pm prompt** Town Moor car park, Narberth SA67 7AG. Derrick Mason 07781 7447069
19th July	**Chiltern Pub Night 8pm-ish** Full Moon, Cholesbury Lane, Hawridge HP5 2UH. P. Barfield 01442 824143 chilternvmcc@hotmail.com
19th July	**Bristol Evening Run 7pm** The Wishing Well, Wapley Road, Codrington, Bristol BS37 6RY. John Beddis 01454 886506
20th July	**West Wiltshire Wandering 12 noon** The Mill, Withington, GL54 4BE. Colin Smith 07778 281332 colin.smith1951@btinternet.com
20th July	**Bedfordshire Midweek Run 10.15am** Shefford Town Memorial Hall, Hitchin Road, Shefford SG17 5JA. Don Mckeand 01525 720629
20th July	**Oxford Thursday Run 10am** Turnpike Pub, Yarnton OX5 1PJ. Maurice Belcher 01865 247823
20th July	**Notts and Derby Evening Run 7.30pm** Ripley Market Place DE5 3BR. Paul Sharman 07929 189886 nottsandderbyvintageclub@outlook.com
20th July	**North Staffs Run to Manifold Inn 7.15pm** Leek Market Place. Terry Barlow 01625 573542

20th July	**Cotswold Section Run 6.30pm** Rising Sun, Moseley Green, Lydney GL15 4HN. 01594 562008 Graham Rowcliffe 07515 288414 grahamrowcliffe58@outlook.com
20th July	**Somerset Evening Meet 7pm** Horse and Jockey, Gurney Slade BA3 3UH. Richard Gray 01934 513910
20th July	**North Cotswold Thursday Pub Meet 12 noon** The Snowshill Arms, Snowshill. Chris Delaney 07966 395032 chrisdelaney650@gmail.com
20th July	**East Yorkshire Goathland Camping Weekend. All weekend** Abbots House Farm, Goathland YO22 5NH. Alan Barker 07887 592400 lindaandalanbarker@hotmail.co.uk
22nd July	**Chiltern Cherry Pie Run 10.30am** Full Moon, Cholesbury Lane, Hawridge HP5 2UH. P. Barfield 01442 824143 chilternvmcc@hotmail.com
22nd July	**Notts and Derby Pie and Pea Run 2.30pm** Butchers Arms, Chesterfield Rd, Oakerthorpe, Alfreton DE55 7LN. Andrew Cooke 07774 442823 nottsandderbyvintageclub@outlook.com
22nd July	**Herefordshire & Mid Wales Trail ride 6 10am** Car park behind Chinese Take Away, Corvedale Rd, Craven Arms SY7 9NE. Mark Evans 07791 241641 mark1ducati@yahoo.co.uk
23rd July	**Worcestershire Vintage Show 10am** Abbey Car Park, Shrewsbury. Richard Caddick 01299 403334
23rd July	**Ironmasters Mystery Tour 10.30am** Long Lane cafe car park A442. Rod Morris 01785 841257
23rd July	**Taverners Founders Day 9am** Stanford Hall, nr Lutterworth, Leicester LE17 6DH. Kev Alexander 07713 908407 gautrek@ntlworld.com
23rd July	**Blackpool & District Lancs Lanes 10am** Butty Hut, A6 Ashmead, New Holly Garage, Lancaster Rd, Preston PR3 0BL. Terry A. Robinson 07960 116769 terry.robinson6@btinternet.com
23rd July	**South Wales Follow the Velo 10am** Venue TBA, see section website calendar. Rob Jones 01685 877212 robejones2@gmail.com
23rd July	**South Hants Pitt Down Run 10.30am** Basingwell Street car park at Bishop's Waltham SO32 1PA. Russell Daysh 01329 311331
23rd July	**Isle of Wight Underpowered Wobble Pt2 2pm** The Old Smithy, High Street, Godshill PO38 3HZ. Andrew Eason 07507 338633 andrew.eason1@btinternet.com
23rd July	**Reivers The Small Run 9am** Railway Inn, Acklington NE65 9HU. Mike Laidler 01670 715537
23rd July	**Dartmoor Club Run to South Hams 10am** Opposite Royal Seven Stars Hotel, The Plains, Totnes TQ9 5DD. Mike Burton 07790 459795
23rd July	**Cyclemotor Founders Day Rally** Stanford Hall, Leicestershire. Alan Hummerstone 01908 262520
23rd July	**Lakeland La'al Ratty ride-in 10.30am** The La'al Ratty Café, Boot Station, Eskdale CA19 1TF. John Silcock 01229 861264
25th July	**Surrey and Sussex Evening Run 6.30pm** Venue TBA. Brian Robins 07901 183181 surreysussexvmcc@gmail.com
25th July	**South Cotswold Tuesday Evening Pub Meet 6.30pm** The Potting Shed at Crudwell SN16 9EW. Jeremy Retford 07831 314884 jeremyretford@btinternet.com
25th July	**West Wiltshire Coffee Morning 10am** Bird & Carter, Fonthill Bishop, Tisbury, SP3 5SF. Kevin Phillips 07952 173693 starfield181@gmail.com
25th July	**Ipswich & Suffolk Evening ride 6.30pm** Ipswich School, Sports Centre, Rushmere St Andrews. Trevor Dickings 01473 798653
25th July	**Devon Evening Pub Meet 6.30pm** The Grampus, Lee, near Ifracombe EX34 8LR. Nick Smiles 07711 444686 nickesmiles@googlemail.com
25th July	**Goodwood Noggin 'n' Natter 8pm** The Red Lion, London Road, Ashington RH20 3DD. Dave Johnson 01243 582074 goodwoodvmcc@aol.com
26th July	**South Wales Evening ride-out 7pm** Home. Bill Phelps 02920 890255 webadmin@southwalessectionvmcc.co.uk
26th July	**Reivers St Mary's Loch Run 9.30am** Vale Cafe, High Street, Rothbury NE65 7TE. Dave Spencer 07907 200883
26th July	**Wakefield and West Yorkshire Scissett Coffee Morning 10am** Mustang Café, Scissett, HD8 9HU. Alistair Durie and Neil Lewis 07483 862303 neil.r.lewis@btinternet.com
26th July	**Herefordshire & Mid Wales Breakfast meet 10am** Sally's Place (British Camp) Wynds Point, Jubilee Drive, Upper Colwall, Malvern WR13 6DW. Geoff McGladdery 07588 559698 geoffmac@globalnet.co.uk
26th July	**North Birmingham Ian's Mid-Week Run 10am** Venue TBA. www.vmcc-nbs.co.uk Ian Goodhall 07804 693917 NorthBirminghamVMCC@outlook.com
27th July	**Worcestershire Bullock's Bridgnorth Bash 9.30am** Cob House, Wichenford WR6 6YE. Richard Bullock 01905 641216
27th July	**East Sussex Rob's Run 10.30am** Lilly's Cafe near Rolvenden. Section secretary 07434 280380 secretary@eastsussexvmcc.co.uk
27th July	**Bristol Lunchtime meet 12 noon** The Plough Inn, Pilning St, Pilning BS35 4JJ. Alan Burton 07774 923721
27th July	**South Dorset Club Night 8pm** The Three Compasses, Charminster DT2 9QT. Martin Figg 07896 507278 figg.martin@gmail.com
27th July	**Cotswold Section Run 6.30pm** Yew Tree, Chaceley Stock, GL18 1JS. 01452 780333 Graham Rowcliffe 07515 288414 grahamrowcliffe58@outlook.com
27th July	**North Cotswold Wrinkly Run 10am** Venue TBA. Chris Delaney 07966 395032 chrisdelaney650@gmail.com
27th July	**Notts and Derby Evening Run 7.30pm** Griffins Head Car Park, Moor Rd, Papplewick, Nottingham NG15 8EN. John Patterson 07946 261247 nottsandderbyvintageclub@outlook.com

27th July	**South Hants Evening Run 7.30pm** Southwick Rd and James Callaghan Drive junction, Portsmouth PO6 3RU. Clive Brown 01329 841920
27th July	**Taverners Evening Run 7.30pm** The Malt Shovel, Barkby Leicester LE7 3QG. Roger Monk 01509 412662
28th July	**Allen House Donington Park Track Day 9am** Donington Park, Castle Donington, Derby DE74 2RP. Classic Bike Track Days 07971 424472 info@classicbiketrackdays.com
28th July	**Central Scottish, Scottish National Rally 8pm** Venue TBA. Brian 01241 853946 snaeventsec@hotmail.com
29th July	**Reivers Back of Yer Leg Run 9am** Blacksith's Cafe, Blagdon NE20 0DU. Mike Coxon 07919 666818
29th July	**Notts and Derby Saturday Afternoon Run** Ripley Market Place DE5 3Br. Graham Franks 07932 954603 nottsandderbyvintageclub@outlook.com
29th July	**Dorset White Horse Run 9.30am** Udder Farm Shop, East Stour SP8 5LQ. Paul Swaddle 07930 300947 secretary@dorsetvmcc.co.uk
30th July	**Bedfordshire Breakfast Meet 10am** Toby Carvery, Goldington Road, Bedford MK41 0DS. Richard Chambers 07905 203823
30th July	**Taverners Steve`s Steam Run 10am** 27 The Heights, Market Harborough LE16 8BQ. Mark McEvoy 07973 142440 mmcevoy@infoteknix.co.uk
30th July	**Somerset Sign Post Rally and Social Run 10am** Creech St Michael Village Hall TA3 5QS. Phil Ham 01278 671626
30th July	**Cheshire and North Wales Wirral Wander/Tiddlers' Run 11am** The Tap, Eastham Ferry, Wirral CH62 0AU. secretary@candnw.vmcc.net Neil Shirley 01352 713204 chairman@candnw.vmcc.net
30th July	**Northampton Oily Rag Run 10.30am** New Inn, Abthorpe NN12 8QR. Alan Berkshire 01604 831584 alberk75@outlook.com
30th July	**Berkshire Girder Fork & Rigid Run 10.30am** West Berkshire Brewery, Yattenden, RG18 0XT. Malcolm White 01344 642866 info@berkshire-vmcc.org.uk
30th July	**Dartmoor Breakfast meet 10am** The Jolly Roger, St John's Lane, Bovey Tracey TQ13 9FF. Derek French 07747 032659
30th July	**Cyclemotor Oily Rag Run 10am** The New Inn, Apthorpe NN12 8QR. Alan Berkshire 01604 831584
30th July	**Worcestershire Roy Lambert Ride in 10am** The Lion, Leintwardine SY7 0JZ. Richard Caddick 01299 403334
30th July	**East Lancs Brownies' Bash 11am** Layby near Petre Garage Langho, Whalley Road BB6 8AB. Brian Settle 07724 671698
30th July	**Banbury Chairman's Run 9.30am** Horsefair. J. Schofield 07830 813865
30th July	**Herefordshire & Mid Wales Roof of Wales ride 10am** Dom's Bike Stop, Stoke Prior Rd, Leominster HR6 0QJ. Chris Richards 07588 559698 geoffmac@globalnet.co.uk
30th July	**Allen House Summer Classic Show & Bike Jumble 9am** Ardingly. Gary Sleeman gary@vmcc.net
30th July	**South Lincs and Peterborough Summer Saunter Run 10.30am** Venue TBA. Gary Sleeman 01733 770241 gary.sleeman1@gmail.com
30th July	**North East Golden Era Run 9.30am** Elvington Air Museum, Halifax Way, Elvinton, York YO41 4AU. Graham Wilson 07772 724078 gericwilson@ntlworld.com
30th July	**North Staffs Afternoon Tea at Tink's Café** Crown Street Car Park, Stone. Tony Melvin 07814 409215
30th July	**Cornwall Rame Head Run 10.30am** Chequered Flag Café, Plymouth Road (A38), Liskeard PL14 5GD. Kelvin Brown 01752 844206

AUGUST

1st August	**Taverners Wrinkly Run 10am** Apple Trees, Bradgate Close, Mountsorrel, Leicester LE12 7DZ. Roger Monk 01509 412662
1st August	**Ipswich & Suffolk Evening ride 6.30pm** Ipswich School Sports Centre. Trevor Dickings 01473 798653
2nd August	**North Birmingham Club Night 8pm** The Round Oak Inn, Ounsdale Road, Wombourne WV5 8BU. David Spencer 07975 629810. NorthBirminghamVMCC@outlook.com
2nd August	**Gwent Baffle Haus Coffee Morning 11am** Baffle Haus, The Cedars, Goytre, Pontypool. Mark Hillier 07870 535933 markhillier61@icloud.com
2nd August	**Bristol Evening meet 7.30pm** The Griffin Inn, London Road, Bridgeyate, Bristol BS30 5JN. Stuart Edwards 07369 249011
2nd August	**Surrey and Sussex Wrinkly Run 10am** Venue TBA. Brian Robins 07901 183181 surreysussexvmcc@gmail.com
2nd August	**Wakefield and West Yorkshire Chairman's Run Around 10.30am** Squires Café, Newthorpe, nr Sherburn in Elmet LS25 5LX. Neil Lewis 07483 862303 neil.r.lewis@btinternet.com
2nd August	**Cotswold Section Run 6.30pm** Butchers Arms, Oakridge, GL6 7NZ. 01285 760371 Graham Rowcliffe 07515 288414 grahamrowcliffe58@outlook.com
2nd August	**East Sussex Secretary's Saunter 10.30am** Heathfield Fire Station car park. Section secretary 07434 280380 secretary@eastsussexvmcc.co.uk
2nd August	**Chiltern Evening Run 7pm** Full Moon, Cholesbury Lane, Hawridge HP5 2UH. P. Barfield 01442 824143 chilternvmcc@hotmail.com
3rd August	**Blackpool & District Wray Bike Night 6.15pm** St. Michael's Village Hall, Blackpool Rd, St Michael's on Wyre, Preston PR3 0UA. Terry A. Robinson 07960 116769 terry.robinson6@btinternet.com
3rd August	**North Cotswold Wrinkly Run 10am** Venue TBA. Chris Delaney 07966 395032 chrisdelaney650@gmail.com
3rd August	**Oxford Thursday Run 10am** Milletts Farm OX13 5HB. Steve Wiggins 01235 528760

3rd August	**South Hants Evening Run 7.30pm** Alresford Station Car Park, Station Rd, Alresford SO24 9JN. Andy Collett 07584 663991
3rd August	**West Wiltshire President's Run 10am** Venue TBA. Tim James 07952 173693 starfield181@gmail.com
3rd August	**Worcestershire Pub Night 7pm** The Berkeley, Egdon WR7 4QL. John Porter 01386 553329
5th August	**Stirling Castle 41st S&T Regularity Run 9am** Cultybraggan Camp, Comrie, Crieff PH6 2AB. Douglas Cowie 07753 656541 douglascowie@btinternet.com
5th August	**South Durham Saunter and BBQ 10am** Cricket Club, Middleton St George. Viv Tubby 07741 472382
5th August	**Dorset Ken's Perambulation 10.30am** Stour Meadows Car Park, Blandford DT11 9LS. Ken Druce 01258 452977 secretary@dorsetvmcc.co.uk
6th August	**Lakeland The Birthday Run 10.30am** Lowther Castle Cafe, Lowther, nr Penrith CA10 2HH. Howard Ostle 01931 713349
6th August	**Flat Tank Severn Saunter 11am** Hamfields Leisure. Charles Wright 01452 790296
6th August	**Isle of Wight Dodge the GGs Breakfast Run 9am** Carisbrooke Nunnery car park, Whitcombe road, Newport PO30 1YS. Ron Wallis 01983 752861 ron.wallis10@gmail.com
6th August	**Worcestershire Herefordshire Secrets 9.30am** Conquest Car Park, Bromyard HR7 4LL. Mike Davies 07967 350254
6th August	**Pennine Roses Run 10.30am** The Comrades Club, Manchester Rd., Shaw, Oldham OL2 8SB. Geoff Green 07817 178287 secretary@penninevmcc.org.uk
6th August	**Mid Lincs Mystery Run 10am** The Happy Cafe, Sandtoft Airfield. DN9 1PN. Peter Gunnee/R. Maw 01652 657169 p.gunnee@talktalk.net
6th August	**Northampton Bill Lacey Run 10.30am** Sixfields car park, Northampton NN5 5QL. Richard Stone 01604 768069 richardstone47@hotmail.co.uk
6th August	**West South Wales Val's Welsh Cake Run 10.30am** Tycroes, Maesybont Nr Crosshands SA14 7HD Mrs Val Newton 07709 928416
6th August	**Somerset Tiddler Run 10am** Cider Farm, Bere, nr Langport TA10 0QX. James Ward 01458 251999
6th August	**Banbury Bill Lacey Run 9.30am** Brackley Market Place. P. Westbrook 01280 704050
6th August	**Anglian Hobbsons Choice Run 10.30am** Orchard Farm, St. Ives Road, Eltisley, St Neots. Martyn Blunt 07880 026257 martynblunt@hotmail.co.uk
6th August	**South Wales Chairman's Run 11am** Caerphilly Mountain Snack Bar, Mountain Road, Caerphilly CF83 1JA. Howard Jayne 02920 868203 howard.jayne@talktalk.net
6th August	**North Cotswold Bill Lacey Run 9am** The Square, Chipping Campden. Chris Delaney 07966 395032 chrisdelaney650@gmail.com
6th August	**King's Lynn Northwold Trundle 10am** Sports and Social Club, Hovell's Lane, Northwold, Thetford IP26 5LX. John Chease 01366 728994 Club Secretary – malcolmrolph@talktalk.net
6th August	**Warwickshire Banbury Re-run Time TBA** British Motor Museum entrance road, Gaydon CV35 0BJ. Barry Heath 07786 718867 b4heath@yahoo.co.uk
6th August	**Essex Bike Day 9.30am** Langford Museum of Power. Dave Iszard 07543 901340 daveandnicki@sky.com
7th August	**North Cotswold Club Night 8pm** College Arms, Lower Quinton. Chris Delaney 07966 395032 chrisdelaney650@gmail.com
8th August	**Herefordshire & Mid Wales Brunch ride-in 11am** Cattle Shed café, Penrhos Court, A44, Kington HR5 3LH. Gary Jones 07870 389317 jgjones@sky.com
8th August	**Ipswich & Suffolk Evening ride 6.30pm** Ipswich School, Sports Centre, Rushmere St Andrews. Trevor Dickings 01473 798653
8th August	**South Cotswold Tuesday Evening Pub Meet 6.30pm** The Carpenters Arms at Miserden GL6 7JA. Jeremy Retford 07831 314884 jeremyretford@btinternet.com
8th August	**Herefordshire & Mid Wales Brunch ride-in 11am** Cattle Shed café, Penrhos Court, A44, Kington HR5 3LH Rob Woodford 07870 389317 07847 098597
9th August	**West Wiltshire Green Lane Run 9am** Venue TBA. Keith Johnstone 07836 376107 keith.johnston55@hotmail.co.uk
9th August	**Northampton Midweek run 10am** Royal Oak, Blisworth NN7 3BU. Trevor Pinfold 01604 859215 trevorpinfold168@btinternet.com
9th August	**South Lincs and Peterborough Wrinkly Run 10.30am** Venue TBA. Gary Sleeman 01733 770241 gary.sleeman1@gmail.com
9th August	**Berkshire Mid-Week Run 10.30am** Venue TBA. Malcolm White 01344 642866 info@berkshire-vmcc.org.uk
9th August	**East Sussex Bill's Wrinkly Run 10.30am** Bowship roundabout. Section secretary 07434 280380 secretary@eastsussexvmcc.co.uk
9th August	**Cyclemotor The Swanbourne Run 10.30am** The Betsy Wynne PH, Swanbourne MK17 0SH. Laurie Erwood 01582 842337
9th August	**Chiltern Mid-week Run 10.30am** Full Moon, Cholesbury Lane, Hawridge HP5 2UH. P. Barfield 01442 824143 chilternvmcc@hotmail.com
9th August	**Wakefield and West Yorkshire Scissett Coffee Morning 10am** Mustang Café, Scissett, HD8 9HU. Alistair Durie and Neil Lewis 07483 862303 neil.r.lewis@btinternet.com
9th August	**North East Lunch Meeting 12 noon** Harewood Arms, Harewood. Steve Rowley 07704 374773 rowley_s2@sky.com
10th August	**North Cotswold Wrinkly Run 10am** Venue TBA. Chris Delaney 07966 395032 chrisdelaney650@gmail.com

10th August	**Blackpool & District Waddington Fell Run 10am** Butty Hut A6, Ashmead, New Holly Garage, Lancaster Rd, Preston PR3 0BL. Terry A. Robinson 07960 116769 terry.robinson6@btinternet.com
10th August	**Herefordshire & Mid Wales Trail ride 7 10am** Coco's Café A4103, Fromes Hill, Ledbury HR8 1HT. THE TANK! Roger Bibbings 01684 540249 rogerbibbings@gmail.com
10th August	**Dartmoor Early Evening Run 6pm** Opposite Royal Seven Stars Hotel, The Plains, Totnes TQ9 5DD. Derek French 07747 032659.
10th August	**South Hants Day Run 10.30am** Basingwell Street Car Park, Bishop's Waltham SO32 1PA. Pete Denham
10th August	**Bristol Breakfast Run 10.30am** New Manor Tea Rooms, Widcombe, Bishop Sutton, Bristol BS40 6HP. Stuart Edwards 07369 249011
10th August	**Taverners Evening Run 7.30pm** Waitrose, Granite Way, Mountsorrel, Leicester LE12 7TZ. Roger Monk 01509 412662
11th August	**Goodwood Friday Run with Tiddlers & 2-Stroke Run 10.30am** The Selsey Arms, Cowfold Road, Coolham, Horsham RH13 8QJ. Dave Johnson 01243 582074 goodwoodvmcc@aol.com
12th August	**Lakeland Motor Museum Ride-in 11am** Lakeland Motor Museum Café, Backbarrow LA12 8TA. John Silcock 01229 861264
12th August	**Taverners Saturday Run 6.30pm** Wistow Park, Kibworth Road, Leicester LE8 0QF. Roger Monk 01509 412662
12th August	**South Dorset Social Breakfast Meet 9.30am** The Three Compasses, Charminster DT2 9QT. Martin Figg 07896 507278 figg.martin@gmail.com
12th August	**Cyclemotor Camping Weekend** Peacehaven Farm, Ickford HP18 9JE. Alan Hummerstone 01908 262520
13th August	**Norwich and District Flixton Aviation Museum Run 10am** The Street, Flixton, Bungay NR35 1NZ. 01986 896644 John Pearson 01603 300945 07712552501 jppearson7@gmail.com
13th August	**East Sussex Stan's Pilot Run 10am** Ravenside car park opposite Esso Garage. Section secretary 07434 280380 secretary@eastsussexvmcc.co.uk
13th August	**Essex Club Run 9.30am** Venue TBA. Dave Iszard 07543 901340 daveandnicki@sky.com
13th August	**Northumbrian Geoff's Cloverleaf Run 10am** Brown Horse, High Stoop. DL13 4HJ. Geoff Grigg 07999940727 g.grigg@sky.com
13th August	**Dorset Border Run 10.30am** Top of Gold Hill, High Street, Shaftesbury, SP7 8JW. Paul Miles 07774 921600 secretary@dorsetvmcc.co.uk
13th August	**North East Topcliffe Run 10.30am** Yorkshire Gliding Club, Sutton Bank, Thirsk YO7 2EY. Steve Rowley 07704 374773 rowley_s2@sky.com
13th August	**North Birmingham Breakfast Run 10am** Venue TBA. www.vmcc-nbs.co.uk Rob Todd 07802 462430 NorthBirminghamVMCC@outlook.com
13th August	**East Lancs Tower Run 10.30am** Churchfield House, Church Street Great Harwood BB6 7RE. Graham Daniels 07952 348339 grahamdaniels9@hotmail.com
13th August	**North Staffs Staffordshire Run 11am** Leek Market Place. Richard Bills 07588 707701
13th August	**Allen House Ace Café 9am** London. Gary Sleeman gary@vmcc.net
13th August	**Blackpool & District Pre-1980 Meet 6pm** St Michael's Village Hall, Blackpool Rd, St Michael's on Wyre PR3 0UA. Terry A. Robinson 07960116769 terry.robinson6@btinternet.com
13th August	**Devon Atlantic Coast Run/Davidstow War Museum 10.30am** Atlantic Village, upper car park, Bideford EX39 3QU. John Young 07847 753725 jebyoung@hotmail.com
13th August	**North Cotswold Graham Hallard Rigid/Girder Run 10am** Pavillion Café, Lighthorne. Chris Delaney 07966 395032 chrisdelaney650@gmail.com
13th August	**Cornwall Girder fork/flat tanker run 10.30am** Quintrell Inn, North Way, Quintrell Downs, Newquay TR8 4LA. Andy Coombe 01872 530647
13th August	**Men of Kent Club Run 10.30am** Tadpole Tearoom, Frog Lane, Bishopsbourne CT4 5HR. Richard Barsby 07989 352990 richardbarsby61@tiscali.co.uk
15th August	**Isle of Wight Good Harvest Lunch Run 11.30am** Hare and Hounds car park, Downend, Arreton PO30 2NU Ron Wallis 01983 752861 ron.wallis10@gmail.com
15th August	**Ipswich & Suffolk Evening ride 6.30pm** Ipswich School, Sports Centre, Rushmere St Andrews. Trevor Dickings 01473 798653
15th August	**Surrey and Sussex Evening Run 6.30pm** Venue TBA. Brian Robins 07901 183181 surreysussexvmcc@gmail.com
15th August	**South Cotswold Tuesday Evening Pub Meet 6.30pm** Kings Head at Kings Stanley GL10 3JD. Jeremy Retford 07831 314884 jeremyretford@btinternet.com
16th August	**East Sussex Tim's Girder Fork Run 10.30am** Brian's Barn, Brownbread Street Ashburnham TN33 9NX. Section secretary 07434 280380 secretary@eastsussexvmcc.co.uk
16th August	**Bristol Evening meet 8pm** The Compton Inn, Compton Dando, Keynsham BS39 4JZ. Stuart Edwards 07369 249011
16th August	**Dorset Mid-Week Run 2pm** Virginia Ash, Henstridge, BA8 0PL. Simon Barker 07745 201512 secretary@dorsetvmcc.co.uk
16th August	**Lakeland Newfield Inn Ride-in 11.30am** Newfield Inn, Seathwaite, South Lakes LA20 6ED. Colin Steer 01768 774536
16th August	**Chiltern Breakfast ride-in 10am** London Gliding club resturant LU6 2JP. P. Barfield 01442 824143 chilternvmcc@hotmail.com

16th August	**Cotswold Section Run 6.30pm** Old Crown, Uley, GL11 5SN. 01453 860502 Graham Rowcliffe 07515 288414 grahamrowcliffe58@outlook.com
16th August	**King's Lynn Ride-a-Bike Night 7pm** Make your own way. Club Secretary 01842 811077 malcolmrolph@talktalk.net
16th August	**Chiltern Pub Night 8pm-ish** Full Moon, Cholesbury Lane, Hawridge HP5 2UH. P. Barfield 01442 824143 chilternvmcc@hotmail.com
17th August	**South Hants Day Run 10.30am** Southwick Rd and James Callaghan Drive junction, Portsmouth PO6 3RU. Maurice Hayman 01329 282058
17th August	**West Wiltshire Wandering 12 noon** The Grill on the Hill, Swanborough, SN6 7RN. Colin Smith 07778 281332 colin.smith1951@btinternet.com
17th August	**North Cotswold Thursday Pub Meet 12 noon** Venue TBA. Chris Delaney 07966 395032 chrisdelaney650@gmail.com
17th August	**Bedfordshire Mid-week Run 10.15am** Shefford Town Memorial Hall, Hitchin Road, Shefford SG17 5JA. Don Mckeand 01525 720629
17th August	**Oxford Thursday Run 10am** Turnpike Pub, Yarnton. OX5 1PJ. Paul Albert 01993 891733
17th August	**Somerset Evening Meet 7pm** King William Inne, Catcott. Mike Chipperfield 01749 679371
17th August	**Notts and Derby Last Ride Run 6.45pm (note early start)** Ripley Market Place DE5 3BR. Graham Bower 07745 888938 nottsandderbyvintageclub@outlook.com
17th August	**Worcestershire Borth Adventure 9am** The Farm Shop, Ludlow SY8 2JR. Mark Evans 07791 241641
19th August	**Reivers Eric's Westwood Ho 10am** Riverside Kitchen, Chollerford NE46 4EW. Eric Bushell 07860 812272
19th August	**Dorset Breakfast Meet 10am** Thorngrove Garden Centre, Common Mead Lane, Gillingham SP8 4RE. Paul Wirdnam 07775 923206 secretary@dorsetvmcc.co.uk
20th August	**Dartmoor Club/Museum Run 9.30am** Bovey Tracey, Town Centre Car park TQ13 9S. Bob Harris 07812 811053
20th August	**North Staffs Peak District Run 11am** Leek Market Place. Terry Barlow 01625 573542
20th August	**Herefordshire & Mid Wales Forest of Dean ride 10am** The Beefeater, Travellers Rest, Ledbury Rd, Ross-on-Wye HR9 7QJ. Mike Bertenshaw 07831 774660
20th August	**North West Mick Bodell's Run 10am** Mere Brow Villiage Hall PR4 6JX. Angie Graham 07773 555819 angiegraham2012@yahoo.co.uk
20th August	**Northampton Little and Old 10.30am** Irchester Country Park Gypsy Lane NN29 7DL. Bob Percival 01933 355617 marleen.percival@yahoo.co.uk
20th August	**Wakefield and West Yorkshire Secretary's Run Around 10.30am** Morrison's, 4 Jubilee Way, Elland HX5 9DT. Alistair Durie and Neil Lewis 07483 862303 neil.r.lewis@btinternet.com
20th August	**Notts and Derby Willingham Woods Run 10.30am** Horse and Groom, Main Street Linby, Notts. Kate Sherras 07961 754780 nottsandderbyvintageclub@outlook.com
20th August	**Norwich and District Castle Acre 10.30am** High Barn, Shipdham Road, Carbrooke IP25 6SY. Steve Hallam 07732 364524 shallam89@gmail.com
20th August	**East Sussex Steve's Summer Sortie 10.30am** Boship Roundabout. Section secretary 07434 280380 secretary@eastsussexvmcc.co.uk
20th August	**South Dorset Club Run 10.30am** The Three Compasses, Charminster DT2 9QT. Martin Figg 07896 507278 figg.martin@gmail.com
20th August	**South Hants The Mid Hants Run 10.30am** The Brickmakers Arms, Church Rd, Swanmore, Southampton SO32 2PA. Russell Daysh 01329 311331
20th August	**Somerset Codgers and Dodgers Run 10am** Rich's Cider Cafe, Watchfield TA9 4RD. Rod Thomas 01934 627358
20th August	**South Lincs and Peterborough High Summer Run 10.30am** Venue TBA. Gary Sleeman 01733 770241 gary.sleeman1@gmail.com
20th August	**Dorset Tortoise & Hare Run 11am** Halsey Arms, Pulham DT2 7DZ. Chris Biddiscombe 01935 427608 secretary@dorsetvmcc.co.uk
20th August	**Surrey and Sussex Sunday Social Run 11am** Venue TBA. Brian Robins 07901 183181 surreysussexvmcc@gmail.com
20th August	**Banbury Wychwood Run 9.30am** Horsefair. D. Clacy 01295 810566
20th August	**Isle of Man Section Trial 1.30pm** Billown Glen. Shaun Seal 07624 485133
20th August	**South Cotswold The Harvest Run 10am** The Rail Yard car park, Tetbury GL8 8EY. Dave Carroll or Jeremy Retford, Jeremy 07831 314884 Dave dodursley@tiscali.co.uk
22nd August	**Devon Evening Pub Meet 6.30pm** Black Cock Inn, Molland, nr South Molton EX36 3NW. John Young 07847 753725 jebyoung@hotmail.com
22nd August	**Goodwood Noggin 'n' Natter 8pm** The Red Lion, London Road, Ashington RH20 3DD. Dave Johnson 01243 582074 goodwoodvmcc@aol.com
22nd August	**South Cotswold Tuesday Evening Pub Meet 6.30pm** The Tipputs Inn GL6 0QE. Jeremy Retford 07831 314884 jeremyretford@btinternet.com
22nd August	**Ipswich & Suffolk Evening ride 6.30pm** Ipswich School Sports Centre, Rushmere St Andrews. Trevor Dickings 01473 798653
23rd August	**Reivers East Border's Run 10am** Riverside Kitchen, Chollerford NE46 4EW. Dave Spencer 07907 200883
23rd August	**Herefordshire & Mid Wales Breakfast meet 10am** Holloways, Glasshouse café, Suckley WR6 5DE. Geoff McGladdery 07588 559698 geoffmac@globalnet.co.uk
23rd August	**North Birmingham Dave's Mid-Week Run 10am** Venue TBA. www.vmcc-nbs.co.uk/ David Spencer 07975 629810 NorthBirminghamVMCC@outlook.com

23rd August	**Men of Kent Bike Night 8pm** The Chance Inn, Guston, nr Dover CT15 5EW. Richard Barsby 07989 352990 richardbarsby61@tiscali.co.uk
23rd August	**North East Dales Run 10.30am** Leathley Farm Shop LS21 2PS (on A658 north of Poole). Graham Wilson 07772 724078
23rd August	**Lakeland Watchtree Café Ride-In 11am** The Café, Watchtree Nature Reserve, nr Wiggonby, Carlisle, CA5 6NL. Eddie Stephenson 07932 544789
23rd August	**Wakefield and West Yorkshire Scissett Coffee Morning 10am** Mustang Café, Scissett, HD8 9HU. Alistair Durie and Neil Lewis 07483 862303 neil.r.lewis@btinternet.com
23rd August	**Cotswold Section Run 6.30pm** Gardeners Arms, Alderton, GL20 8NL. 01242 620257 Graham Rowcliffe 07515 288414 grahamrowcliffe58@outlook.com
23rd August	**Isle of Man International Manx Rally 9am** Laxey Prom. Gary Corlett 07624 496672
24th August	**Bristol Lunchtime meet 12 noon** The Anchor Inn, Epney, Saul GL2 7LN. Alan Burton 07774 923721
24th August	**South Hants Day Run 10.30am** Southwick Rd and James Callaghan Drive junction, Portsmouth PO6 3RU. Dave Tanner 01329 827262
24th August	**North Cotswold Wrinkly Run 10am** Venue TBA. Chris Delaney 07966 395032 chrisdelaney650@gmail.com
24th August	**South Dorset Club Night 7.30pm** The Three Compasses, Charminster DT2 9QT. Martin Figg 07896 507278 figg.martin@gmail.com
25th August	**Allen House Castle Coombe Track Session 9am** Castle Coombe Race Circuit, Castle Combe, Chippenham SN14 7EY. Annie Durrant 01283 540557 events@vmcc.net
26th August	**Worcestershire Breakfast Meet 10am** Lucksall Caravan Park Eatery HR1 4LP. Richard Caddick 01299 403334
27th August	**Bedfordshire Summer Saunter and Breakfast Meet 10am breakfast, 10.30am run** Jordans Mill, Holme Mills, Langford Road, Biggleswade SG18 9JX. Bryan Marsh 07309 731191 bryan.marsh@btinternet.com
27th August	**Ironmasters Last Summer Run 10.30am** Atcham Bridge layby, B5061. Rob Sawyer 01785 841257
27th August	**Wakefield and West Yorkshire Netherton Car Show Around 10.30am** Netherton Sports and Social Club WF4 4HQ. Duncan Long 07384 330702 neil.r.lewis@btinternet.com
27th August	**East Lancs Pendle Hill Run 10.30am** East Lancs Railway car park, Rawtenstall. David Prismall 01706 217572 davidprismall@hotmail.com
27th August	**Herefordshire & Mid Wales Tiny Tots and Old Pots 10am** Croft Farm, Knapton Green, Herefordshire HR4 8ER Mike Smith 07785 368635
27th August	**Berkshire August Amble 10.30am** Venue TBA. Malcolm White 01344 642866 info@berkshire-vmcc.org.uk
27th August	**North Cotswold Tiddlers Run 10am** Venue TBA. Chris Delaney 07966 395032 chrisdelaney650@gmail.com
27th August	**Dartmoor Breakfast meet 10am** The Jolly Roger, St John's Lane, Bovey Tracey TQ13 9FF. Derek French 07747 032659
27th August	**East Yorkshire The Sunk Island Run 10.30am** The Haven Arms, Hedon, HU12 8HH. Brian Springett 07889 799028 bspringett1954@gmail.com
27th August	**Dorset August Run 11am** Virginia Ash, Henstridge BA8 0PL. Andy Grew 01935 595096 secretary@dorsetvmcc.co.uk
27th August	**South Durham Baydale Run 10am** Cricket Club Middleton St George. Bobby Robinson 01325 380293
27th August	**Blackpool & District BVPG Stanley Park Show 9.30am** Stanley Park, Blackpool. Terry A. Robinson 07960 116769 terry.robinson6@btinternet.com
27th August	**Cornwall Restormel Run 10.30am** East Taphouse Hall A390, Liskeard PL14 4TA. Peter Kempen 07929 026928
28th August	**Chiltern Quainton Run 10.30am** Full Moon, Cholesbury Lane, Hawridge HP5 2UH. P. Barfield 01442 824143 chilternvmcc@hotmail.com
29th August	**South Cotswold Tuesday Pub Meet 6.30pm** The Anchor Inn at Epney GL2 7LN. Jeremy Retford 07831 314884 jeremyretford@btinternet.com
29th August	**Ipswich & Suffolk Evening ride 6.30pm** Ipswich School Sports Centre, Rushmere St Andrews. Trevor Dickings 01473 798653
29th August	**West Wiltshire Coffee Morning 10am** Sleight Valley Golf Cafe, Sleight Lane, Devizes SN10 3HW. Kevin Phillips 07952 173693 starfield181@gmail.com
30th August	**South Wales Wednesday evening ride-out 7pm** Your home. Bill Phelps 02920 890255 webadmin@southwalessectionvmcc.co.uk
30th August	**Cotswold Section Run 6.30pm** Carpenters Arms, Miserden GL6 7JA. 01285 821283 Graham Rowcliffe 07515 288414 grahamrowcliffe58@outlook.com
31st August	**Worcestershire Breakfast Meet 9.30am** The Colliers Arms, Rock DY14 9HA. Les Bennett 07981 550982
31st August	**Oxford Thursday Run 10am** Turnpike Pub, Yarnton OX5 1PJ. Geoff Dee 01865 375133
31st August	**South Hants Day Run 10.30am** Basingwell St Car Park, Bishop's Waltham SO32 1PA. Dave Bettridge 02380 464822
31st August	**Taverners Evening Run 7pm** County Hall, Glenfield Road, Leicester. Roger Monk 01509 412662
31st August	**South Hants Day Run 10.30am** Portchester Castle Car Park, Church Ln, Portchester, Fareham PO16 9QW. Clive Brown 01329 841920

AUTUMN RIDES
SEPTEMBER – OCTOBER

Over 150 runs, rides and socials listed

Photo: Steve Joyce

AUTUMN

SEPTEMBER

2nd September — **Auld Reekie Scottish Gathering 10.30am**
Venue TBA. Ralph White 07535 603370

3rd September — **King's Lynn Norfolk Coast Run 10am**
The Butter Cross (Market Place) Swaffham,
Norfolk. Brian Robinson 01842 810307
Club Secretary malcolmrolph@talktalk.net

3rd September — **North Staffs Darren's First Run 11am**
Moorville Hall Hotel. Darren Johnson 07737 306856

3rd September — **Dorset Big Road Run 11am**
Cranborne Garden Centre BH21 5PP. Bernard Jones
01258 472554 secretary@dorsetvmcc.co.uk

3rd September — **Somerset West Somerset Run 10am**
Willowbrook Garden Centre,
nr Wellington TA2 9HX. Mark Peel 01934 813638

3rd September — **Warwickshire Genteel Run Time TBA**
Long Itch Diner, Southam Rd, Long Itchington,
Southam CV47 9QZ. Barry Heath 07786 718867
b4heath@yahoo.co.uk

3rd September — **Cotswold Summer Wandering 12 noon**
Walwyn Arms, Much Marcle, Ledbury HR8 2LY
(SO 656 333). 01531 660601
Peter Kent 01452 610375

3rd September — **Bristol Bill Shepherd Memorial Run 9.30am**
The Jubilee Inn, Main Road, Flax Bourton,
Bristol BS48 3QX. Duncan Venison 07970 689624.

3rd September — **Clyde Valley Kirkcudbright Run 10am**
Route 74 Truckstop, Teiglum Road, Lesmahagow.
Bob Irvine 07873 787813 sshirv@outlook.com

3rd September — **South Hants Stuart Walbridge Run 10.30am**
The Square, Wickham, Fareham PO17 5JT.
Russell Daysh 01329 311331

3rd September — **North Cotswold River Run 10am**
Venue TBA. Chris Delaney 07966 395032
chrisdelaney650@gmail.com

3rd September — **Notts and Derby Ridges Run 10am**
Yondermann Café, A623 Wardlow Mires,
Derbyshire SK17 8RW. Mike Ransom
07704 943795 nottsandderbyvintageclub@outlook.com

3rd September — **Men of Kent Dickie Dunster Memorial Run 10.30am**
Blue and White Cafe, A20 Smeeth nr Ashford
TN25 6SP. Richard Barsby 07989 352990
richardbarsby61@tiscali.co.uk

3rd September — **Devon Three Tors Run 9am**
Torrington Common, Station Hill, Great Torrington
EX38 8DL. Nick Smiles 07711 444686
nickesmiles@googlemail.com

3rd September — **Lakeland Ride-In 11am**
Stott Park Bobbin Mill, Finsthwaite LA12 8AX.
John Silcock 01229 861264

3rd September — **Northampton Navigation Rally 9am**
Earls Barton Cricket Club, Northampton Rd,
Earls Barton NN6 0HF. Trevor Pinfold
01604 859215 trevorpinfold168@btinternet.com

3rd September — **Allen House Copdock Classic Motorcycle Show 9am**
Ipswich. Gary Sleeman – gary@vmcc.net

3rd September — **Worcestershire Worcester OTT 9.30am**
Cob House, Wichenford WR6 6YE.
Richard Caddick 01299 403334

3rd September — **Isle of Wight End of Summer breakfast run 9am**
Carisbrooke Nunnery car park, Whitcombe Road,
Newport PO30 1YS. Ron Wallis 01983 752861
ron.wallis10@gmail.com

3rd September — **Northumbrian Bob Rawlings Run 10am**
Kiln Pit Hill, Consett DH8 9SG. Pete Bagnall
07968 646357 petebagnall44@hotmail.com

3rd September — **East Lancs Hills n' Hairpins Run 10.30am**
East Lancs Railway car park, Rawtenstall.
David Prismall 01706 217572
davidprismall@hotmail.com

3rd September — **Essex End of Summer Run 9.30am**
Venue TBA. Dave Iszard 07543 901340
daveandnicki@sky.com

5th September — **Ipswich & Suffolk Evening ride 6.30pm**
Ipswich School Sports Centre, Rushmere St Andrews.
Trevor Dickings 01473 798653

6th September — **Cotswold Section Run 6.30pm**
Yew Tree, Chaceley Stock GL18 1JS.
01452 780333 Graham Rowcliffe 07515 288414
grahamrowcliffe58@outlook.com

6th September — **North Birmingham Club Night 8pm**
The Round Oak Inn, Ounsdale Road,
Wombourne WV5 8BU. David Spencer
07975 629810 NorthBirminghamVMCC@outlook.com

6th September — **Norwich and District The Kingfisher 12 noon**
CJ Ball M/Cycle,,s Salhouse Road Norwich NR7 9AB.
John Pearson 07712 552501 jppearson7@gmail.com

6th September — **Gwent Baffle Haus Coffee Morning 11am**
Baffle Haus, The Cedars, Goytre, Pontypool.
Mark Hillier 07870 535933 markhillier61@icloud.com

6th September — **East Sussex Tim's Wrinkly Run 10.30am**
Brian's Barn, Brownbread Street, Ashburnham
TN33 9NX. Section secretary 07434 280380
secretary@eastsussexvmcc.co.uk

6th September — **Wakefield and West Yorkshire Scissett Coffee Morning 10am**
Mustang Café, Scissett, HD8 9HU.
Alistair Durie and Neil Lewis 07483 862303
neil.r.lewis@btinternet.com

6th September — **Gwent Baffle Haus Coffee Morning 11am**
Baffle Haus, The Cedars, Goytre, Pontypool.
Mark Hillier 07870 535933 markhillier61@icloud.com

7th September — **Dartmoor Early Evening Run 6pm**
Opposite Royal Seven Stars Hotel, The Plains,
Totnes TQ9 5DD. Dave Wills 01803 812830

7th September — **Blackpool & District Wray Bike Night 5pm**
St Michael's Village Hall, Blackpool Rd,
St Michael's on Wyre, Preston PR3 0UA.
Terry A. Robinson 07960 116769
terry.robinson6@btinternet.com

7th September — **West Wiltshire Mid-Week Run 10am**
Fox & Hounds, Acton Turville. Derek Daniels
07952 173693 starfield181@gmail.com

7th September	**North Cotswold Wrinkly Run 10am** Moreton in Marsh. Chris Delaney 07966 395032 chrisdelaney650@gmail.com
8th September	**Touring Section ISDTW of Mid Wales 10.30am each day** Howey village hall car park. Rob Woodford 07847 098597 robwoodford1@hotmail.co.uk
9th September	**Flat Tank Mid-Wales Girder Fork Experience 10am** Cilmery, Powys. Rob Woodford 07847 098597 robwoodford1@hotmail.co.uk
9th September	**Reivers Tiddler Run 9am** Railway Inn, Acklington. NE65 9HU. Mike Laidler 01670 715537
9th September	**Reivers Rover 10am** Blacksmiths Cafe, Belsay NE20 0DU. Jon Hill 07811 333359
9th September	**South Dorset Social Breakfast Meet 9.30am** The Three Compasses, Charminster D2 9QT. Martin Figg 07896 507278 figg.martin@gmail.com
9th September	**North Birmingham Clun Run 10am** Venue TBA. www.vmcc-nbs.co.uk Brian Jones 07791 898563 NorthBirminghamVMCC@outlook.com
9th September	**Notts and Derby Coffee Run 10am** Ripley Market Place DE5 3BR. Graham Bower 07745 888938 nottsandderbyvintageclub@outlook.com
9th September	**Central Scottish The Wee Run Frae The Doc's Auld Hoose 10am** Emma Terrace, Blairgowrie, Perthshire PH10 6JA. Alistair Huddleston 07788 475849 Ali_Hud1966@yahoo.com
10th September	**Lakeland Mike Bond Memorial Run 10.30am** Market Square, Milnthorpe, LA7 7PP. Cliff Robinson 01524 735554
10th September	**Devon Dartmoor Run 11am** Whiddon Down Services EX20 2QT. John Young 07847 753725 jebyoung@hotmail.com
10th September	**Dorset Last of the Summer Wine Run 10.30am** Hinton St Mary Village Hall DT10 1NB. Phil Allen 07584 078338 secretary@dorsetvmcc.co.uk
10th September	**Banbury Anniversary Run 9.30am** Venue TBA. C. Butler 07557 272153
10th September	**Norwich and District Gt Ouse and Cam Run 10am** Acacia, Queen Street, Spooner Row NR18 9JU. Richard Mack 07860 208045 newimpboy@gmail.com
10th September	**Northampton Canal run 10.30am** Brixworth Country Park Pitsford Reservoir NN6 9DG. Peter Tomkins 07917 407400 peter_james_tomkins@yahoo.co.uk
10th September	**Blackpool & District BVPG Lytham Fairhaven Show 9.30am** Lytham Green. Terry A. Robinson 07960 116769 terry.robinson6@btinternet.com
10th September	**Taverners Sporting Trial 10am** Venue TBA. Mark McEvoy 07973 371349 mmcevoy@infoteknix.co.uk
10th September	**King's Lynn 5th Classic Bike and Vehicle Show 11am till late** The Recreation Field, Hovell's Lane, Northwold, Thetford IP26 5LX. Dick Fendick 01366 728852 Club Secretary – malcolmrolph@talktalk.net
10th September	**North Staffs Kate's Canter 11.30am** Strongford Layby, A34 Trentham. Kate Wain 07561 530136
10th September	**South Wales Vale of Glamorgan run 11am** Llanharry Workingmen's Club, Elm Road, Llanharry CF72 9HR. Howard Jayne 02920 868203 howard.jayne@talktalk.net
11th September	**North Cotswold Club Night 8pm** College Arms, Lower Quinton. Chris Delaney 07966 395032 chrisdelaney650@gmail.com
11th September	**East Yorkshire Bangers & Cash Run 10.30am** Mishka Pub/Frankies Cafe, Riverhead, Driffield YO25 6NX. Alan Barker 07887 592400 lindaandalanbarker@hotmail.co.uk
12th September	**Taverners Wrinkly Run 10am** Apple Trees, Bradgate Close, Mountsorrel, Leicester LE12 7DZ. Roger Monk 01509 412662
12th September	**Surrey and Sussex Evening Run 5.30pm** Copthorne Social Club, Copthorne, Crawley RH10 3RE. Brian Robins 07901 183181 surreysussexvmcc@gmail.com
12th September	**South Cotswold Tuesday Evening Pub Meet 6.30pm** The Anchor Inn at Thornbury BS35 1JY. Jeremy Retford 07831 314884 jeremyretford@btinternet.com
12th September	**Herefordshire & Mid Wales Brunch ride-in 11am** The Seasons Café, Caersws, SY17 5SA. Gary Jones 07870 389317 jgjones@sky.com
12th September	**Ipswich & Suffolk Evening ride 6.30pm** Ipswich School Sports Centre, Rushmere St Andrews. Trevor Dickings 01473 798653
13th September	**Chiltern Mid-week Run 10.30am** Full Moon, Cholesbury Lane, Hawridge HP52UH. P. Barfield 01442 824143 chilternvmcc@hotmail.com
13th September	**King's Lynn Ride a Bike Night 7pm** Make your own way. Club Secretary 01842 811077 malcolmrolph@talktalk.net
13th September	**Men of Kent Fish and Chip Run 7pm** Village Hall, Dunkirk, nr Faversham ME13 9LF. Frank Mitchell 07837 918087 richardbarsby61@tiscali.co.uk
13th September	**Northampton Mid-week run 10am** Royal Oak, Blisworth NN7 3BU. Trevor Pinfold 01604 859215 trevorpinfold168@btinternet.com
13th September	**South Lincs and Peterborough Wrinkly Run 10.30am** Venue TBA. Gary Sleeman 01733 770241 gary.sleeman1@gmail.com
13th September	**Wakefield and West Yorkshire Dam Buster's Run Around 10.30am** Mustang Café, Scissett, HD8 9HU. Alistair Durie and Neil Lewis 07483 862303 neil.r.lewis@btinternet.com

13th September	**Cotswold Section Run 6.30pm** The Shutters, Gotherington, GL52 9EZ. 01242 300240 Graham Rowcliffe 07515 288414 grahamrowcliffe58@outlook.com
13th September	**Warwickshire Club night 8pm** Kenilworth Rugby Club, Glasshouse Lane, Kenilworth CV8 2AJ. Barry Heath 07786 718867 b4heath@yahoo.co.uk
13th September	**Berkshire Mid-Week Run 10.30am** Venue TBA. Malcolm White 01344 642866 info@berkshire-vmcc.org.uk
13th September	**West Wiltshire Green Lane Run 9am** Venue TBA. Keith Johnstone 07836 376107 keith.johnston55@hotmail.co.uk
13th September	**North East Lunch Meeting 12 noon** Harewood Arms, Harewood. Steve Rowley 07704 374773 rowley_s2@sky.com
14th September	**Worcestershire Breakfast Meet 9.30am** Hotspur Cafe, Shobdon Airfield HR6 9NR. Les Bennett 07981 550982
14th September	**Devon Evening Pub Meet 6.30pm** Poltimore Arms, Yarde Down, nr Brayford, EX36 3HA. John Young 07847 753725 jebyoung@hotmail.com
14th September	**Oxford Thursday Run 10am** Steventon Village Hall OX13 6RR. Barry Winter 01235 531402
14th September	**North Cotswold Wrinkly Run 10am** Ellendon Farm Shop. Chris Delaney 07966 395032 chrisdelaney650@gmail.com
15th September	**West South Wales Saundersfoot 10am** Coppet Hall beach centre car park SA69 9EY (just outside Saundersfoot village). Chris Thomas 07974 373987
15th September	**Goodwood Friday Run 10.30am** Venue TBA. Dave Johnson 01243 582074 goodwoodvmcc@aol.com
16th September	**Herefordshire & Mid Wales Trail ride 8 10am** Barrow Wake – just off A417, nr Air Balloon car park (OS sheet 163 SO154933; GL4 8JX). Geoff Brown 07746 377075 geoff.brown8m@btopenworld.com
16th September	**Lakeland Uldale Café Ride-In 11am** Maes Tearooms, Uldale, nr Ireby, CA7 1HA. Eddie Stephenson 07932 544789
16th September	**Allen House Cadwell Moto 9am** Cadwell Park Circuit, Louth LN11 9SE. Classic Bike Track Days 07971 424472 info@classicbiketrackdays.com
16th September	**Dorset Breakfast Meet 10am** Thorngrove Garden Centre, Common Mead Lane, Gillingham SP8 4RE. Paul Wirdnam 07775 923206 secretary@dorsetvmcc.co.uk
16th September	**Allen House Kop Hill 9am** Princes Risborough. Gary Sleeman gary@vmcc.net
17th September	**Northampton Autumn Leaves Run 10.30am** Tove Short Stay car park, Towcester NN12 6LD. Ian Townsend 01604 859215 iantownsend@enterprisecontrol.co.uk
17th September	**Blackpool & District Rivington Barn Run 9.30am** A6 layby adj to Barton Hall, Broughton. Terry A. Robinson 07960 116769 terry.robinson6@btinternet.com
17th September	**North East Scottish Royal Deeside Pre-75 Run 10.30am** Banchory, Aberdeenshire. Tony Mortishire 07887 740396 mortishire@btinternet.com
17th September	**South Durham Beamish Trophy Trial 9am** The New Board Inn Esh DH7 9RL Tom Norman 07951 746362
17th September	**Taverners 66th Road Trial 8.30am** The Castle Inn, Main Street, Caldecott Corby, Market Harborough LE16 8RT. Mick Bemrose 07747 805531 mike.bemrose@ntlworld.com
17th September	**South Dorset Club Run 10.30am** The Three Compasses, Charminster DT2 9QT 10.30am. Martin Figg 07896 507278 figg.martin@gmail.com
17th September	**North Cotswold Japanese Bike Run 10am** Venue TBA. Chris Delaney 07966 395032 chrisdelaney650@gmail.com
17th September	**South Cotswold Sunday Café Meet 12 noon** Cotswold Waterpark Gateway Cafe GL5 7TL. Jeremy Retford 07831 314884 jeremyretford@btinternet.com
17th September	**Isle of Man Section Trial 1.30pm** Venue TBA. Shaun Seal 07624 485133
17th September	**Dartmoor Run to the Sun 10.30am** Fox Tor Cafe, Princetown PL20 6QS. Steve Carr 07800 631271
17th September	**Warwickshire Afternoon Tea and Cake Run 2pm** Hatton Layby A4177 Hatton (52.30060818836583, -1.6405068132106515). Barry Heath 07786 718867 b4heath@yahoo.co.uk
17th September	**East Lancs Blackburn Run 10.30am** Layby near Petre Garage at Langho, Whalley Road BB6 8AB. Graham Daniels 07952 348339 grahamdaniels9@hotmail.com
17th September	**Surrey and Sussex Sunday Social Run 11am** Venue TBA. Brian Robins 07901 183181 surreysussexvmcc@gmail.com
17th September	**Cyclemotor Radcot Run 10.30am** Ye Olde Swann PH, Radcot Bridge, nr Bampton OX18 2SX. Frank Chapman 07780 967014
17th September	**Notts and Derby Roaches Run 10.30am** Layby A6 south of Whatstandwell. Kate Sherras 07961 754780 nottsandderbyvintageclub@outlook.com
17th September	**Worcestershire Pete's Perambulation 9.30am** Market Square, Bromyard HR7 4BP. Pete Howells 01886 853293
19th September	**South Cotswold Tuesday Evening Pub Meet 6.30pm** The Ship Inn at Brimscombe GL5 2QN. Jeremy Retford 07831 314884 jeremyretford@btinternet.com
20th September	**Dorset Mid-Week Run 2pm** Hambro Arms, Milton Abbas DT11 0BP. Paul Wirdnam 07775 923206 secretary@dorsetvmcc.co.uk
20th September	**Essex Mid-week Run 9.30am** Venue TBA. Dave Iszard 07543 901340 daveandnicki@sky.com
20th September	**Bristol Under 125cc tiddler and low power girder fork run 10am** The Plough Inn, Piling St, Pilning, Bristol, BS35 4JJ. Rod Western 07778 704097.

20th September	**Cotswold Section Run 6.30pm** Anchor Inn, Epney GL2 7LN. 01452 740433 Graham Rowcliffe 07515 288414 grahamrowcliffe58@outlook.com
20th September	**East Sussex Richard's Wrinkly Run 10.30am** Brian's Barn, Brownbread Street, Ashburnham TN33 9NX. Section secretary 07434 280380 secretary@eastsussexvmcc.co.uk
20th September	**Chiltern Breakfast ride-in 10am** London Gliding club restaurant LU6 2JP. P. Barfield 01442 824143 chilternvmcc@hotmail.com
20th September	**Wakefield and West Yorkshire Scissett Coffee Morning 10am** Mustang Café, Scissett, HD8 9HU. Alistair Durie and Neil Lewis 07483 862303 neil.r.lewis@btinternet.com
20th September	**Chiltern Pub Night 8pm-ish** Full Moon, Cholesbury Lane, Hawridge HP5 2UH. P. Barfield 01442 824143 chilternvmcc@hotmail.com
20th September	**Cyclemotor Feeble Machine Run 10am** Ye Olde Swann PH, Radcot Bridge, nr Bampton, OX18 2SX. Rod Weston 07778 704097
21st September	**Devon AGM 7.30pm** Town Arms, East Street, South Molton EX36 3BU. John Young 07484 753725 jebyoung@hotmail.com
21st September	**Bedfordshire Mid-week Run 10.15am** Shefford Town Memorial Hall, Hitchin Road, Shefford SG17 5JA. Don Mckeand 01525 720629
21st September	**North Cotswold Girder/Rigid Run 10am** Tredington. Chris Delaney 07966 395032 chrisdelaney650@gmail.com
21st September	**West Wiltshire Wandering 12 noon** Thames Head, Coates, GL7 6NZ. Colin Smith 07778 281332 colin.smith1951@btinternet.com
21st September	**Herefordshire & Mid Wales Black Mountain Run 10am** Brycheiniog Car Park, Brecon canal basin. Gary Jones 07870 389317 jgjones@sky.com
22nd September	**Isle of Wight September 4pm** The Orchards Holiday Park, Main Road, Newbridge, Yarmouth PO41 0TS. Ron Wallis 01983 752861 ron.wallis10@gmail.com
23rd September	**Reivers Howard's Run 9.30am** Spurreli Cafe, Coquet St, Amble, Morpeth NE65 0DJ. Howard Perrin 07981 700179
23rd September	**Notts and Derby Saturday Afternoon Run 2pm** The Triangle, Belper Mill Junction, DE56 1BJ Jim Bradley 0115 9329049 nottsandderbyvintageclub@outlook.com
23rd September	**Lakeland South Lakes Mountain Weekend 10am Sat, 10.30am Sun** The Wilson Arms, Torver, nr Coniston LA21 8BB. Colin Steer 01768 774536
24th September	**North East Boroughbridge Run 10.30am** Coronation Hall, Boroughbridge. Keith Hudson 07835 995059
24th September	**East Sussex Blackboys Steam Rally Run 10am** Heathfield Fire Station. Section secretary 07434 280380 secretary@eastsussexvmcc.co.uk
24th September	**Dartmoor Breakfast meet 10am** The Jolly Roger, St John's Lane, Bovey Tracey TQ13 9FF. Derek French 07747 032659
24th September	**Isle of Man Road Run 2pm** Venue TBA. Gary Corlett 07624 496672
24th September	**Gwent Leap Year Run 10am** Abergavenny Bus Station. Mark Hillier 07870 535933 markhillier61@icloud.com
24th September	**Berkshire Mystery Run 10.30am** Venue TBA. Malcolm White 01344 642866 info@berkshire-vmcc.org.uk
24th September	**Bedfordshire Breakfast Meet 10am** Scald End Farm Tea Room, Mill Road, Thurleigh MK44 2DP. Richard Chambers 07905 203823
24th September	**Dorset Veteran & Vintage Run 10.30am** Leigh Village Hall DT9 6HL. Rod Hann 01935 872528 secretary@dorsetvmcc.co.uk
24th September	**Ironmasters Mike's Meander 10.30am** Priorslee Lake Jnt4 M54. Mike Instone 01785 841257
24th September	**North Birmingham Levis Road Trial 10am** The Lenchford Inn, Shrawley, nr Worcester. Martyn Round 0121 5501547 NorthBirminghamVMCC@outlook.com
24th September	**Norwich and District The Crumble 10.30am** High Barn, Shipdham Road, Carbrooke IP25 6SY. Steve Hallam 07732 364524 shallam89@gmail.com
24th September	**South Lincs and Peterborough Founders Run 10.30am** Venue TBA. Gary Sleeman 01733 770241 gary.sleeman1@gmail.com
24th September	**North East Boroughbridge Run 10.30am** Coronation Hall, Boroughbridge. Keith Hudson 07835 995059
24th September	**Banbury Harvest Run 9.30am** Horsefair. M. Phipps 07985 035502
24th September	**Northampton Wrong Way Round Run 10am** Billing Garden Village NN3 9EX. Trevor Pinfold 01604 859215 trevorpinfold168@btinternet.com
26th September	**Goodwood Noggin 'n' Natter 8pm** The Red Lion, London Road, Ashington RH20 3DD. Dave Johnson 01243 582074 goodwoodvmcc@aol.com
26th September	**West Wiltshire Coffee Morning 10am** Compton Abbas Airfield Cafe, Compton Abbas SP5 5AP. Kevin Phillips 07952 173693 starfield181@gmail.com
26th September	**South Cotswold Tuesday Evening Pub Meet 6.30pm** The George Inn at Cambridge GL2 7AL. Jeremy Retford 07831 314884 jeremyretford@btinternet.com
27th September	**South Wales Wednesday evening ride-out 7pm** Your home. Bill Phelps 02920 890255 webadmin@southwalessectionvmcc.co.uk
27th September	**Cotswold Section Run 6pm** Carpenters Arms, Miserden, GL67JA. 01285 821283 Graham Rowcliffe 07515 288414 grahamrowcliffe58@outlook.com
27th September	**Herefordshire & Mid Wales Breakfast meet 10am** The Potting Shed, Kirby's Yard, Whitchurch, Ross-on-Wye HR9 6DJ. Geoff McGladdery 07588 559698 geoffmac@globalnet.co.uk
28th September	**Bristol Lunchtime 12 noon** Lamb Inn, Wotton Road, Iron Action, Bristol BS37 9UZ. Alan Burton 07774 923721

28th September	**Worcestershire Breakfast Meet 10am** Wheelhouse Cafe, Upton on Severn WR8 0PB. Les Bennett 07981 550982
28th September	**South Dorset Club Night 8pm** The Three Compasses, Charminster DT2 9QT. Martin Figg 07896 507278 figg.martin@gmail.com
28th September	**Oxford Thursday Run 10am** Milletts Farm OX13 5HB. Cyril Barrett 01865 390868
30th September	**Clyde Valley The John Macmillan Early Motor Bicycle Run 10.30am** Lochside Caravan Park, Castle Douglas, DG7 1EU. John Harper 07770 647799 john@cathburn.com
30th September	**Dorset Autumn Run 11am** Toy Barn, Blackmarsh Farm, Sherborne DT9 4JX. Andy Grew 01935 595096 secretary@dorsetvmcc.co.uk
30th September	**Notts and Derby Coffee Run** Griffins Head Car Park, Moor Rd, Papplewick, Nottingham NG15 8EN. Graham Bower 07745 888938 nottsandderbyvintageclub@outlook.com

OCTOBER

1st October	**Notts and Derby Dukeries Run 10.30am** Horse and Groom, Main Street, Linby NG15 8AE. Bruce Phillips 07442 168932 nottsandderbyvintageclub@outlook.com
1st October	**Cyclemotor The Vincent Run 10am** Fairlands Valley Park off Six Hills Way, Stevenage SG2 0BL. Chris Sawyer 01438 723142, 07950 903794
1st October	**Flat Tank Belt and Braces Run 9.30am** Bealesville, A48 Hartland Hill, Minsterworth, Glos. Dennis Beale 01452 750424
1st October	**West South Wales EJW Run 10.30am** Tycroes, Maesybont SA14 7HD Carm's. Val Newton 07709 928416
1st October	**North Cotswold Windmill Run 10am** College Arms, Lower Quinton. Chris Delaney 07966 395032 chrisdelaney650@gmail.com
1st October	**Worcestershire Tour about Evesham 9.30am** Pinvin Services WR10 2DT. Andrew Fitzpatrick 07813 845894
1st October	**Isle of Wight Autumn Leaves Breakfast Run 9am** Carisbrooke Nunnery car park, Whitcombe road, Newport PO30 1YS. Ron Wallis 01983 752861 ron.wallis10@gmail.com
1st October	**Essex Lely Run 9.30am** Venue TBA. Lesley Willmore 07971 266167
4th October	**North Birmingham Club Night 8pm** The Round Oak Inn, Ounsdale Road, Wombourne WV5 8BU. David Spencer 07975 629810 NorthBirminghamVMCC@outlook.com
4th October	**Gwent Baffle Haus Coffee Morning 11am** Baffle Haus, The Cedars, Goytre, Pontypool. Mark Hillier 07870 535933 markhillier61@icloud.com
4th October	**Surrey and Sussex Wrinkly Run 11am** Venue TBA. Brian Robins 07901 183181 surreysussexvmcc@gmail.com
4th October	**Lakeland Café Ride-In 11am** Threlkeld Café, Main Street, Threlkeld CA12 4RX. David Weeks 01768 772315
4th October	**East Sussex Secretary's Autumn Saunter 10.30am** Brian's Barn, Brownbread Street, Ashburnham TN33 9NX. Section secretary 07434 280380 secretary@eastsussexvmcc.co.uk
5th October	**Herefordshire & Mid Wales Let There be Dragons 1.30pm** Bringsty Vintage Café, Bringsty Common, Worcester WR6 5UJ. Geoff McGladdery 07588 559698 geoffmac@globalnet.co.uk
5th October	**West Wiltshire Mid-Week Run 10am** Venue TBA. Peter Fielding 07952 173693 starfield181@gmail.com
7th October	**Norwich and District Letheringsett Watermill 10.30am** Acacia, Queen Street, Spooner Row, NR18 9JU. Richard Mack 07860 208045 newimpboy@gmail.com
7th October	**Notts and Derby Saturday Afternoon Run 2pm** The Triangle, Belper Mill Junction, DE56 1BJ. Clive Russell 01335 390369 nottsandderbyvintageclub@outlook.com
8th October	**Warwickshire Autumn Leaves Run 10am** Long Itch Diner, Southam Rd, Long Itchington, Southam CV47 9QZ. Barry Heath 07786 718867 b4heath@yahoo.co.uk
8th October	**Northampton Cold, wet, short, fun Run 10.30am** Super Sausage A5, NN12 7QD. Ray Cobley, John Lourie Ray 07831 228550, John 01908 567418 johnlourie@outlook.com, raycobley@aol.com
8th October	**Banbury Conker Run 9.30am** Horsefair. J. Harris 01295 721282
8th October	**East Lancs Memorial Run 10.30am** Layby near Petre Garage Langho, Whalley Road BB6 8AB. David Prismall 01706 217572 davidprismall@hotmail.com
8th October	**East Yorkshire Autumn Ramble 10.30am** The Tea Pot Cafe, Fimber YO25 3HG. Dudley Wilson 07592 035482 dudley_wilson@hotmail.com
8th October	**King's Lynn Pre-'31 Run 10am** Venue TBA. Club Secretary 01842 811077 malcolmrolph@talktalk.net
8th October	**North Birmingham Autumn Run 10am** Venue TBA. www.vmcc-nbs.co.uk John Williams 07866 796841 NorthBirminghamVMCC@outlook.com
8th October	**Pennine Autumn Run 10.30am** The Comrades Club, Manchester Rd., Shaw, Oldham OL2 8SB. Geoff Green 07817 178287 secretary@penninevmcc.org.uk
8th October	**Northumbrian Colonial Run 9.30am** High House Farm Brewery, Matfen, Newcastle upon Tyne NE20 0RG. Andreas Schrocksnadel 07973 318210
8th October	**Devon Ruby Run 11am** Jonesy's Cafe, Winkleigh EX19 8EZ. Nick Smiles 07711 444686 nickesmiles@googlemail.com
8th October	**Cyclemotor 100-Mile Run 9am** Quainton Memorial Hall Station Road, Quainton, Bucks HP22 4BW. Malcolm Tappin 01494 672459

8th October	**North Staffs Autumn Leaves Run 12 noon** Yew Tree Inn, Cauldon, ST10 3EJ. Ian Pettifor 07760 346003
8th October	**Somerset Autumn Leaves Run 10.30am** New Manor Farm Shop, Bishop Sutton BS40 6HW. Colin Bentham 01761 241516
9th October	**North Cotswold Club Night 8pm** College Arms, Lower Quinton. Chris Delaney 07966 395032 chrisdelaney650@gmail.com
10th October	**Herefordshire & Mid Wales Brunch ride-in 11am** Kirsty's café, New Street, Bishop's Castle SY9 5DQ. Gary Jones 07870 389317 jgjones@sky.com
11th October	**South Lincs and Peterborough Wrinkly Run 10.30am** Venue TBA. Gary Sleeman 01733770241 gary.sleeman1@gmail.com
11th October	**North East Lunch Meeting 12 noon** Harewood Arms, Harewood. Steve Rowley 07704 374773 rowley_s2@sky.com
11th October	**Berkshire Mid-Week Run 10.30am** Venue TBA. Malcolm White 01344 642866 info@berkshire-vmcc.org.uk
11th October	**West Wiltshire Green Lane Run 9am** Venue TBA. Keith Johnstone 07836 376107 keith.johnston55@hotmail.co.uk
11th October	**Northampton Mid-week run 10am** Royal Oak, Blisworth NN7 3BU. Trevor Pinfold 01604 859215 trevorpinfold168@btinternet.com
11th October	**Chiltern Mid-week Run 10.30am** Full Moon, Cholesbury Lane, Hawridge HP5 2UH. P. Barfield 01442 824143 chilternvmcc@hotmail.com
12th October	**Oxford Thursday Run 10am** Steventon Village Hall OX13 6RR. Chris Green 01235 210761
12th October	**Herefordshire & Mid Wales Trail ride 9 10am** Regent House Filling Station, Clyro HR3 5SB. Paul Farley 01874 610303 palmag@btinternet.com
12th October	**Worcestershire Haven't we been here before? 9.30am** Cob House, Wichenford WR6 6YE. Howard Williams 07864 567705
13th October	**Goodwood Friday Run 10.30am** Venue TBA. Dave Johnson 01243 582058 goodwoodvmcc@aol.com
14th October	**Lakeland Shap Ride-In 11am** Shap Chippy/Café, Main Street, Shap CA10 3JS. Eric Stephenson 01900 824898
14th October	**South Dorset Social Breakfast Meet 9.30am** The Three Compasses, Charminster DT2 9QT. Martin Figg 07896 507278 figg.martin@gmail.com
14th October	**Allen House Classic Motorcycle Mechanics Show 9am** Stafford Showground. Gary Sleeman – gary@vmcc.net
15th October	**Dartmoor End of Season Run 10.30am** Opposite Royal Seven Stars Hotel, The Plains, Totnes TQ9 5DD. Mike Burton 07790 459795
15th October	**Northampton Gold & Brown Run 10.30am** Venue TBA – see latest issue of What's On. Chris Towell 07860 719363 chris@cltowellandson.co.uk
15th October	**South Dorset Club Run 10.30am** The Three Compasses, Charminster DT2 9QT. Martin Figg 07896 507278 figg.martin@gmail.com
15th October	**South Durham Anniversary Run 10am** The Crown, Manfield. Mike Carruthers 01325 254195
15th October	**Herefordshire & Mid Wales Bredon Hill and Winchcombe 9.30am** Ledbury Market Hall, High St, Ledbury HR8 1DS. Geoff McGladdery 07588 559698 geoffmac@globalnet.co.uk
15th October	**Isle of Man Section Trial 1.30pm** South Barrule. Shaun Seal 07624 485133
15th October	**Taverners Sporting Trial 10am** Venue TBA. Mark McEvoy 07973 142440 mmcevoy@infoteknix.co.uk
15th October	**North Cotswold Idiots' Run 10am** Venue TBA. Chris Delaney 07966 395032 chrisdelaney650@gmail.com
15th October	**South Cotswold Sunday Café Meet 12 noon** Whistlestop Café, Tetbury Goods Shed GL8 8EY. Jeremy Retford 07831 314884 jeremyretford@btinternet.com
15th October	**Dorset Autumn Leaves Run 11am** Virginia Ash, Henstridge BA8 0PL. Bernard Jones 01258 472554 secretary@dorsetvmcc.co.uk
17th October	**Taverners Wrinkly Run 10am** Apple Trees, Bradgate Close, Mountsorrel, Leicester LE12 7DZ. Roger Monk 01509 412662
17th October	**Isle of Wight Muddy Lanes Lunch Run 11.30am** The Hare and Hounds car park, Downend, Arreton PO30 2NU. Ron Wallis 01983 752861 ron.wallis10@gmail.com
18th October	**Chiltern Pub Night 8pm-ish** Full Moon, Cholesbury Lane, Hawridge HP5 2UH. P. Barfield 01442 824143 chilternvmcc@hotmail.com
18th October	**Reivers Season's End Run 10am** Nelson's Cafe, Swarland NE65 9BQ. Dave Spencer 07907 200883
18th October	**Chiltern Breakfast ride-in 10am** London Gliding club resturant LU6 2JP. P. Barfield 01442 824143 chilternvmcc@hotmail.com
19th October	**Bedfordshire Mid-week lunch 12 noon** Cross Keys, 13 High St, Pulloxhill, Beds MK45 5HB. Richard Chambers 07905 203823
19th October	**Devon Club Night 7.30pm** Town Arms, East Street, South Molton EX36 3BU. John Young 07484 753725 jebyoung@hotmail.com
19th October	**West Wiltshire Wandering 12 noon** The Wheatsheaf Inn, Crudwell SN16 9ET. Colin Smith 07778 281332 colin.smith1951@btinternet.com
19th October	**Flat Tank Silver Fox Run 11am** Silver Fox Cafe, Broadoak A48. Charles Wright 01452 790296

21st October	**Worcestershire Grand House Tour 11am** Discovery Centre Cafe SY7 9RS. Richard Caddick 01299 403334
21st October	**Chiltern Autumn Run 10.30am** Full Moon, Cholesbury Lane, Hawridge HP5 2UH. P. Barfield 01442 824143 chilternvmcc@hotmail.com
21st October	**Dorset Breakfast Meet 10am** Thorngrove Garden Centre, Common Mead Lane, Gillingham, SP8 4RE. Paul Wirdnam 07775 923206 secretary@dorsetvmcc.co.uk
21st October	**Bedfordshire Autumn Gold Run 9.45am breakfast, 10.30am run** Jordans Mill, Holme Mills, Langford Road, Broom SG18 9JY. Bryan Marsh 07309 731191 bryan.marsh@btinternet.com
22nd October	**Cheshire and North Wales End of season lunch run-out 12.00 rendezvous** The Telford Inn, New Road, Trevor, LL207TT secretary@candnw.vmcc.net Neil Shirley 01352 713204 chairman@candnw.vmcc.net
22nd October	**Goodwood Pumpkin Run 10.30am** The Forge, Slindon, Reynolds Road, Slindon BN18 0QT. Dave Johnson 01243 582074 goodwoodvmcc@aol.com
22nd October	**Surrey and Sussex Practice Trial (in aid of NSPCC) 10.30am** Selah Clayton Hill Hassocks, West Sussex BN6 9PQ. Chris Brown 01342 834744 guvbrown@btinternet.com
22nd October	**West Wiltshire Autumn Leaves Run 10am** Fox & Hounds, Acton Turville. Jim Gaisford 07952 173693 starfield181@gmail.com
22nd October	**Warwickshire Antelope Ride-in. 12 noon** The Antelope, The Green, Lighthorne, Warwick CV35 0BX. Barry Heath 07786 718867 b4heath@yahoo.co.uk
22nd October	**Berkshire Autumn Frolic 10.30am** Venue TBA. Malcolm White 01344 642866 info@berkshire-vmcc.org.uk
22nd October	**Cotswold Winter Wandering 12 noon** Halfway House Inn, Kineton, nr Cheltenham GL54 5UG (SP 097 265). 01451 850344 Peter Kent 01452 610375
22nd October	**South Lincs and Peterborough Autumn Leaves Run 10.30am** Venue TBA. Gary Sleeman 01733 770241 gary.sleeman1@gmail.com
22nd October	**Ironmasters Fowl Weather Run 10.30am** Redhill cafe lay-by, A5. John Carter 01785 841257
22nd October	**Banbury Autumn Amble 9.30am** Horsefair. C. Mant 01869 340232
22nd October	**Gwent Des James Run 10am** Abergavenny Bus Station. Mark Hillier 07870 535933 markhillier61@icloud.com
24th October	**Goodwood Noggin 'n' Natter 8pm** The Red Lion, London Road, Ashington, West Sussex, RH20 3DD. Dave Johnson 01243 582074 goodwoodvmcc@aol.com
25th October	**Bristol Annual Dinner and Prize Giving Begbrook Social Club. 7.00 for 7.30 pm** Prompt Begbrook Social Club, Frenchay Park Road, frenchay, Bristol, BS16 1HY. Brenda Foot / Stuart Edwards. 01249 720172 / 07369 249011
25th October	**Herefordshire & Mid Wales Breakfast meet 10am** The Lion, Leintwardine SY7 0JZ. Geoff McGladdery 07588 559698 geoffmac@globalnet.co.uk
25th October	**Essex End Of Season Run 9.30am** Venue TBA. Dave Iszard 07543 901340 daveandnicki@sky.com
26th October	**Oxford Thursday Run 10am** Turnpike Pub, Yarnton OX5 1PJ. Neil Kerr 01993 705179
26th October	**Devon Planning Meeting 7.30pm** Venue TBA. John Young 07484 753725 jebyoung@hotmail.com
26th October	**Worcestershire Breakfast Meet 9.30am** Cleobury Golf Club DY14 8HQ. Richard Caddick 01299 403334
26th October	**South Dorset Club Night 8pm** The Three Compasses, Charminster DT2 9QT. Martin Figg 07896 507278 figg.martin@gmail.com
26th October	**North Cotswold Wrinkly Lunch 12 noon** Venue TBA. Chris Delaney 07966 395032 chrisdelaney650@gmail.com
28th October	**Allen House National Motorcycle Museum 9am** Birmingham. Gary Sleeman gary@vmcc.net
28th October	**Dorset Halloween Run 11am** Coffee House, Kings Stag DT10 2AY. Simon Barker 07745 201512 secretary@dorsetvmcc.co.uk
29th October	**King's Lynn, Halloween Run 10am** Venue TBA (Watton area). Steve Jones 01953 884070 Club Secretary – malcolmrolph@talktalk.net
29th October	**Bedfordshire Breakfast Meet 10am** Danish Camp Riverside Visitor Centre, Chapel Lane, Willington MK44 3QG. Richard Chambers 07905 203823
29th October	**Dartmoor Breakfast meet 10am** The Jolly Roger, St John's Lane, Bovey Tracey TQ13 9FF. Deark French 07747 032659
29th October	**North East Section Meeting 2pm** Coronation Hall, Boroughbridge. Steve Rowley 07704 374773 rowley_s2@sky.com
29th October	**West South Wales Charity run 10.30am** 12 Llys y Nant, Llandybie SA18 2TL (between Llandeilo & Ammanford). Allan & Rhian Thomas 01269 851171 07800 741896
29th October	**Worcestershire Llandovery Tour 10am** Oakchurch HR4 7NH. Alan Williams 01432 275395
29th October	**Notts and Derby Autumn Road Run 10.30am** Layby A6 1 mile south of Whatstandwell. Graham Bower 07745 888938 nottsandderbyvintageclub@outlook.com
31st October	**West Wiltshire Coffee Morning 10am** Orchid Cafe, Holt Road, Bradford on Avon BA15 1TS. Kevin Phillips 07952 173693 starfield181@gmail.com

WINTER RIDES
NOVEMBER – DECEMBER

Over 100 runs, rides and socials listed

WINTER

NOVEMBER

1st November — Surrey and Sussex Wrinkly Run 11am
Venue TBA. Brian Robins 07901 183181
surreysussexvmcc@gmail.com

1st November — Lakeland Coniston Speed Week Ride-In 11am
The Bluebird Café, Coniston LA21 8AN.
John Silcock 01229 861264

1st November — North Birmingham Club Night 8pm
The Round Oak Inn, Ounsdale Road,
Wombourne WV5 8BU. David Spencer 07975 629810
NorthBirminghamVMCC@outlook.com

2nd November — West Wiltshire New Forest Run 10am
The former Chocolate Poodle Pub
(A360 south of West Lavington). Peter Fielding
07952 173693 starfield181@gmail.com

2nd November — Worcestershire Breakfast Meet 10am
The Den, Stanford Bridge WR6 6SP.
Les Bennett 07981 550982

4th November — Somerset Autojumble 9.30am
Bath and West Showground,
Shepton Mallet BA4 6QN.
Dave Atterbury 01297 32853

4th November — North Birmingham Winter Wander 10am
Tony's Diner, Quatford, nr Bridgnorth WV15 6QL.
David Spencer 07975 629810
NorthBirminghamVMCC@outlook.com

5th November — Norwich and District Guy Fawkes Run 10.30am
Old Buckenham Airfield, Abbey Road,
Old Buckenham NR17 1PU.
Stephen Lee 07768 088740
strathearnhouse@btinternet.com

5th November — Banbury Guy Fawkes Run 10am
Brackley Market Place. T. White 01280 841816

5th November — Worcestershire Drovers' Delights 9.30am
The Farm Shop, Ludlow SY8 2JR.
Mark Evans 07791 241641

5th November — Northampton Guy Fawkes Run 10.30am
Venue TBA – see latest issue of What's On.
Chris Towell 07860 719363
chris@cltowellandson.co.uk

5th November — Devon Guy Fawkes Run 11am
Quay Cafe, Velator, Braunton EX33 2DX.
Nick Smiles 07711 444686
nickesmiles@googlemail.com

5th November — Somerset Guy Fawkes Run 10am
Cheddar Garden Centre, Cheddar BS27 3RU.
Richard Gray 01934 513910

5th November — North Staffs Guy Fawkes Run 10.30am
Leek Market Place. Simon Feeney 07976 165587

5th November — Isle of Wight No Fireworks Breakfast Run 9am
Carisbrooke Nunnery car park, Whitcombe Road,
Newport PO30 1YS. Ron Wallis 01983 752861
ron.wallis10@gmail.com

8th November — Chiltern Mid-week Run 10.30am
Full Moon, Cholesbury Lane, Hawridge HP5 2UH.
P. Barfield 014428 24143 chilternvmcc@hotmail.com

8th November — North East Lunch Meeting 12 noon
Harewood Arms, Harewood.
Steve Rowley 07704 374773 rowley_s2@sky.com

9th November — Herefordshire & Mid Wales Trail ride 10 10am
Just off A465 near Pandy, grid ref SO334221.
Paul Farley 01874 610303 palmag@btinternet.com

10th November — Goodwood Friday Run 10.30am
Venue TBA. Dave Johnson 01243 582074
goodwoodvmcc@aol.com

11th November — South Dorset Social Breakfast Meet 9.30am
The Three Compasses, Charminster DT2 9QT.
Martin Figg 07896 507278 figg.martin@gmail.com

11th November — Dorset Memorial Run 11am
Shell Service Station nr ALDI SP8 5FB.
Ray Dickinson 07414 289472
secretary@dorsetvmcc.co.uk

12th November — Notts and Derby Sunday Lunch Meet 12 noon
Grindleford Station Café, Upper Padley,
Grindleford S32 2JA.
Graham Bower 07745 888938
nottsandderbyvintageclub@outlook.com

12th November — East Sussex Brian's breakfast run 9.30am
Brian's Barn, Brownbread Street, Ashburnham
TN33 9NX. Section secretary 07434 280380
secretary@eastsussexvmcc.co.uk

12th November — Herefordshire & Mid Wales
Autumn lunch ride 9.30am
Starbucks A49, Woofferton, Ludlow SY8 4AL.
Geoff McGladdery 07588 559698
geoffmac@globalnet.co.uk

12th November — Cyclemotor Last of the Year Run/AGM 10.30am
Peacehaven Farm, Ickford HP18 9JE.
Malcolm Tappin 01494 672459

13th November — North Cotswold Club Night 8pm
College Arms, Lower Quinton.
Chris Delaney 07966 395032
chrisdelaney650@gmail.com

15th November — Lakeland Wal Handley Memorial Ride-In Time TBA
Wal Handley Memorial, Fingland, nr Wigton CA7
5EN. Bob Mayow 01946 822580

15th November — Berkshire Mid-Week Run 10.30am
Venue TBA. Malcolm White 01344 642866
info@berkshire-vmcc.org.uk

15th November — Chiltern Pub Night 8pm-ish
Full Moon, Cholesbury Lane, Hawridge HP5 2UH.
P. Barfield 01442 824143 chilternvmcc@hotmail.com

15th November — West Wiltshire Green Lane Run 9am
Venue TBA. Keith Johnstone 07836 376107
keith.johnston55@hotmail.co.uk

15th November — Chiltern Breakfast ride-in 10am
London Gliding club resturant LU6 2JP. P. Barfield
01442 824143 chilternvmcc@hotmail.com

16th November — North Cotswold Wrinkly Lunch 12 noon
Venue TBA. Chris Delaney 07966 395032
chrisdelaney650@gmail.com

16th November	**West Wiltshire Wandering 12 noon** The Three Magpies, Sells Green SN12 6RN. Colin Smith 07778 281332 colin.smith1951@btinternet.com
16th November	**Bedfordshire Mid-week lunch 12 noon** Scald End Farm Tea Room, Mill Road, Thurleigh MK44 2DP. Richard Chambers 07905 203823
16th November	**Devon Club Night 7.30pm** Town Arms, East Street, South Molton EX36 3BU. John Young 07484 753725 jebyoung@hotmail.com
18th November	**Dorset Breakfast Meet 10am** Thorngrove Garden Centre, Common Mead Lane, Gillingham SP8 4RE. Paul Wirdnam 07775 923206 secretary@dorsetvmcc.co.uk
18th November	**Worcestershire Gentle Gliding to the Rudges 9.30am** Cob House, Wichenford WR6 6YE. Richard Caddick 01299 403334
19th November	**South Cotswold Sunday Café Meet 12 noon** The Highfield Garden Centre Cafe, Whitminster GL2 7PB. Jeremy Retford 07831 314884 jeremyretford@btinternet.com
19th November	**South Dorset Club Run 10.30am** The Three Compasses, Charminster DT2 9QT. Martin Figg 07896 507278 figg.martin@gmail.com
19th November	**Cotswold Winter Wandering 12 noon** Seven Tuns Inn, Chedworth, nr Cheltenham GL54 4AE (SP 052 119). 01285 720630 Peter Kent 01452 610375
19th November	**Taverners Sporting Trial 10am** Vickers Farm. Mark McEvoy 07973 142440 mmcevoy@infoteknix.co.uk
19th November	**Isle of Man Section Trial 1.30pm** Dhoon Quarry. Shaun Seal 07624 485133
19th November	**Northampton Brass Monkey Run 10.30am** Tove Short Stay car park, Towcester NN12 6LD. Ian Townsend 01604 859215 iantownsend@enterprisecontrol.co.uk
21st November	**Isle of Wight Grey Skies Lunch run 11.30am** Hare and Hounds car park, Downend, Arreton PO30 2NU. Ron Wallis 01983 752861 ron.wallis10@gmail.com
23rd November	**Oxford Thursday Run 10am** H Café, Dorchester on Thames OX10 7LY. Rob Harris 01865 730109
23rd November	**South Dorset Club Night 8pm** The Three Compasses, Charminster DT2 9QT. Martin Figg 07896 507278 figg.martin@gmail.com
26th November	**Worcestershire Brewery visit 12 noon** The Ludlow Brewery SY8 2PQ. Richard Caddick 01299 403334
26th November	**North East Annual General Meeting 2pm** Coronation Hall, Boroughbridge. Steve Rowley 07704 374773 rowley_s2@sky.com
26th November	**Notts and Derby Sunch Lunch Meet 12 noon** Yondermann Café, A623 Wardlow Mires, Derbyshire SK17 8RW. Graham Bower 07745 888938 nottsandderbyvintageclub@outlook.com
26th November	**Bedfordshire Breakfast Meet 10am** Flitvale Garden Centre, Flitwick Road, Westoning MK45 5AA. Richard Chambers 07905 203823
26th November	**Dartmoor Breakfast meet 10am** The Jolly Roger, St John's Lane, Bovey Tracey TQ13 9FF. Derek French 07747 032659
28th November	**West Wiltshire Coffee Morning 10am** Ship Inn Cafe, Luckington SN14 6PA. Kevin Phillips 07952 173693 starfield181@gmail.com
29th November	**Warwickshire Christmas Lunch Time TBA** Leamington Golf Club, Golf Ln, Whitnash, Leamington Spa CV31 2QA. Barry Heath 07786 718867 b4heath@yahoo.co.uk
30th November	**Worcestershire Breakfast Meet 10am** The Farm Shop, Chadbury WR11 4TD. Richard Caddick 01299 403334

DECEMBER

2nd December	**North Cotswold Annual Awards Dinner 7pm** Village Hall, Weston sub Edge. Chris Delaney 07966 395032 chrisdelaney650@gmail.com
3rd December	**Isle of Wight Ron's Christmas Pudding Run 1.30pm** Carisbrooke Nunnery car park, Whitcombe road, Newport PO30 1YS. Ron Wallis 01983 752861 ron.wallis10@gmail.com
3rd December	**Worcestershire Breakfast Meet 9.30am** Cob House, Wichenford WR6 6YE. Richard Caddick 01299 403334
3rd December	**Dorset Mince Pie Run 11am** Marsh & Ham Car Park, Blandford DT11 7AW. Phil Allen 07584 078338 secretary@dorsetvmcc.co.uk
3rd December	**Banbury Early Christmas Run 10am** Horsefair. G. Wheeler 07850 052423
6th December	**North Birmingham Club Night 8pm** The Round Oak Inn, Ounsdale Road, Wombourne WV5 8BU. David Spencer 07975 629810 NorthBirminghamVMCC@outlook.com
6th December	**Surrey and Sussex Wrinkly Run 11am** Venue TBA. Brian Robins 07901 183181 surreysussexvmcc@gmail.com
8th December	**Goodwood Winter Wobble 10.30am** The Forge, Reynolds Lane, Slindon BN18 0QT. Dave Johnson 01243 582074 goodwoodvmcc@aol.com
8th December	**South Cotswold Christmas Meal 7pm** Venue TBA. Jeremy Retford 07831 314884 jeremyretford@btinternet.com

9th December	**South Dorset Social Breakfast Meet 9.30am** The Three Compasses, Charminster DT2 9QT. Martin Figg 07896 507278 figg.martin@gmail.com
9th December	**Notts and Derby Saturday Run 11am** Layby A6 south of Whatstandwell. Gordon Milburn 07800 826733 nottsandderbyvintageclub@outlook.com
10th December	**Taverners Sporting Trial 10am** Venue TBA. Mark McEvoy 07973 142440 mmcevoy@infoteknix.co.uk
10th December	**Notts and Derby Sunday Lunch Meet 12 noon** The Old Smithy Cafe, Church Street, Monyash DE45 1JH. Graham Bower 07745 888938 nottsandderbyvintageclub@outlook.com
10th December	**Cotswold Winter Wandering 12 noon** Red Hart Inn, Blaisdon, Longhope GL17 0AH (SO 702 169). 01452 831717 Peter Kent 01452 610375
11th December	**Worcestershire Christmas Event 7.30pm** The Bell, Lower Broadheath WR2 6QG. John Porter 01386 553329
11th December	**North Cotswold Club Night 8pm** College Arms, Lower Quinton. Chris Delaney 07966 395032 chrisdelaney650@gmail.com
13th December	**North East Lunch Meeting 12 noon** Harewood Arms, Harewood. Steve Rowley 07704 374773 rowley_s2@sky.com
13th December	**West Wiltshire Green Lane Run 9am** Venue TBA. Keith Johnstone 07836 376107 keith.johnston55@hotmail.co.uk
14th December	**South Dorset Club Night 8pm** The Three Compasses, Charminster DT2 9QT. Martin Figg 07896 507278 figg.martin@gmail.com
14th December	**Worcestershire Breakfast Meet 10am** Bringsty Cafe WR6 5UJ. Les Bennett 07981 550982
16th December	**Dorset Breakfast Meet 10am** Thorngrove Garden Centre, Common Mead Lane, Gillingham SP8 4RE. Paul Wirdnam 07775 923206 secretary@dorsetvmcc.co.uk
17th December	**South Dorset Club Run 10.30am** The Three Compasses, Charminster DT2 9QT. Martin Figg 07896 507278 figg.martin@gmail.com
17th December	**Isle of Man Section Trial 1.30pm** Knock Froy. Gary Corlett 07624 496672
17th December	**South Cotswold Sunday Café Meet 12 noon** The Jet Age Museum Cafe GL2 9QL. Jeremy Retford 07831 314884 jeremyretford@btinternet.com
19th December	**West Wiltshire Coffee Morning 10am** The AV8 Café, Cotswold Airport GL7 6BA. Kevin Phillips 07952 173693 starfield181@gmail.com
21st December	**Bedfordshire Mid-week lunch 12 noon** Toby Carvery, Goldington Road, Bedford MK41 0DS. Richard Chambers 07905 203823
21st December	**Devon Mince Pies and Natter 7.30pm** Town Arms, East Street, South Molton, EX36 3BU. John Young 07484 753725 jebyoung@hotmail.com
26th December	**Taverners Boxing Day Run 11am** Victoria Park Car Park, Granville Road, Leicester LE1 7RY. Roger Monk 01509 412662
26th December	**Herefordshire & Mid Wales Brass Monkey Ride 11am** The Moon, Mordiford HR1 4LW. Geoff McGladdery 07588 559698 geoffmac@globalnet.co.uk
26th December	**East Sussex Boxing Day Run 11.30am** Boship Roundabout. Section secretary 07434 280380 secretary@eastsussexvmcc.co.uk
26th December	**South Cotswold Boxing Day lunchtime gathering 12 noon** The Tipputs Inn (on A46 south of Nailsworth) GL6 0QE. Jeremy Retford 07831 314884 jeremyretford@btinternet.com
26th December	**Surrey and Sussex Boxing Day Run 11am** Copthorne Social Club, Copthorne, Crawley RH10 3RE. Brian Robins 07901 183181 surreysussexvmcc@gmail.com
26th December	**Bristol Boxing Day Meet 12 noon** Wishing Well, Wapley Road, Codrington, Bristol BS37 6RY. Stuart Edwards 07369 249011
26th December	**West South Wales Boxing Day Run 10.30am** Tirdail, Nantgaredig Carm's SA32 7NH. Chris & Eirios Thomas 07974 373987
26th December	**Chiltern Boxing Day Run 10.30am** Subject to review. P. Barfield 01442 824143
26th December	**South Durham Boxing Day Run 10.30am** Market Place, Darlington town centre. Brian Smith 01325 286623
26th December	**Cotswold Boxing Day Gathering 12 noon** Tipputs Inn, Tiltups End, nr Nailsworth GL6 0QE (ST 844 972). 01453 834365 Peter Kent 01452 610375
27th December	**South Lincs and Peterborough Chilly Willie Run 10.30am** Venue TBA. Gary Sleeman 01733 770241 gary.sleeman1@gmail.com
27th December	**Northampton Ring Out the Old 12 noon** Stags Head, High St, Great Doddington NN29 7TQ. Richard Stone 01604 768069 richardstone47@hotmail.co.uk
27th December	**Somerset Ashley's Run 10.30am** Pecking Mill Inn, Evercreech BA4 6PG. Dave Boon 01749 672672
27th December	**Worcestershire Boxing Day+1 Meet 12 noon** Lion, Clifton on Teme WR6 6DH. Pete Howells 01886 853293
27th December	**South Wales Day after Boxing Day Run 12.30pm** Your home. Howard Jayne 02920 868203 howard.jayne@talktalk.net
27th December	**Banbury Ring Out the Old 10am** Horsefair. Follow the leader 07850 052423
31st December	**Bedfordshire Breakfast Meet 10am** Jordans Mill, Holme Mills, Langford Road, Broom SG18 9JY. Richard Chambers 07905 203823
31st December	**Dartmoor Breakfast meet 10am** The Jolly Roger, St John's Lane, Bovey Tracey TQ13 9FF. Derek French 07747 032659

CHARTERHOUSE
Auctioneers & Valuers

1974 Ducati 750 GT

Classic & Vintage Motorcycle Auction
Thursday 30th March 2023

At Haynes International Motor Museum, Sparkford
Viewing Wednesday 29th March 9.30am-4.30pm

Late entries invited, call George Beale 07808 159149
or email images to bikes@charterhouse-auction.com

The Long Street Salerooms Sherborne DT9 3BS
01935 812277   www.charterhouse-auction.com

Getting on the Road

You've bought a classic, but it's not running – OLIVER HULME shows how to get it on the road

Check front fork play

Getting on the Road

So, your classic has arrived. Let's assume it doesn't need a complete restoration and no parts are missing, but it hasn't been used for a while and does need recommissioning. The temptation is to try and start it straight away but it's best to check it over first.

Nothing should be done in a rush. Unless you know the previous owner very well, take anything they've told you with a large pinch of salt. Nobody will ever admit to a bodge. First, get the battery on charge, making sure you make a note of whether the bike is positive or negative earth. Clean each area you are going to work on thoroughly.

Tyres

How old are the tyres? You can find this out by looking at the sidewalls. The production date of any tyre made since 2000

Tyres – if they are as old as this, change them

can be found on one of the sidewalls, at the end of the 'DOT' (Department of Transport) code. The last four figures – typically after other letters and numbers – show the production date. The first two are the week it was made, and the last are the year. If the code is only three numbers, the tyre is very old indeed and needs replacing. Check for cuts, splits, worn tread and perishing. Fortunately, classic bike tyres are much cheaper than those for modern sports bikes.

Wheels

Has the bike been standing? The chances are that it has, and that the inside of the brake drums have some corrosion. The wheels will need to come off so you can clean things out. While they're off, grease the wheel bearings and if they feel lumpy or rough, they'll need to be changed too. When refitting or replacing caged bearings, pop them in your freezer compartment for an hour first to make refitting easier.

Refit your cleaned up wheels. Check spokes for corrosion and make sure none are loose. Be extra careful when refitting a front wheel as some motorcycle forks have soft aluminium threads that can easily strip under pressure. On bikes with bolt-on end caps on the bottom of forks, make sure the caps go back on the correct way round and don't overtighten them, as these can fracture easily. This is where your camera will help during the dismantling process.

Bleeding the brakes

If the bike has hydraulic brakes, change the fluid. You can do this from the caliper end to make bleeding easier later on. For this you will need some of the correct fluid, a length of clear pipe and a clear container. Slacken off the bleed nipple and attach the clear pipe to it, pumping the lever to get the old fluid out. Then remove the reservoir cap and soak up any old

Budget priced grease gun will do nicely

A Halford professional ¼ drive set – a bargain at £19.99

An impact driver. Ideal for undoing clutch nuts and the like

Cheap fuel pipe will perish, and quickly

fluid in a rag or tissue, taking care not to let the fluid spill onto the paintwork. Fill the reservoir with fresh brake fluid, then bleed the brakes.

There are many different methods of doing this, and clever tools to make it easier, though the old milk bottle full of fluid and clear pipe works 80% of the time. If your bleed nipple is seized it may snap off, so be careful. If it looks like it is not going to budge, removing the caliper and heating it up with a hot air gun or in front of a fire may help as the two metals (steel nipple and alloy calliper) expand and contract at different rates. Use copper or aluminium grease on the nipple threads and banjo bolt when refitting to prevent future seizures.

Steering head bearings

With the front wheel off the ground, grab hold of the front forks and pull backwards and forwards. If the bottom of the forks move but the top doesn't, your internal fork bushes need attention. If the whole fork moves or clunks, the head bearing adjustment needs sorting. The adjustment is correct if there is no play and the forks will move from lock to lock after a light push from one side. To adjust, tighten the central steering head bolt until all the play is removed but the forks still move smoothly from side to side. Any notchiness in the travel indicates that the ball bearings or the races they run in are worn and need replacing. Replacement taper-roller bearings are cheap and easy to fit and set up, if available for your bike.

Check the Chain

There should be 15-20mm of up and down movement on the chain. First of all, clean the chain with degreaser or paraffin and check the condition of both the sprockets to make sure there is no excessive wear. Too much side-to-side movement on the sprocket indicates that the cush drive rubbers may be excessively worn. To adjust the chain, slacken the axle nuts just a little and loosen the brake torque arm where it attaches to the rear brake. Slacken off any locknuts on the adjuster, push the wheel so the adjuster screws sit firmly onto the end of the swing arm, then using an appropriate spanner, tighten or loosen the adjusters. Do this a half turn at a time, equally on both sides and swapping between each side until the tension is correct. Tighten up the axle and the adjuster screw locknuts and check the tension again. Tighten up the torque arm nut and fit a new split pin to stop it coming loose. Use a good chain lube – heavy duty gearbox oil will work too but does fly off.

Clean the chain and sprocket so you can check their condition

Try for movement at the swing arm

Swing Arm

Grease/lubricate the swing arm bushes if there are grease nipples. Different nipples need different grease gun fittings, and some older machines use heavy oil rather than grease. Simply attach the grease gun and pump in grease/oil until you see old lubricant coming out of the other side of the bushes. With the bike on a stand, give the swing arm a tug and see if there is any movement. If there is an appreciable amount, it might be worth replacing the swing arm bearings, which means taking out the swing arm and pressing in some new ones. If in doubt, once the bike is running take it down to your local MOT station and ask their advice.

Changing the Oil

On a British motorcycle this involves draining the oil tank properly – the existing oil might look okay on the surface, but can hide a multitude of sins. An AMC single I bought had been sitting for decades and the oil looked fine, but I found around two inches of thick tarry gloop where the oil had settled at the bottom of the tank.

To drain the tank, unscrew the drain plug (if there is one) and tank feeds and let the oil drain away. Clean out the feeds with a degreaser or paraffin and refit, changing any gaskets as needed. There may be a sump plate, and inside that will be a gauze filter. Undo the bolts holding it on and clean the filter, checking for bits of metal that can signify trouble to come. Refit with new gaskets. Replacement sump plates are available for many models with integral drain plugs, which can be handy later on. Some owners will have fitted external oil filters in the return feed. These are an excellent mod that make the filter change easy and increase oil capacity, with the Morgo offerings about as good as you can get. Also drain the gearbox oil and refill.

Japanese engines are easier to work on in this department. There's usually a single drain plug and a replaceable filter somewhere behind a cover. The alloy can be soft, so be very careful not to strip a thread. Most Japanese bikes used 10w-40 oil when new and there's no harm in continuing to use that, changing it regularly. I always buy oil from my local bike shop – it might be a few pounds more expensive but supporting your local shop will benefit you in the long run.

On BMWs, there's a drain plug at the back of the sump plate, and a paper filter inside the front of the engine. Moto Guzzis use a canister filter, but it's inside the engine and the only way to replace it is to pull the sump off. Early Ducati V-twins had a gauze filter attached to the sump plug while later models had a paper filter inside a housing on the crankcase. Always replace any sump plug washers with new.

Which Oil?

Now that's a question which has many answers. Have a look at a manual for the original recommendation and ask a fellow owner what they use now. Just as important, change the oil every 1000 miles, or every year, whichever comes sooner. Oil isn't that

Oil – other brands are available... etc.

The two oil feeds on the bottom of the tank will need removing and cleaning

expensive and fresh lube will always be a good thing. I use Pennine 20w-50 in my '70s Triumph, Motul 10w-40 semi-synthetic in my Yamaha and 50-weight Silkolene monograde in my AJS.

Sorting the Fuelling

Drain the petrol tank. On British bikes you will find two taps, one on either side, that are simply on/off. Pull the fuel pipe from the tap and turn it on, allowing that stinky old petrol to drain away... but not down the drain. If you have a petrol car, add it to the tank, or keep the old fuel as a cleaning agent.

Check the condition of the fuel line. If it's perished replace it with new, good quality pipe from a bike shop or reputable supplier. Take the tank off, add some fresh petrol, swirl it around and pour it out. Refit the tank.

Have the carbs been sitting with old petrol in them? If so, they'll need cleaning out. Removing the carbs, stripping them out and cleaning them is not hard on British and European bikes,

First thing, charge the battery

Don't just check the oil – drain, clean out and refill with fresh

Nice new banjo bolt and brake hose on his calliper

which tend to have one carb per cylinder, or less, but banks of four carbs on a Japanese machine are trickier to handle. Ultrasonic cleaning of each carb is a good idea, and there are specialists who can do this for you at around £35 per carb. Or buy your own ultrasonic cleaner from around £150, which is worth considering.

Resetting cleaned out carbs can be a long job, so have patience. The ultimate answer is to use your bike regularly and keep refreshing the fuel. A new gasket for your filler cap will stop moisture getting into the petrol from outside.

Controls

Check the condition of any cables, and if there are loose strands, replace the cable. If you can't find complete replacements, Venhill will make up a cable or supply a kit for you to make it yourself. Lubricate and adjust the clutch and the brake cables – you can buy cable oilers for this. Finally, adjust the cable making sure there is a small amount of play at the lever or throttle end.

Final Adjustments

We're getting close to the moment of truth now – starting up for the first time. Fit new spark plugs – I use Brisk plugs from F2 Motorcycles as they seem more resistant to fouling. Refit the charged battery and add half a gallon of clean, fresh petrol to the tank. Clean the coil terminals if you have contact breaker ignition, remove the points cover, and rotate the engine until the points are closed. Turn on the ignition and open and close the points with an insulated screwdriver – there should be a spark. Remember to turn off the ignition afterwards, as leaving it on may burn out your coil.

Adjust the points gap

Remove the spark plug(s) and rotate the engine until the points are in the fully open position. Slacken the plate that the points sit on by loosening the retaining screw and, sliding a feeler gauge of the correct size between the points, move the plate backwards or forwards until the gap is correct. Movement of the feeler gauge with a tiny amount of resistance is what you are looking for.

Start Me Up!

With the ignition off, kick the engine over a few times to get the oil circulating. On an electric start machine, flip the kill switch and thumb the button a few times. Pull on the choke lever(s) if fitted, or on a bike with Amal carbs, hold the tickler button on the carb down, which allows fuel to flood the float

A proper workshop

Moment of truth – will it start?

chamber and trickle into the carb inlet. When the fuel dribbles out around the tickler, release the button. On an old British single, use the decompressor (if there is one), and find top dead centre. Twins don't need this. Then turn on the ignition and kick the bike over. If there is no sign of life at all after half a dozen kicks, there may be problems you have not diagnosed. Remember the golden rule: If you think the problem is with the ignition, it's probably the fuelling. If you think it's the fuelling, it's probably the ignition.

After Starting

Hurrah, your newly fettled motorcycle is running! But the job isn't over yet. On a dry sump British motorcycle, check the oil is circulating. Does it have an oil pressure warning light? If it does, this should go off straight away. Check circulation by removing the oil filler cap and peering inside – oil should be spurting from the return feed pipe back into the tank. If it isn't, turn off the engine immediately and find out why.

If that's all good, check the battery is charging. Turn on the headlight and rev the engine. If the light glows brighter, the system is charging. British bikes sometimes have an ammeter, which will have a positive reading when charging, and negative when the system is under load with lights on. To reduce load on the system, fit good LED headlight and tail light bulbs. Not only do they use less current for the same or better illumination, but they are more resistant to vibration.

Ready for the Road

Now your classic is running, it's time to finally hop on and go for a ride. A little ride round the block is in order, just to try it out, and perhaps book it in for a MoT even if it doesn't legally need one, so everything can be checked over. Then, enjoy! ∎

What Tools do I Need?

Someday, you too can have a toolbox like this, if you're not careful

A dirt cheap essential, the £8 multimeter

For home servicing, you will need some extra tools. A camera or camera phone will be useful to photograph every stage of the work, so you know where parts go. Also a torch to probe all nooks and crannies and a notepad for remembering stuff.

A good copper/hide or plastic hammer or two will be a boon, as will one of those telescopic magnetic picker-uppers. An old-fashioned oil can with a long spout will be more useful than all manner of sprays. A grease gun and blowtorch or heat gun will help. And you will bless the day you bought some big rolls of paper wipes.

A solid workbench with a decent vice on it is almost essential and an electrical multimeter will come in handy for checking charging and the completeness of circuits. A bike lift will save your back, and a purpose-made oil drainer comes in handy, as anyone who has tipped the contents of an old roasting tin full of dirty engine oil onto a workshop floor will tell you. Old carpet or purpose made workshop mats will make your stay in the workshop more comfortable, and will stop dropped nuts from bouncing into another dimension.

If your classic is Japanese or European, spanners and sockets must be metric. For British motorcycles up until the mid-1960s, you'll need British Standard/Whitworth, while late '60s bikes are going to be a mixture of Whitworth and AF. Brits from the '70s should be all AF, except for extremely small nuts and bolts which will be BA. A good quality set of 1/4 and 3/8-inch drive sockets will be the most useful. While metric and AF sockets are going to be available from your local tool shop, the older stuff will be harder to find – jumbles are a good source for these.

Good screwdrivers are essential. Japanese bikes use screws that are Japanese Industrial Standard, which look similar to Philips and Posidrive but are slightly different and fit Japanese crossheads perfectly. A good set of JIS screwdrivers will pay for themselves in saved screws when working on an old Yamaha or Honda.

British bikes use more special tools than Japanese machines, and you'll find a use for all manner of flywheel pullers. If you have space, a bench grinder and a pillar drill will be useful, but not essential – you can do a lot of jobs with a battery-powered drill, some decent files and a hacksaw or two. A simple impact 'rattle' gun will be handy too, as will a Dremel type multitool.

Finally, a kettle. This is for boiling water to soften rubber components in. More importantly, for making the tea.

JOIN US!

Come and join the VMCC – the motorcycle club which hosts over 1000 rides a year

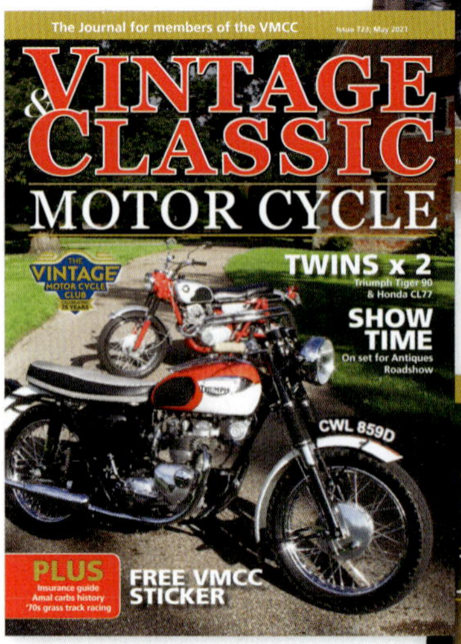

- Unrivalled programme of runs, meets and socials
- Monthly glossy magazine
- Club insurance scheme to save you money
- Huge motorcycle archive open to all members
- DVLA registration service
- The biggest old bike club in the world – over 13,000 members
- All powered two/three wheelers over 25 years old welcome

Join the VMCC and be part of a massive motorcycle community – from c1900 pioneers to 1990s sports bikes and everything in between.

We're the international club with local links – wherever you live, you won't be far from one of our 85 sections who organise runs, meets and social events. Our racing arms – British Historic Racing, Grasstrack and Speedway – run many vintage race events through the year.

Want to enjoy your bike with like-minded people? That's us.

E: membership@vmcc.net T: 01283 495100

www.vmcc.net

H J Pugh & Co

LEDBURY
01531 631122
www.hjpugh.com

HAZLE MEADOWS AUCTION CENTRE,
LEDBURY, HEREFORDSHIRE, HR8 2LP

28th/29th APRIL

2 DAY SALE OF OVER 200 VINTAGE AND CLASSIC MOTORCYLES, PROJECTS AND BRITISH MOTORCYCLE SPARES

THE SALE INCLUDES- A collection from a deceased estate of Vincent Rapide projects and spares and a large quantity of Norton international projects and 100 lots of Ariel spares

1950 Vincent Comet

Triumph Tiger 90

1955 Triumph 650

1965 Triumph Trophy 650

ACCEPTING ENTRIES NOW

Transport and storage can be arranged for whole collections. No storage fees
Our auctions are - Live and Online - Over 85% sale success rate - International buyers – Nationwide collection service available And a stunning new auction centre that can hold up to 300 motorcycles

Call us on 01531 631122 www.hjpugh.com

NEW Free Catalogue subscription and email sale notification service.
www.hjpugh.com
If you have a single item or whole collection to sell please contact us.

ON SITE PRE SALE ADVICE AVAILABLE. SINGLE ITEMS AND WHOLE COLLECTIONS UNDERTAKEN.
ALL ENQUIRIES TREATED IN CONFIDENCE. www.hjpugh.com

Available in our National Motorcycle Museum Auction, 29th March 2023:

1936 Indian 4

Est: £54,000 - £58,000*

Trusted Motorcycle Auctioneers for 30 Years

To consign your motorcycle or scooter to this iconic venue please contact H&H Classics today

sales@HandH.co.uk | 01925 210035 | HandH.co.uk

*All hammer prices are subject to the following Buyer's Premium: Motorcycles & Scooters - 15% plus VAT

29th March 2023 - National Motorcycle Museum

Including

 An Auction of Classic Motorcycles

 An Auction of Vintage Scooters